DENOMINATIONALISM
DENOMINATIONALISM
DENOMINATIONALISM
DENOMINATIONALISM

edited by
Russell E. Richey

ABINGDON
Nashville

DENOMINATIONALISM

Library of Congress Cataloging in Publication Data

Denominationalism.

1. Sects—United States—Addresses, essays, lectures.
I. Richey, Russell E.
BR516.5.D45   280'.0973   76-49103

ISBN 0-687-10469-6
ISBN 0-687-10470-X pbk.

MANUFACTURED BY THE PARTHENON PRESS AT
NASHVILLE, TENNESSEE, UNITED STATES OF AMERICA

To My Parents

Contents

Foreword

The denomination is one of the most familiar, enduring, and important aspects of American religion. It is, however, less understood and more maligned than almost any other religious institution. Slurs on the denomination and on denominationalism recur throughout religious literature, made as though they were so self-evident as to require no elaboration. Such bad press would be of little concern were the denominations possessed of visible direction, purpose, and self-understanding. Instead, however, malaise prevails—not a crisis, but a gnawing sense of unease and indirection. A variety of signs of uncertainty about the nature, meaning, and purpose of denominations have emerged: a slowed growth or actual loss of membership (resulting in program cutbacks, retrenchments on administrative levels, and general economies) with little convincing explanation being offered as to why the decline is occurring or what might be done about it; an increase in ministerial careerism or professionalism, seemingly a quest for meaning among the clergy; a rapid growth of competitive conservative and sectarian movements on the periphery of denominational Christianity; an abandonment of ecumenical ventures which had once provided worthy goals for some denominational leaders; the existence of antibureaucracy movements within denominations; and the prevalence of civil-religious and folk-religious sentiments providing rationale for membership among some persons. Recent structural reforms, the vocal prominence of women's and minority groups, and lingering polarization on social issues increase the pressure for denominational self-understanding. Each problem tests denominational will and invites restatement of denominational identity and purpose. At no other time have the denominations had a greater need for clarity about themselves and been less able to achieve it.

This collection of essays on the denomination and on the perplexing fact of the organization of religious movements in denominations (denominationalism) should serve as an important resource for those seeking definition of denominational purpose. It is intended also for the student and teacher of American religion, American history, and sociology. On the scholarly level the topic has been given attention, but an incoherence about the denomination and denominationalism is apparent here as well. The absence of focus derives in part from the fact that the denomination has been explored under a variety of rubrics and through several disciplines. The denomination, like other subjects, suffers from the boundaries drawn between disciplines. This volume will not resolve the confusion. It may, however, help to clarify some of the perspectival options. Its particular historical approach is distinctive, in fact, and ought to be contrasted with the dominant methods of studying the denomination. Five major approaches have been utilized to date. Most familiar are denominational history[1] and the sociologist's method of ideal typology (frequently church, sect, and denomination).[2] Less well known are studies that conceive of the denomination as voluntary association,[3] as organization,[4] and as ethnic group.[5]

These five approaches have the denomination as their subject; that is, they tend to be concerned with a particular denomination or with the denomination in particular, and generally ignore the overall pattern of denominationalism. Insofar as denominationalism is treated, it is as composite— as the assemblage of denominations, the pattern created by competitive denominations, the common mold into which the religious spirit is poured to form and cool, the accident of pluralism and religious freedom, or the unhappy result of voluntarism and individualism. There is an integrity and intellectual safety in such reluctance to concede reality to denominationalism. Denominations are observable social structures; denominationalism is more ineffable and insubstantial. Might it be reification, a conferring of substantiality on a word, or merely a term referring to the fact of pluralism and mutual tolerance? Or is it a euphemism for sectarianism, a surrogate for the moral indignation against schism, uncharitableness, and division in Christianity?

Such possibilities are given some plausibility by the most widely appreciated assessment of denominationalism, H. Richard Niebuhr's *Social Sources of Denominationalism.* Niebuhr's work does not fit neatly into the typology of approaches just mentioned; it borrows freely from several, especially sociology; and it is in a class by itself. Despite the implication of its title, it uses these approaches to analyze denominations; denominationalism is characterized by the several conditions that produce and sustain denominations. The conditions which create denominations are the social factors of the modern world—class, caste, race, region, nationality—that channel the religious impulse, particularize religious movements, and render them indifferent to the ideals of the gospel—love, unity, and brotherhood. The analysis is carried out with great subtlety but also with ethical and theological passion:

> For the denominations, churches, sects, are sociological groups whose principle of differentiation is to be sought in their conformity to the order of social classes and castes. It would not be true to affirm that the denominations are not religious groups with religious purposes, but it is true that they represent the accomodation of religion to the caste system. They are emblems, therefore, of the victory of world over the church, of the secularization of Christianity, of the church's sanction of the divisiveness which the church's gospel condemns.
>
> Denominationalism thus represents the moral failure of Christianity.[6]

Denominationalism is for Niebuhr a moral failure. But is it a sociological reality? Its sociological status would seem to be derivative, epiphenomenal, and tenuous. Denominationalism is a theological-sociological judgment based on the fact that denominationally divided Christianity is the result of the common capitulation of religious movements to social factors. Denominationalism is that hypocrisy, that divided state of the church created by the compromises and institutionalizations of the several denominations. "Compromise," "hypocrisy," "evil," "moral failure"—denominationalism seems to have a privitive substantiality, and like evil in some theological systems it seems to exist as a negation of the proper ecclesiastical unity and brotherhood. Or to put it in terms of disciplines, "denomination" is given historical and sociological scrutiny by Niebuhr; "denominationalism" seems to be a category of ethics and of theology. Niebuhr's analysis lends plausibility to the notion that "denominationalism" is a word with an uncertain referent that ought to be used with caution.

Such a warning ought to be kept in mind during the reading of this volume; for this collection of essays concerns itself with both the denomination and denominationalism. The intention, in fact, is to explore denominationalism, and the emphasis of the volume falls on denominationalism. Formative in shaping discussions on "denominationalism" and in shaping this collection are the efforts of two historians, Winthrop Hudson and Sidney Mead, who address themselves to the question, "What is denominationalism?" To their (differing) estimates are joined others—additions, elaborations, illustrations, alternatives, criticisms of the theories. While the volume includes critical opinion in line with the five approaches and the underlying assumption already mentioned, the assumption of this volume is the reverse of that assumption. The possibility is entertained that there is such a thing as denominationalism, of which the particular denominations are parts and representatives. This volume, then, takes a somewhat different tack on one of the most well-known aspects of American religion. The approach is not novel, however, and its unfamiliarity says more about the mood of American Protestantism than it does about the arguments of the essays. American Protestantism has been through a period in which the norms of ecumenism and the theology of neo-orthodoxy made pluralism and denominationalism suspect. Earlier, however—for much of the nineteenth century—pluralism in religion, like social and political pluralism, was highly valued both in itself and as a precondition of religious and civil freedom. The literature on denominations as voluntary associations manifests such an appreciation. Furthermore, as several of the essays included here show, the pluralism evident in denominationalism was held to be congruent with a certain unity in the church (among evangelical Protestants). Essays in this volume, in examining the pluralism in unity of denominationalism, discuss and in some cases are in substantial agreement with nineteenth-century perceptions of denominationalism. They bring to the subject not only an alternative to the approaches already mentioned and the theological-ecumenical dismissal of denominations, but also an important resource for understanding the denomination and the possibilities of ecumenism within it.

How might the essays be characterized? They are, for the most part, historical essays. Even the two essays that come from nonhistorians (Frazier and Niebuhr) are in fact historical in character and devoted to a particular period. The essays provide a roughly chronological treatment of the denomination and denominationalism. The focus of the volume is, however, on the origins and essence of denominationalism. This focus and the historical methodology (and considerations of space) have produced a concentration on the nineteenth century. This does result in neglect of the very important twentieth-century developments in the denomination—the growth of bureaucracy and adjustment to institutionalized cooperation among denominations, for instance. However, the decisive changes that prepared the way for these developments are examined. And the twentieth-century changes in denominationalism are simply in need of historical attention. The appropriateness of the concentration on the nineteenth century should become apparent as the essays are read; the denomination, it is argued, is a nineteenth-century artifact. To live with it and to understand it in the twentieth century requires confronting it as a legacy of the nineteenth century.

The essays are arranged and introduced so as to accent their scholarly differences with respect to denominationalism. It is noteworthy that though differences on denominationalism are quite real and the implications of these differences of some import for denominational self-understanding, program structuring and restructuring in the present, there has been little real debate. The denomination has not merited a full-scale historical discussion. In fairness it should be observed that church history has so far proved itself immune to the paradigmatic formulation of major issues that Thomas Kuhn and others have argued constitute a discipline. But even allowing for the state of the discipline, it is remarkable that there is not more debate on denominationalism and the denomination. The five major approaches and sister disciplines have not generated much more discussion. Even within sociology little real debate on the denomination has taken place; on sect, yes, and on the typology as a whole, yes, but not really on the denomination except as it has been required in these and other discussions. The volume, then, does not sample a wide-ranging discussion but may provide some basis for one.

The selections are limited to Protestantism and mainly to evangelical Protestantism. By adopting one of the other approaches to the denomination a broader range of issues can be brought into view. Gibson Winter in *Religious Identity* quite successfully compares the organizational development of Protestantism, Catholicism, and Judaism. His book might well be read in conjunction with this volume. The sharp focus of this book is quite as important. The concentration on denominationalism, rather than on religious organization or even more broadly on voluntary societies, permits the historical work to serve theological and practical ends as well. The book brings into view what is called the denominational theory and pattern of the church. It is this theory and pattern represented fully by the several denominations together and only partially within the experience of a single denomination that constitutes a Protestant, American, and Evangelical contribution to the history of Christianity. Martin E. Marty observed that this development is the most basic administrative change in the church in fourteen hundred years.[7] The essays in this volume concern themselves with the nature and meaning of that important change. To be sure, the denomination needs to be understood genetically through denominational history; comparatively and structurally, as voluntary association, organization, and ethnic group. The sociological

approach through ideal types provides an important access to the denomination as a form of the church. But denominationalism—the denominational theory and pattern of the church—must also be treated as a whole, directly, and in its historical context. The historical efforts to accomplish this undertaken so far and represented here focus on emergent denominationalism—in evangelical Protestantism. The limitation to evangelical Protestantism is appropriate to the subject and the state of the discussion.[8] Aside from its scholarly utility, such a focus and approach should allow those within denominations to appreciate most fully the nature of the denomination and denominationalism as expressions of the church. The editor nourishes the hope that greater understanding of denominationalism may serve ecumenical, reforming, and invigorating interests.

It may surprise some readers that a collection on the denomination would contain no selections devoted to the relation of the denomination to the sect. There are several reasons for this. In the first place the collection contains primarily historical treatments of the denomination, and historians seem to prefer historical generalizations to the sociological ideal types. Second, typology and discussion of sectarianism by historians occur mainly in the examination of single denominations. Here even in essays on particular denominations the attention is to the form itself. Finally, since the focus is on the denominational form and on denominationalism, the interest here is less on how and why a sect becomes a denomination than on the emergence of the denominational form that makes the development of the sect a historical possibility. It is of note that historians locate the reasons for the appearance of the form not so much in the institutional and authority dilemmas of sectarianism as in broader historical currents. The issue is, in part, a perspectival one. The reader interested in a sociological reading of the emergence of the denomination should consult some sociological literature.[9] In particular this volume may be fruitfully read along with H. Richard Niebuhr's *Social Sources of Denominationalism*; the two represent contrasting but perhaps complementary approaches to denominationalism.

I

The Denominational Theory of the Church

1
Introduction

Winthrop Hudson's article has become a classic. The conception of denominationalism advanced within it has been imbedded in later works by Hudson, notably *American Protestantism* and *Religion in America*. It has been adopted by other major interpreters of American religious history, most recently by Martin E. Marty in *Righteous Empire* and *Protestantism* and by Sydney E. Ahlstrom in *A Religious History of the American People*. It is sanctified by inclusion in *The Westminster Dictionary of Church History*.[1] While opposing and alternative explanations exist, in this volume represented by the selections of Timothy Smith, Sidney Mead and H. Richard Niebuhr, Hudson's argument has earned the status of a major theory.

Hudson insists that the denomination and denominationalism are not to be explained as accidents of religious liberty and disestablishment, or as functions of social factors like class and caste. Rather, underlying denominationalism is a new theory or theology of the church. There is theological legitimacy for denominationally divided Christianity. Implicit in the theology of the Reformers, this theory of the church was most fully worked out within the Puritan movement by the Independents (Congregationalists). In defense of their congregational practice the Independents articulated a theory of the church which predicated a unity and reality to the church transcending the emerging party differences in Puritanism. The neutral term "denomination" later employed to convey this understanding, though applied to distinct movements and institutions, signified that these were but "differing attempts to give visible expression to the life of the church in the life

1. Hudson, *American Protestantism* (Chicago: University of Chicago Press, 1961), pp. 33-48; *Religion in America* 2nd ed. (New York: Charles Scribner's Sons, 1973), pp. 80-82. Marty, *Righteous Empire* (New York: Dial Press, 1970), p. 69; *Protestantism* (New York: Holt, Rinehart and Winston), pp. 137-38. Ahlstrom, *A Religious History of the American People* (New Haven: Yale University Press, 1972), pp. 381-82. Jerald C. Brauer, ed., *The Westminster Dictionary of Church History* (Philadelphia: The Westminster Press, 1971), s.v. "Denominationalism."

of the world." Adopted and popularized by Pietists and Evangelicals, this theory of the church provided the theological rationale for American denominationalism.

Hudson's essay draws attention to theological dimensions in denominationalism. It also suggests the importance of the European intellectual and institutional background for American religious development. At the same time Hudson's theory invites certain questions. To what extent is denominationalism informed by a theology of the church? At what points in the American development is such a theology articulated; by whom is it articulated; and with what effect? Was such a theology really embodied within the denominations? How widely? Has it influenced the ways in which denominations interacted? In short, has the denominational theory of the church really functioned? If so, when? During the revivals only or also in periods of institutional consolidation? A second major line of questioning can be suggested by noting two other possible sources for such denominational theory. One was the conception of the church as a voluntary society made influential through the writings of John Locke and articulated in his *Letters Concerning Toleration*. Denominationalism was here prefigured by the insistence that toleration was one of the marks of the gospel and that the church was "a free and voluntary society." [2] A second possible source was "catholic" Protestantism, a small band of irenic souls, who sought unity among Protestants. Typically Erasmian in spirit they had confidence in reason, expected diversity in the church, sought truth through discussion, emphasized charity among Protestants differing in views, and predicated a unity in the church on fundamentals or on essentials. [3] Since both Locke

2. *A Letter Concerning Toleration* in *The Works of John Locke*, 10 vols. (London, 1823), 6: 9, 13.

3. The "catholic" tradition was a small but illustrious company, numbering among its adherents such sixteenth-century giants as Martin Bucer, Philip Melanchthon, perhaps John Calvin, and certainly Theodore Beza and Jacobus Acontius. In the seventeenth century, the French Protestants Philip du Plessis Mornay, Moise Amyraut, Isaac Casaubon; the Lutheran George Calixtus; the Silesian Reformed Pietist David Pareus; the Moravian John Amos Comenius; the Scot John Dury; the Dutch Arminians (Hugo Grotius and others); and among the English, William Chillingworth, the Latitudinarians, the Cambridge Platonists, certain Puritans, and those designated by W. K. Jordan as "English Moderates" and "Lay Thinkers." See W. K. Jordan, *The Development of Religious Toleration in England*, 4 vols. (Cambridge, 1932–1940) and John T. McNeill and James Hastings Nichols, *Ecumenical Testimony* (Philadelphia, 1974). This tradition was transmitted to the American scene by such "catholic" Christians as Richard Baxter, Cotton Mather, Philip Doddridge, Isaac Watts, Daniel Neal and Samuel Davies.

and the catholic Christians espoused tolerance, expected divisions, and sought a unity amid disagreement, Hudson's insistence on the Independents as the source for denominational theory may be open to question. If they were an important source, what were the lines of transmission to the American Evangelicals? If they were not the sole source, how might the denominational theory be modified to reflect elements included from other sources? A third set of questions might be raised concerning implications of Hudson's theory for the present. What strategies for church renewal, for ecumenical efforts, for theologies of the church might be derived from Hudson's insights? And finally, does Hudson's theory of the church provide criteria for judging denominational policies, present and past?

1

Denominationalism as a Basis for Ecumenicity: A Seventeenth Century Conception

Winthrop S. Hudson

The use of the word "denomination" to describe a religious group came into vogue during the early years of the Evangelical Revival. Typical of the mood which gave currency to the new term are John Wesley's oft-quoted words; "I . . . refuse to be distinguished from other men by any but the common principles of Christianity. . . . I renounce and detest all other marks of distinction. But from real Christians, of *whatever denomination*, I earnestly desire not to be distinguished at all. . . . Dost thou love and fear God? It is enough! I give thee the right hand of fellowship." The word "denomination" was adopted by the leaders of the Evangelical Revival, both in England and America, because

Reprinted, footnotes omitted, with the permission of Church History and the author. Footnotes available in Church History, 24 (1955), 32-50.

it was a neutral term which carried with it no implication of a negative value judgment.

Denominationalism is the opposite of sectarianism. The word "denomination" implies that the group referred to is but one member of a larger group, called or denominated by a particular name. The basic contention of the denominational theory of the church is that the true church is not to be identified in any exclusive sense with any particular ecclesiastical institution. The outward forms of worship and organization are at best but differing attempts to give visible expression to the life of the church in the life of the world. No denomination claims to represent the whole church of Christ. No denomination claims that all other churches are false churches. No denomination claims that all members of society should be incorporated within its own membership. No denomination claims that the whole of society and the state should submit to its ecclesiastical regulations. Yet all denominations recognize their responsibility for the whole of society and they expect to cooperate in freedom and mutual respect with other denominations in discharging that responsibility.

The denominational theory of the church was popularized by the leaders of the eighteenth century awakening, but it was a theory which had been hammered out by a group of Puritan divines in the preceding century and which had won sufficiently widespread acceptance so that its theological justification could largely be taken for granted. As a consequence, the Evangelical leaders were not compelled to construct a systematic defense of the conception of the church which was common to them all. To discover their fundamental presuppositions, which they betray only in incidental remarks and observations, one must go back to the seventeenth century divines who first formulated the denominational theory of the church.

Actually, the denominational theory of the church was implicit in the thinking of the Protestant Reformers. The true church, they affirmed, is not an institution, although in the life of the world it must assume institutional form. But the church must not and cannot be identified in any exclusive sense with any particular institution. There are many, John

Calvin confessed, who "are not satisfied unless the church can always be pointed out with the finger." But, said he, that is something that cannot be done in any final sense. The whole question as to the dimensions, the boundaries, the limits of the church of Christ must be left to God, "since he alone 'knoweth them that are his.'" Thus the Reformers recognized as true churches all churches which possessed an essentially common faith, whether they were Lutheran churches as in Germany and Scandinavia; Reformed churches as in Switzerland, Holland, and Scotland; or an Anglican church as in England. All these churches in their various geographical areas were different manifestations of the whole church of Christ which embraced them all.

The new element which was to be introduced into this type of thinking was the application of the basic convictions of the Reformers to a situation in which religious diversity existed within a particular geographical area rather than between different geographical areas. Formerly it had been a question as to whether or not a church in England could be and was in communion with a church in Holland. The answer of Protestantism in general had been that they both could be and were in communion with one another. In seventeenth century England, it was to be suggested that this was equally true of Anglican, Presbyterian, Congregational, and Baptist churches when they were located on opposite corners in the same city. Each could be and should be regarded as constituting a different "mode" of expressing in piety, thought, and organization that larger life of the church in which they all shared.

I

The real architects of the denominational theory of the church were the seventeenth century Independent divines within the Church of England, whose most prominent representatives were the Dissenting Brethren in the Westminster Assembly. The initial concern of the Independents some decades before had been to carry out a liturgical reformation that would make the worship of the church express more adequately and convey more clearly the fundamental theological conviction they held concerning the nature and the implications of the Christian faith. Unfortunately an increasing pressure to secure liturgical conformity made it progressively more difficult for these men to maintain the liturgical reforms which they had introduced in their parishes and pushed them in the direction of Separatism. Yet, even when the force of circumstance compelled them to establish a separate worship, they were unwilling to adopt the Separatist contention that the conforming churches were to be disowned as false churches, and they continued to maintain communion, so far as they were able, with their former parish churches. Of one of their leaders, William Bradshaw, it was said: "He had learned Christ better than for difference of opinion in such points to make schisms and divisions, as their [the Separatists'] manner is, with all those that do not in all things concur with them and subscribe to what they say." The worship and even the government of the conforming churches might be defective and corrupt to varying degrees, but to regard them as false churches without any valid ordinances and devoid of true Christians would be to divide the body of Christ, to unchurch the martyrs of former generations (such as Cranmer, Ridley, Latimer, and Hooper), and to run counter to one of the deepest convictions of the Independents concerning the economy of Christ in the life of the world.

During the early sessions of the Westminster Assembly, the Dissenting Brethren had objected to the establishment of a national church on a Presbyterian model. Charged with being obstructionists, they sought to justify their position by issuing *An Apologetical Narration*. There were two major principles, they asserted, upon which they had proceeded in their thinking concerning the outward arrangements of the church.

"The supreme rule," which they had followed, ". . . was the primitive pattern and example of the churches created by the Apostles." They are willing to concede, as Henry Burton was later to acknowledge, that "no such model is left in the New Testament as was given to Moses in the Old;" yet they could not "but imagine that Christ hath ever been as exact in setting forth the true bounds and limits of whatever portion of power he hath imparted unto any (if we of this age could attain rightly to discern it) as he hath been in ordering what kind of censures and for what sins, . . . which we find he hath been punctual in."

When they had gone into exile abroad, they had been forced to inquire into the positive part of church government, and they believed that this circumstance of being completely on their own had served to free them from bias and thus had allowed them to search out the pattern of the primitive church impartially, being guided only by the "light and touch" of God's Spirit.

We had, of all men, the greatest reason to be true to our own consciences in what we should embrace, seeing it was for our conscience that we were deprived at once of whatever was dear to us. We had no new commonwealths to rear to frame church government unto . . . to cause the least variation by us from the primitive pattern. We had no state-ends or political interests to comply with; no kingdoms in our eye to subdue to our mold . . . ; no preferments or worldly respects to shape our opinion for. We had nothing else to do but simply and singly to consider how to worship God acceptably and so most accordingly to his Word.

"Although we cannot profess that sufficiency of knowledge as to be able to lay forth all those rules therein . . . , yet we found principles enough, . . . to us clear and certain, and such as might well serve to preserve our churches in peace and from offense and would comfortably guide us to heaven in a safe way."

The second principle upon which they had proceeded "was not to make our present judgment and practice a binding law unto ourselves for the future."

We had too great an instance for our own frailty in the former way of our conformity, and therefore . . . we kept this reserve . . . to alter and retract (though not lightly) whatever should be discovered to be taken up out of a misunderstanding of the rule.

The keeping of a "reserve to alter and retract" is reflected again and again in the writings of the Independents. The elders of the churches in New England in 1639, responding to an inquiry concerning their practice, had phrased it thus:

We see as much cause to suspect the integrity of our own hearts as yours; and so much the more, as being more privy to the deceitfulness of our own hearts than to yours . . . , which causeth us with great reverence to accept and receive what further light God may be pleased to impart unto us by you. But as we have believed, so have we hitherto practiced. . . . If anything appear to be unsound, and dissonant from the Word, which we for our parts cannot discern, we shall willingly attend to what further light God may send unto us by you.

In the same year, the anonymous author of *The Saints' Apology* had written in similar vein:

I have in my plain way endeavored to express my judgment in these particulars, desiring to be always ready to open mine eyes to receive further light from whomsoever it shall be showed unto me. In the meantime, I must walk according to that I have. . . . If there be any begged principles or grounds wanting proof or anything inferred from grounds too weak to maintain the same . . . , make that appear unto me, and I shall either make them good . . . (at least to my apprehension) or quit them.

Thomas Hooker put it even more vividly when he wrote:

My only aim . . . is to lay down . . . the grounds of our practice according to that measure of light I have received. . . . The sum is, we doubt not what we practice, but it's beyond all doubt that all men are liars and we are in the number of those poor feeble men; either we do or may err, though we do not know it; what we have learned we do profess, and yet profess still to live that we may learn.

Hooker's hope was that he "might occasion men eminently gifted to make further search and to dig deeper that, if there be any vein of reason which lies yet lower, it might be brought to light." "We profess and promise," he continued, "not only a ready ear to hear it, but a heart willing to welcome it."

It was this type of thinking which led the Independents to oppose the establishment of a national church on a Presbyterian model. They felt certain, as Henry Burton declared, that they could "prove our way with all our practices in every particular out of God's Word," and they also felt sure that this the others could not do. Yet, knowing the deceit that lurked within their own hearts, they were aware that they might be wrong. Thus they objected not only to the Presbyterian claim that the system of church government which they proposed was *jure divino* but were equally unwilling to make such a claim for their own proposals.

Beyond this fundamental disagreement as to the extent to which divine sanction could be claimed for a particular ecclesiastical structure, the difference between the two parties was not great. Charles Herle, a moderate Presbyterian, summarized the difference in this fashion:

Our difference 'tis such as doth at most but ruffle a little the fringe, not any way rend the garment of Christ. 'Tis so far from being a *fundamental* that 'tis scarce a *material* one. Nay not so much as the *form*. 'Tis but the better or worse way for the exercise of the same form of discipline that is in question. *That it be* and *What it be* and *Which it be* is agreed on amongst us. 'Tis but the *Whose it be* we differ in, and herein not so much *Whose* neither, as *Where it be*, whether in every congregation apart or of the same men joined with the like of other congregations in a synod?

The specific issue around which the controversy centered was where the power of the keys—the power to excommunicate and deliver unto Satan—was to reside. The one thing which their experience had taught the Independents was that the authority of the church could be utilized by men to hinder and obstruct God's people from yielding full obedience to God's will as it had been made known to them. This possibility they wished to reduce to a minimum.

One cannot escape the feeling, as one reads the literature of the time, that the Independents regarded the act of excommunication as involving, in the last analysis, an act of intolerable presumption on the part of those called upon to judge, but they could not deny its obvious Scriptural warrant. They could find in Scripture, however, no basis for a synod having the authority to deliver anyone to Satan, and they were convinced that it was highly dangerous to grant such power to such a body. Consequently, they insisted that if a person was to receive that dreadful sentence, it should be pronounced by those who knew him, by the members of his own congregation, and not by a distant tribunal dependent solely upon second-hand reports of his character, conduct, and opinions. Even those threatened with the lesser penalties of civil tribunals, they pointed out, could claim the right to be judged in their own community by a jury of their peers.

As the discussions continued it became clear that the Independents would be content with an accommodation which would permit them to follow the leading of God's Spirit as it was disclosed to them in Scripture.

I shall tell you in a word what will content all the Independents in England. 'Tis this: They desire neither more nor less than what the Puritans desired of Queen Elizabeth and King James; viz. an entire exemption from the jurisdiction of all prelates and ecclesiastical officers other than such as themselves shall choose; . . . to be as free to choose their own company, place, and time, with whom, where, and when to worship God as they are in the choice of their wives; for a forced marriage will not hold.

Or, as the Dissenting Brethren phrased the demand: "If in a parish it happen there be a considerable number of such as cannot partake in the sacraments with the minister and people, they shall have liberty to dispose of themselves as a distinct church and to choose a minister or ministers at their own charge to be maintained, to be their pastor." This, in essence had been the Independent position from the beginning. Henry Jacob had written years before:

We believe concerning mixtures of the open profane with some godly Christians in a visible church, though at once it doth not destroy essentially nor make void the holiness of that whole assembly, yet truly it putteth that whole assembly into a most dangerous and desperate estate . . . by such extreme peril of further infection. . . . Insomuch that what soul soever in such a church state desireth to be in safety ought with all diligence to leave that spiritual society . . . and join to a better, seeing under the gospel there are more free societies at Christians, more visible churches politic, than one in a country, and some more sincere than some. . . . We ought to leave the worse society and enjoy one that is and may be sincere.

This meant, as Jeremiah Burroughes readily acknowledged, that "we must grant that liberty to our brethren we would have ourselves."

II

There were good theological reasons for the Independents to adopt the position that men should be as free in the choice of the forms of worship as they are in the choice of their wives.

Jeremiah Burroughes, the most influential spokesman of the Dissenting Brethren, pointed out that there always had been divisions in the church and that, "so long as we live here in this muddy world," there will continue to be divisions even among the godly. "If we consider things wisely," he suggested, "we have no cause to wonder that godly men in this their estate of imperfection should differ so much one from another as they do." There are several reasons for this:

First, every godly man prizes and seeks after knowledge. Others mind little but their own profit and pleasure. They trouble not themselves about knowing the things of God, except ambition puts them upon it. They care not which way truths go. But the godly man prizes every truth at a high rate, worth the contending for to the uttermost. In the dark, all colors be alike; but in the light, they appear diverse. ... When men discuss things and desire to see farther in them, it is impossible, considering the weakness of the best and the variety of men's apprehensions, but there must needs to be much difference in men's judgments. And then, considering [that] their consciences are engaged in it, that everything they apprehend to be a truth (at least thus far) that they must not deny it for a world, this puts men's spirits at a distance although both be godly, both love the truth equally.

Secondly, godly men are free men. Christ made them so, and requires them not to suffer themselves to be brought under bondage. They must not, cannot submit their consciences to the opinions, determinations, decrees of any men living. They cannot submit to any as lords over their faith. This others can do. As for points of religion, say some, let the learned men judge of them; we will not be wiser than they; we will submit and others must submit to what they shall determine. This makes quick work of divisions, but this those who fear God cannot do. They must see everything they own as a truth with their own light . . . received from Jesus Christ. Though they reverence men of greater parts, deeper learning, yet they have the charge of Christ upon them not to acknowledge it as truth till they understand it to be so. This causes much contention among good men through their weakness and corruption of their hearts. . . . Thirdly, godly men give up themselves to the strictest rules of holiness. They walk in the narrow way of Christ. It is broad enough to the spiritual part, but in regard of our corruptions it is a narrow pent way. They dare not give way to themselves . . . to gratify others, . . . but most keep themselves to the straight rule. . . . Hence there is a clashing, everyone not having the same thoughts of the rule and way that others have. Those who walk by loose rules in ways that are broad . . . can suit themselves one to another easily. They can gratify their friends, yea, the corruptions of their friends, more than others can do. Godly men cannot yield for peace sake to such terms as other men can.

Fourthly, the things that the Saints are conversant about are great things, things of a high nature, about their last end, their eternal estate. Hence everyone is very chary and careful and strongly set to maintain what he apprehends. Those who understand not the infinite consequence of those things, who have not had the fear of them fall upon their hearts, they wonder at the stiffness of men's spirits that they can be brought to yield no more in such things than they conceive they might yield in. Where there are different apprehensions of those things that concern men's eternal estates, even among godly men, they must needs stand out one against the other, till God causes one of them to see things otherwise than he now doth.

Fifthly, the things of religion are hidden mysteries. They are the secrets of God. They are hard to be understood. God reveals them in a differing way. They are not ordinarily so clearly revealed but that the apprehensions of them are like to be different. . . .

Sixthly, the Saints are bound to watch over one another. Each is his brother's keeper. They ought to advise, admonish, reprove one another. . . . Now this, through our corruption, is very displeasing. We do not love to be meddled with, to be crossed in what we have a mind to. Other men can better preserve their own quiet by letting their brethren alone. . . . Hence it is that they many times live more quietly with one another than godly men do. Yet this is a great evil, a shame to those who are godly, that it should be so upon any terms.

Thus you see it is no wonder why there are dissentions among men that fear God.

Denominationalism as a Basis for Ecumenicity

Several years earlier, William Bradshaw's editor had noted the lack of unanimity among the godly, pointing out that "it is well known that there is and hath been no small diversity of judgment between our nonconformists among themselves; some condemning some rites but allowing others, and some condemning those also which others allow; some esteeming the things simply evil in themselves, some only as inexpedient . . . ; some excepting against some passages in our liturgy which others of them stick not at; and the like." He then went on to observe that, "considering the wants and weaknesses that do ordinarily attend men's apprehensions . . . in such things as are not clearly evident of themselves, for a multitude of men of divers parts, abilities, dispositions, and endowments to concur and agree in every particular doubt or debate, question or controversy, . . . might justly be deemed rather a conspiracy than an uniformity of judgment."

While Burroughes readily acknowledged that the divisions among Christians were due to human weakness and sin, he also insisted that God makes use of them for his own purposes. In these divisions, "God is working out ends above our reach for his glory and the good of his Saints." For one thing, God uses these divisions for "the discovery of men's spirits that they which are approved may be made manifest."

The melting of the metal discovers the dross, for they divide the one from the other. These are melting times and thereby discovering times. If reformation had gone on without opposition, we had not seen what drossie spirits we had amongst us. Those who have kept upright without warping in these times are honorable before God.

God also uses these divisions to exercise the graces of his servants.

A little skill in a mariner is enough to guide his ship in fair weather; but when storms arise, where the seas swell and grow troublesome, then his skill is put to it. In these stormy troublesome times, there had need be much wisdom, faith, love, humility, patience, self-denial, meekness. All graces are put to it now! They had need put forth all their strength; act with all their vigor. Our graces had need be stirring, full of life and quickness, now! God prizeth the exercise of the graces of his Saints at a very high rate. He thinks it worth their suffering much trouble.

But above all, Burroughes asserts,

God hath a hand in these divisions to bring forth further light. Sparks are beaten out by the flints striking together. Many sparks of light, many truths, are beaten out by the beatings of men's spirits one against another. If light be let into a house, there must be some trouble to beat down [a place in the wall for] a window. A child thinks the house is beating down, but the father knows the light will be worth the cost and trouble. If you will have the cloth woven, the woof and warp must be cast cross one to another. If you will have truths argued out, you must be content to bear with some opposition for the time. They who are not willing to bear some trouble, to be at some cost to find out truth, are unworthy of it. . . . We may well behold men's weakness in these divisions, but [we may] better admire God's strength and wisdom in ordering them to his glory and his children's good.

John Goodwin, making use of a text which the Independents repeatedly cited, declared: "The Holy Ghost, speaking (doubtless) of these times, prophesied long ago that *many should run to and fro*, and (by this means) *knowledge shall be increased.*" Goodwin went on to point out that "in times of Popery men generally stood still, made no inquiries beyond the lips of their teachers, and knowledge then was at a stand and advanced not." On the other hand, it seemed equally obvious that "since God hath been pleased to put it into the hearts of men to conceive . . . that there may be tracts or regions of knowledge beyond the line of the . . . discoveries of their teachers, and have made many studious expeditions themselves to find them out, knowledge hath increased; yea, and will increase daily more and more, if we relapse not into the lethargie of Popish slothfulness and servility, and suffer our teachers to exercise dominion over our faith."

This, quite obviously, is no doctrine of relativity so far as truth itself is concerned; the relativity is in terms of one's apprehension of truth. "Truth is a daughter of time was the saying of old," wrote Thomas Hooker, "and our daily experience gives in evidence and proof hereof. . . . Not that there is any change in truth, but the alteration grows according to men's apprehensions, to whom it is more or less discovered according to God's most just judgment and their own deservings." Praisegod Barebones phrased it in this fashion: "About the measuring of which things ["the Temple, the Altar, and them that worship therein"], though the truth and true measure be one, yet the persons measuring are very various and much differing, not only concerning the right understanding of the measure, but also concerning the things measured. Hence it is that [there are] diversity of opinions and practices amongst persons concerning matters of religion and godliness."

It was because of this uncertainty regarding men's apprehension of truth that John Cook insisted that assent must not be required even to such propositions "as the greatest number of wise and learned men shall agree upon." The reason why such assent must not be required, he continued, is easily given. It is "because in very many councils, Jesus Christ hath been out-voted by anti-Christ."

Let the rigid Presbyterians in the Assembly but answer me this question: Whether two parts at least in three of all the ministers in this kingdom be not for a moderated episcopacy and the Common Prayer Book? If ever it come to a National Assembly, differences must be ended by a major vote.

In similar vein, John Goodwin asked: "Can that in reason be thought to be the Way of God which seemeth so only in the eyes of a few inconsiderable and for the most part illiterate persons? . . . Do not wise men see more than those that are weak, and many more than a few?" The answer to such questions as these, said Goodwin, was given long ago by Solomon when he pointed out that the race is not always won by the swift nor the battle by the strong, for "time and chance" frequently determine the outcome. By which Solomon meant that "God still reserves a liberty to himself to interpose and to carry the issues and events against all advantages . . . , when and where and as oft as he pleaseth."

Though God be at liberty to make the first discovery or communication of the light of his truth unto the world by greater numbers of men and those learned and in high esteem for wisdom . . . , as well as by one or fewer . . . , yet by the more frequent experience of all ages it appeareth that he taketh pleasure in this latter way rather than in the former.

It is for this reason, Goodwin asserted, that any "reformation according to the Word of God must give leave to the wind to blow where it listeth and give liberty to the Spirit of God to do with his own what he pleaseth; to make what discovery of truth he pleaseth and to what persons and when and where he pleaseth; and must not confine him to his market or compel him to traffic only with councils and synods for his heavenly commodities."

In the light of this fundamental contention, it would seem clear that the Independents did not plead for the right of people to differ and disagree and establish separate forms of worship simply because they themselves were a minority in the Assembly. Indeed, the only point at which they registered a fundamental dissent from the majority was precisely at the point of their unwillingness to agree to the establishment of any over-all instrument of coercion which could be utilized to secure conformity to opinions and practices which were in essential harmony with their own. They insisted that "no coactive violence" be "used against such men who carry themselves religiously and peaceably in their differences from others," because they remembered that "not long since we were ourselves of another mind." "My sin" of conforming in an earlier time, said Burroughes,

makes me to be of the more forebearing spirit towards those who now differ from me. I see now what I did not; . . . Why, then, should . . . I fly upon our brethren because they see not what we think we see? O how unbeseeming it is for . . . [men] to be harsh and bitter in the least degree against their brethren who differ from them, when they do differ so much from what they were themselves but a while since.

"I profess," said Burroughes, ". . . that were my judgment presbyterial, yet I should preach and plead as much for the forebearance of brethren differing from me, not only in their judgment but in their practice." The only alternative to such forebearance would be to require that men "put out their own eyes" and see only "by the spectacles of other men in point of God's service and worship."

John Saltmarsh, who in a sense stood outside both camps, summarized "the whole difference" in point of view in these words.

They of the presbytery would say to the state: We humbly petition you that heretics and schismatics (we believing all that differ from us to be so) may have your power inflicted upon them, whether to fines, imprisonment, or banishment. The Independents, on the contrary, would say: We humbly petition that you will not hazard nor endanger your civil power of the state to help our opinions against our brethren, for we are not *infallible* nor *apostolical; we see but in part;* and that you will not punish any of our brethren presbyterial or others for what they believe or differ from us in things of outward order in the gospel.

III

While the Dissenting Brethren were ready to defend diversity, it must not be supposed that these men who had been so reluctant to separate themselves from communion with their parish churches viewed the divisions among Christians with equanimity. They were, in fact, dismayed and distressed by the divisions and by the bitterness of the controversy which these divisions had aroused. As for themselves, they said that they had made little or no attempt, after their return from exile, "to make and increase a party." Books were written against them by men of "much worth, learning, and authority," but, said they,

we knew and considered that it was the second blow that makes the quarrel, and that the beginning of strife would have been as the breaking in of the waters, and the sad and conscientious apprehension of the danger of rending and dividing the godly Protestant party in this kingdom that were desirous of reformation and [the danger] of making several interests among them in a time when there was an absolute necessity of their nearest union and conjunction ... [have] prevailed with us to occasion the least disturbance among the people.

This account of their irenic behaviour is somewhat idealized, but it is true that a major portion of their attention was directed to the problem of healing the breaches and making real the unity they all had in Christ.

Perhaps the most complete statement of the Independent position as it related to the problem of sectarian conflict is to be found in a treatise by Jeremiah Burroughes with the rather formidable seventeenth century title, *Irenicum, to the Lovers of Truth and Peace Heart-Divisions Opened in the Causes of Evils of Them, with Cautions that We May Not Be Hurt by Them, and Endeavors to Heal Them.* Describing "heart-divisions" as the great "evil of our times," Burroughes proceeds to detail both the ill effects and the sinfulness of divisions among Christians. They destroy our peace and quiet, they hinder our sleep, they spoil our judgment, they absorb our time, they hinder our prayers, they hinder the use of our graces, they divert attention from more important matters. They are against the command of Christ, they are against the prayer of Christ, they are dishonorable to Christ, they grieve the Holy Spirit, they stir up corruption, they harden men in sin, they tend to void God's covenant of grace. In brief, he concludes, "our divisions are against the very character of Christianity." "We are wrangling, devising, plotting, working against one another, minding nothing but to get the day of one another," whereas "love and unity are Christ's badge, the arms of a Christian, whereby he shows of what house he is."

It is an unhappy fact, says Burroughes, that

we are divided notwithstanding we are all convinced of the evil of our divisions. We cry out exceedingly against them. We tell one another that of all the tokens of God's displeasure amongst us, these are the greatest. Yet scarce a man does anything . . . towards any help against divisions or furtherance of our union. Every man cries out at the thief, but who stops him? We all say we would have peace . . . , but where is the man who is willing to be at any cost for it.

It would be easy enough, of course, to secure unity "if those who differ from others would give up their judgments and practices to them, to believe what they believe, and to do what they do." But how is this to be achieved? "Christ hath laid this charge upon [his followers] . . . that they must not believe or practice anything in matters of religion but what they shall first see ground for out of his Word." A Christian is "not to alter his judgment or practice till, in the use of [all the means he can], he should receive further light from Him." Consequently, says Burroughes, "you would not have them give up their judgments or practices . . . till they know they are right; and how can that be till they, by discussing, praying, reading, meditating, find that out? If some men had certainly found out the right, and other men knew certainly that they had done so, then the work were at an end."

The problem was to find a way to unity when Christians do not all agree. "If we stay for peace and love till we come to the unity of the faith in all things, we must stay, for ought I know, till we come to another world. . . . The unity of the faith and the perfect man will both be together." The plain fact which must be faced, Thomas Goodwin reminded the members of Parliament, is that "providence hath disposed it so that they [the Saints] do and will differ in judgment. The Apostles, who were oracles infallible, could not in their times wholly prevent it. And differing thus in judgment, they will hardly ever of themselves agree." And yet, the great need of the kingdom is that animosities shall be allayed and that Christians shall be united and reconciled to one another. "It is your work and will be your honor," he informed the Commons, ". . . to find out ways whereby this may be done, notwithstanding these their differences."

IV

If Christians are to be united, "notwithstanding their differences," there are several fundamental truths which these seventeenth century divines insisted must be recognized and accepted.

First of all, it is necessary to recognize that diversity will continue and that "love and peace" among Christians, therefore, cannot be procured without "liberty of conscience."

"When we complain of our divisions for making much against the cause of Christ," said Burroughes, "we do not complain against men because they cannot all understand all things alike." What we do complain of is "that they have not joined to study what ways and means may be found out to ease the consciences one of another, to bear with one another as far as Christ would have them." It is certain that Christ would not "be pleased with such a reformation wherein the lesser part should give up their consciences and practices to the judgments of the greater," and it is equally certain that such a procedure would not succeed in bringing about unity.

It is a wonder of first magnitude how men come to have so much ground of hope . . . of composing differences and distractions . . . throughout the nation by exalting one way of discipline, of church government, for the treading down and trampling under foot of all others. . . . Undoubtedly that Way whose hand shall be against every [other]Way, will find the hand of every [other] Way will be against it, and then what manner of peace can reasonably be expected?

"A peaceable, humble, and quiet discussing of things" will contribute to understanding and thus lead toward agreement, but the resort to coercion when differences exist will only serve to arouse antagonism and aggravate differences.

It is necessary to recognize, in the second place, the unity that does exist among Christians.

There hath been much ado to get us to agree. We labored to get our opinions into one, but they will not come together. It may be [that] in our endeavors for agreement we have begun at the wrong end. Let us try what we can do at the other end. It may be that we shall have better success there. Let us labor to join our hearts, to engage our affections, one to another. If we cannot be of one mind that we may agree, let us agree to be of one heart.

We must not forget that, while "godly people are divided in their opinions and ways, . . . they are united in Christ."

Though our differences are sad enough, yet they come not up to this to make us men of different religions. We agree in the same end, though not in the same means. They are but different ways of opposing the common enemy. The agreeing in the same means, in the same way of opposing the common enemy, would be very comfortable. It would be our strength. But that cannot be expected in this world.

The actual fact is that "our divisions have been and still are between good men," and it is equally true that "there are as many godly Presbyterians as Independents." This means that, "though we are fully persuaded by God's Word and Spirit that this our Way is Christ's Way, yet we neither do nor dare judge others to be reprobates that walk not with us in it, but leave all judgment to God, and heartily pray for them."

It should be recognized, in the third place, that the mere fact of separation does not of itself constitute schism. "Though they may be divided from such a particular society, yet they are not divided from the Church," for "the true nature of schism is . . . an uncharitable, unjust, rash, violent breaking from union with the church or members of it."

To those who cried out against every separation, even when "loving and peaceable," as constituting schism, Burroughes made a lengthy and detailed reply.

Suppose the Nonconformists or those of the Scottish nation who lived in the City in former times, who could not acknowledge the bishops' authority nor communicate in the sacraments in the parishes where they lived without sin to them, still acknowledging them to be true churches, yet if Parliament made an Act whereby they should have two or three places in the City appointed for them, wherein all that could not conform . . . should have . . . the sacraments and other church ordinances . . . by themselves, freed from the burden of ceremonies and episcopal authority, would they not have blessed God for this liberty?

Would they have been guilty of schism to take advantage of this liberty? It is certain that "the allowance of the state" does not "alter the case." For, "if it be schism . . . without the allowance of the state, . . . it is schism when the state does allow it." In many instances, the state has granted such liberty. How are we to regard those who availed themselves of it?

Where the Lutherans and Calvinists have liberty to live in one country together, and yet not communicating with one another, are all the Lutherans or all the Calvinists schismatics? . . . Many of the French and Dutch churches who live in our parishes, though they understand our language well enough, yet would not communicate in the parishes where they live because of the ceremonies and subjection to bishops, were they all schismatics too?

Furthermore, it is perfectly lawful for a man, for "the enjoyment of the ordinances that he cannot have in the church he formerly liveth in," to move from that parish to another where he can enjoy those ordinances. In this instance, no cry of schism is raised. But, "what if his dwelling be not removed to the other side of the street, does that make it schism?" Yet there are those who will brand as a schismatic any man who "lives in a parish and does not join in church fellowship in that parish." To defend the one practice and to condemn the other, Burroughes insisted, was not only illogical but unjust and unfair. It permits those who can afford it the liberty of choosing their church by choosing their dwelling, but it denies liberty to those who are in more restricted circumstances. John Goodwin makes the point even more vividly:

This liberty of choosing pastors only by choosing houses is so conditioned that it smiles only upon the rich (and that but somewhat faintly) but frowns upon the poor, and so is partial and therefore not Christian. He that hath enough of . . . all things may probably be able to accommodate himself within the precincts of what parish he pleaseth . . . by buying out some inhabitant or by purchasing ground and building upon it . . . , but the case of the poor man is many times such that he cannot tell where to find another hole in all the world to hide his head in besides that wherein it is hid already.

It was difficult for the Independents to believe that these arguments which laid so much stress on the place of birth and place of residence were to be taken seriously. Much more defensible, it seemed to them, was the position which Burroughes outlined in a sentence which was distinguished by its careful qualifications. "When men, who give good testimony of their godliness and peaceableness, . . . cannot without sin to them (though it be through weakness) enjoy all the ordinances of Christ and partake in all the duties of worship as members of that congregation where their dwelling is, they therefore in all humility and meekness . . .

join in another congregation, yet . . . not condemning those churches they join not with as false but still preserve all Christian communion with the Saints as members of the same body of Christ, of the Church Catholic, and join also with them in all duties of worship that belong to particular churches so far as they are able—if this be called schism, it is more than yet I have learned."

Thus the Dissenting Brethren were pleading not only for "the peaceable practices of our consciences which the Reformed churches abroad allowed us," but for that which to them was much more important; namely the establishment of the type of relationship among the churches in England which had existed between the Independents and the Reformed churches abroad, among whom they had been cast to live, where "we both mutually gave and received the right hand of fellowship," recognizing, as Henry Burton put it, that "the Catholic Church . . . includes all true churches throughout the world."

Christians can live together in love and peace, "notwithstanding their differences," if they will grant liberty of conscience to those who disagree with them, if they will keep ever in mind the very real unity they have in Christ, and if they will cease to regard all other churches as false and schismatic. But beyond this, it should also be recognized that those of the various Ways can cooperate for common ends. All who "profess godliness" both can and must join together "in opposing that which they [all] believe cannot stand with godliness" and in promoting "those ways of godliness which they are convinced to be so." If this is done lack of agreement at other points need not be disastrous. After all, is it not true that "soldiers who march against a common enemy all under the same captain, who follow the same colors in their ensign and wear them upon their hats or arms, may get the day though they be not all clothed alike, though they differ in things of less concernment?" What must be done, then, is to "join with all our might in all we know, and with peaceable, quiet, humble spirits seek to know more and in the meantime carry ourselves humbly and peaceably toward those we differ from, and Christ will not charge us at the Great Day for retarding his cause."

V

The Restoration of the Stuarts marked the collapse of the attempt by the Independent divines to secure peace and unity among Christians by a frank recognition that no particular ecclesiastical structure could be identified in any exclusive sense with the whole church of Christ. Nevertheless, the defeat was only temporary. The fundamental convictions of the Independents concerning the nature of the church penetrated the thinking even of members of the episcopate; and as a result of the Act of Toleration of 1689, the establishment was given the formal status only of the greatest of the denominations. So thoroughly was the victory won that the leaders of the Evangelical Revival in England and America could take the denominational conception of the church largely for granted. By the twentieth century, with the exception of the Eastern Orthodox churches and some Anglo-Catholics, no serious dissent would be registered by members of the World Council of Churches to the observation by a Roman Catholic that, "when they speak of 'the Church,' documents emanating from the World Council . . . see this Church alike in each and every one of the various Christian denominations of which the Church is, as it were, the soul and, we might say, the sum total."

II

New Forms for a New Nation: Evangelical Denominationalism

2
Introduction

Recent studies of colonial America, aided by computer techniques and sociological and psychological theory, are providing tantalizing insights into early American social history. Works by Kenneth Lockridge, John Demos, Philip Greven, Richard Bushman, and others, while acknowledging the importance of the intellectual histories written and spawned by Perry Miller, have insisted that explanation of American life and institutions must rest on thorough analysis of the socio-dynamics of immigration, settlement, mobility, population growth, conflict, family life, and economic development. Timothy Smith's discussion of congregation and denomination brings such concerns to bear on the development of American religious institutions. Just as Winthrop Hudson's essay suggests levels of theological meaning in denominations which have often gone unacknowledged, so Smith's essay calls attention to a variety of social needs and social meanings that underlie the emergence of congregations initially and later denominations.

The article overflows with suggestions and theories that invite further exploration. He argues, as had William Warren Sweet earlier in relation to frontier religious bodies, that the fragile congregations erected in early American society were fundamental stabilizing institutions for communities and immigrant groups. Their significance is not exhausted by their maintenance of theological view, ecclesiastical form, and liturgical practice, nor by their nurturance of the religious life. These specifically "religious" factors were intimately related to a variety of social needs often not articulated except in religious form yet frequently met in religious life. New settlements, particularly outside New England—whether created by immigration from abroad or within the colonies—searching for resources of meaning, stability, communal discipline, education, reinforcement of family and community structure, relief from isolation and loneliness discovered that congregations and denominations voluntarily erected and maintained would have to suffice.

Denominationalism

The congregations and denominations came to bear functions—in addition to the religious and social ones they had performed in Europe—that in European society were carried out by kin-groups, the village, local religious and civil authorities, the state, and the culture. These voluntary institutions were forged by group after group as attempts to meet the fundamental social needs through colonial civil authorities and European religious authorities proved insufficient. The American voluntaristic religious patterns were largely the unintended religious solution to primary social needs of immigrant communities.

Smith's essay makes the denomination, then, a significant part of the process of creating society in America. It suggests that the primary religious institution was the congregation and that denominations were the necessary creation of congregations for their service. These insights have been obscured, mainly it would seem, by denominational self-conceptions honored by historians in the writing of denominational history. Those with congregational polity (Baptists, Disciples, and Congregationalists) have been reluctant to recognize their actual and needed denominationalism. The connectionalists (Episcopalians, Presbyterians, and Methodists) have been unwilling to understand the congregationalism that lurked within to challenge polity claims. Together such biases have clouded the primacy of the congregation and the functionality of the denomination. Ecclesiastical practice and theology have, of course, been significant realities in denominational life. They do need to be balanced by examination of the initial and changing social functions of both congregation and denomination and of the congregation-denomination relationship. Finally, Smith suggests that even revivalism is to be understood in terms of congregational formation and reinforcement.

Smith's intriguing theses should be explored, their implications for historical understanding and present strategies assessed, and their bearing on alternative theories examined. Are the theories of Winthrop Hudson and Timothy Smith, for instance, at odds or compatible? Has Smith minimized unnecessarily the theological or religious factors involved in denominational development? Are the social needs met by congregations and denominations relatively common and uniform? Do the primacy of the congregation and the derivative character of the denomination remain intact once revivalistic itinerancy and expansive evangelicalism appear? Do the Awakenings blur into the larger social process of community formation as Smith seems to imply? And, finally, how are Smith's theories reinforced by his other essay in this volume?

2

Congregation, State, and Denomination: The Forming of the American Religious Structure

Timothy L. Smith

The history of religion in America has seemed to most of its students a story best told in terms of the differences among denominations. To Philip Schaff's generation of church historians these differences seemed the outcome of varying doctrinal traditions. The Presbyterians were Calvinists, the Methodists Arminian; Baptists insisted upon a believer's church, while Anglicans revered the apostolic succession; hence the variations in their development. Shortly after World War I, another group of students set out to explain denominational patterns by means of sociological and economic analysis, following the example of the German scholar Ernst Troeltsch. They identified as "right wing" communions those in which liturgy and confessionalism were predominant—Roman Catholic, Lutheran, Anglican, and German Reformed. These represented the old social classes whose status, whether gentlemen, yeomen, or peasants, had traditionally been determined by their relationship to land. The Presbyterians, Congregationalists, and Friends, by contrast, ministered to the rising bourgeoisie, and the Methodists and the Baptists to the workers whom the commercial revolution had deprived of both status and property.

More recently still, Winthrop Hudson and Sidney Mead have proposed a context of interpretation which places the emphasis upon the emergence of denominationalism itself. First in Cromwell's England but more dramatically in colonial America, they have told us, Protestant dissenters

Reprinted, footnotes omitted, from the *William and Mary Quarterly*, 3rd ser., 25 (1968), 155-76 by permission of the author. Copyright 1968 by Timothy L. Smith. Footnotes available in *William and Mary Quarterly*.

came to see their communions not as established "churches" on one hand, or "sects" on the other, but as members of a family of related religious bodies called "denominations." All were heirs of a common faith and a common duty, and after the War for Independence all became partners in the task of remaking American society in the image of evangelical Protestantism. Denominationalism, thus conceived, is the opposite of sectarianism; for it admits no claim to an exclusive possession of saving truth.

Mead and others have explained the origin of this new system of religious order as in some degree a necessary adjustment of religious traditions to the fact of cultural diversity, as in part a response to the enactment of legal toleration, and, finally, as an effort to find a common front against the threat of barbarism and infidelity on the frontier. My aim in this essay is a modest one, namely, to show how denominations emerged out of the needs of congregations in a society where mobility even more than diversity made voluntary association the rule of religious life. Indeed, I think that all three of the denominational interpretations of American church history described above would gain new usefulness and precision from a fresh consideration of the nature, problems, and role of religious congregations in New World communities.

A combination of factors drew the European peasants away from their ties to heath and cottage, to village custom and parish church. The commercial revolution, beginning in the fourteenth and fifteenth centuries, transformed agriculture, affecting first the lower Rhine Valley and southern England, then, in widening circles century by century, the rest of Europe. An immense growth of population at the same time pressed in upon the available space. Poverty became a spreading plague which respected no national boundaries. The sons of both yeomen and gentry who lost out in the scramble for land at home slowly turned toward vacant territories elsewhere: east beyond the Elbe, west to North Ireland, the West Indies, and the continent of North America, and later, to South America, Africa, and Australia. Those who joined the great migrations were not simply lured by free land. The world of their fathers had begun to come apart long before, laying upon them the insecurity and the restless ambition that prepared them for the exodus. America was only one of several promised lands which beckoned to such men. Some of them saw the vision of Canaan earliest in spiritual or apocalyptic form, as Karl Mannheim has made plain in *Ideology and Utopia*. It ought not to surprise us, therefore, that when John Bunyan's England and the Rhineland which still remembered Muenster sent pilgrims to the American wilderness, they journeyed with both earth and heaven in view.

The ambitions and decisions of individuals distinguished this migration sharply from the *Volkwanderungen* of the Middle Ages. Single persons and small family units floated free of the web of community which had once enfolded their lives. Young people, more young men than women, and the landless ones at that, chose colonization most readily, whether in desperation to escape the clutch of poverty or in the hope of finding a better chance beyond the seas. What they seem to have wanted most was not the New Jerusalem but the old village and the familiar community their fathers had known, but reconstituted in such a way as to enable each man to own land outright, as his more fortunate cousins in Europe had managed to do. In the seventeenth century, on both sides of the Atlantic, peasants strove to become free farmers, yeomen to become gentlemen. Neither class realized how much and how long such strivings had contributed to the disruption of traditional patterns of life in the Old World, and how much more difficult they would make the task of creating stable communities in the New.

Family life in the early American settlements was especially lonely and insecure. In Virginia, it hardly existed at all at the beginning, since few women went to the colony until after the leaders of the London Company realized that their chance for profit lay in agriculture and trade, not gold. They hastened then to encourage families to emigrate, and sent out for the single men already there a shipload of at least technically marriageable maids. The "families" which some of these began at once to rear were not children of their own, but youngsters twelve years of age and older gathered off the streets of London and sent out at the same time to be apprenticed to planters in Virginia. Additional cargoes of both women and apprenticed children came in succeeding seasons, to form perhaps the most artificially contrived families known to history. One is not surprised to find how few of the women survived. Of 140 brought over in the years 1620–1622, 105 were in their graves by 1625. In New England, also, disease and unmanageable anxiety took a pathetic toll. Fifty of the passengers of the *Mayflower* died within seven months of their departure from Old Plymouth, among them all but a handful of the women and 14 of the 26 married men. In Charlestown, a little later, the children whom John Winthrop's diary praised for showing neither "fear or dismayedness" during the long voyage, and who joyfully gathered strawberries and wild roses the June afternoon they came off the ships, found their summer days filled with weary toil and their nights with multiplying fears. With winter came illness and death. "There is not a house," Thomas Dudley wrote, "where there is not one dead."

With the loneliness and the danger came also to these fragmented families what seemed by Old World standards an oppressive burden of hard work. Gone was the material heritage of the European village—the cottages and garden plots, the dam and the mill, the oven and threshing floor, the sheds and fences, roads and bridges which man and beast required. Even if the land had not lured tradesmen from their crafts, reconstructing the specialization of skills and the extensive division of labor that the colonists had known in Europe would have taken a generation. Nor had they found room aboard the ships for many of the tools and utensils they required. Homes had to be built at once, and crude furnishings—if possible, at least, a bed—fashioned out of materials found nearby. Fields must be cleared and planted and laboriously tended, and boats built by unaccustomed hands for fishing and for trade. They must soon begin the arduous toil of making linen cloth, using spinning wheels and looms also constructed on the spot. These would replace the garments which, brought over from Europe or meted out by masters at the end of the servant's term of indenture, were so quickly worn to shreds. The tasks of the family had thus multiplied enormously, but the hands to perform them were fewer. The old people and the maiden aunts who might have borne a share had not ventured across the sea. And the servants whom better-off families brought along struck out on their own as soon as law and circumstances permitted.

Little wonder that when respite came briefly from loneliness, danger, and toil, or when illness interrupted the busy round of life, weary minds threw a bridge of memory across the Atlantic and longed for the order and security of the villages they had left behind. In such moments was bred a deep hunger for kinship and community in the new settlements which they now must call home. But how did one create community, when the only kind he had known seemed a natural inheritance, not a human contrivance? The pattern of life in the European village and town had been marvelously intricate. Habits so deeply ingrained as to require little conscious thought regulated word, work, and worship. To each person and family belonged usually a status in the neighborhood, and a set of duties and privileges to fit it. To fashion new and equally secure relationships in the American wilderness seemed a task beyond mere human capacity. Simply to sign a compact aboard the *Mayflower*, or to create by decree a parish in Virginia, or to plat a Swiss township in Carolina, was not enough.

To men reared in an age of faith, this crisis of community inevitably seemed a religious one. They took it for granted that the church congregation must be the nucleus of all their new associations. Awe and reverence alone seemed to them able to generate the mystic force required to knit erstwhile strangers into units of belonging. They simply could not have dealt with the problem in a purely instrumental way, as modern Americans do, when with all the paraphernalia of P.T.A.'s, community centers, Kiwanis clubs, and backyard barbecues we lace ourselves into suburban togetherness.

Herein lies the meaning of the exaggerated emotions which characterized congregational life in the New World. In Virginia, it was not simply the heritage of reformation piety which, as Perry Miller has suggested, turned men's minds to God. The anxieties awakened by their taking leave of England and their arrival in America, strangers to one

51

another and in a strange land, also played a part. Likewise in New England, the solemn ceremonies of church founding and church joining bespoke a search for long lost community as well as a testimony to new-found grace. Later, Pennsylvania pietism, though originally imported from Europe, was nurtured by the need which both British and German immigrants felt for personal identity, for recognition and response, in a threatening wilderness.

John Winthrop's account of the troubles in the church at Watertown in 1631 and 1632 makes plain how the search for brotherly fellowship initially took precedence even over the concern for Puritan orthodoxy. The trouble began when Elder Richard Brown maintained, after a debate and decision of the congregation to the contrary, that "the churches of Rome were true churches." The people of Watertown invited Winthrop and other of the magistrates to sit with them in council on the matter. After a lengthy discussion, the divided flock "agreed to seek God in a day of humiliation, and so to have a solemn uniting." Meanwhile, they permitted the elder to retain both his opinions and his office. The strife continued, however, and the next year the congregation gave those who refused to take communion with Brown the choice of submission or excommunication. Eventually, to be sure, Brown was discharged from the eldership—not for his opinions, however, but on account of "his passion and distemper in speech, having been oft admonished."

In all the colonies, the early congregations were exceedingly fragile institutions. They were too new in their personnel, and too unstable in their structure to bear unaided the responsibility laid upon them to nurture a sense of spiritual kinship in the neighborhood or to provide for the education of children. None was, as far as I have been able to discover, a bodily transplantation from Europe, with pastor, elders, or deacons, and lesser officers intact and with each communicant bearing in his heart the memory of his place in the village status system at home. Those about whose history this legend clings—as, for example, the founders of Plymouth and Dorchester in early Massachusetts, the Baptist company which settled first in Rehoboth and then in

Swansea after the Restoration, or the Welsh Friends who a bit later colonized Merion, Pennsylvania—were at most only fragments of churches recently "gathered" in Europe. More typical, indeed, was a great diversity of background, especially in the larger towns like Boston, New Amsterdam, Philadelphia, and Charleston.

The Boston church, organized in midsummer 1630 among the ill and troubled settlers who were soon to flee the reeking squalor of Charlestown Hill, received new members each time a ship from England anchored in the harbor. John Cotton arrived in 1633, with some of his former parishioners as well as others from East Anglia, desiring to "sit down where they might keep store of cattle." Their pastor was soon persuaded to become teacher in the church at Boston, however, and to allow his own flock to be scattered throughout the town. Cotton began his ministry in the Puritan city with a brave statement on the sovereignty of the congregation. He wound up some years later at the head of the movement which imposed synodical order on the New England churches. In the interim, of course, Mistress Anne Hutchinson had arrived and, gathering about herself a coterie of true believers, had nearly torn the Boston congregation and community to shreds. Her movement, and the response of the clergy and magistrates to it, reflected both the consistencies and the contradictions between Puritan ideals of social order and personal religious experience, to be sure. But it also owed something, I believe, to the simple fact that this and other Massachusetts congregations were composed of persons new to one another, and in a new land. Many were profoundly disturbed by the hazards, known and unknown, which lay before them, and by the memory of the ordeal of migration which they had just passed through. They fell easy prey to the emotionalism and the egotism of the magnetic personalities whose teachings highlighted their sense of social and spiritual estrangement.

The situation in New Amsterdam was even more confused, but completely typical of the tenuous character of congregational life in the Middle Colonies. When Jonas Michaelius administered the first communion on Manhattan

Island in 1628, the fifty whom he admitted to the sacrament were a motley group indeed. Part were Dutch and part French-speaking Walloons. Some came on their first confession of faith and some by church certificate. A large number, however, having either misplaced their certificates of membership or neglected to bring them to America, "not thinking that a church would be formed and established here," were admitted on the testimony of persons who had known them in Europe. Matters improved but slowly in succeeding years, chiefly because the Dutch West India Company persisted for two decades more in policies suitable only for the operation of a trading post. All the residents were under contract to the company, and enjoyed none of the municipal liberties which in Holland were the backbone of Dutch freedom. The discontinuity between congregation and community proved disastrous. Little sense of social unity developed, and almost no commitment to a common dream of the colony's future. The education of children and young people inevitably suffered.

The Friends and other dissenters who first settled West New Jersey were chiefly English in origin and shared a similar religious outlook. But the individual members of each congregation were drawn from widely separated villages and towns in Britain. Similarly, at Germantown, the Mennonite Francis Daniel Pastorius found the problem of establishing a sense of community among the mechanics and weavers who comprised the original settlement almost unmanageable. They were natives of various localities in the Rhineland and represented every shade of religious opinion. Pastorius described the ship on which he came over as a veritable "Noah's Ark" of different faiths. In his own household of servants were those who clung, he said, "to the Roman, to the Lutheran, to the Calvinistic, to the Anabaptist, and to the Anglican church, and only one Quaker." The legal bond to the community which he tried to fashion was William Penn's rule requiring corporate settlement. Its spiritual heart proved to be nationality—Pastorius's accent on German municipal law and the use of the German language in church, school, and social discourse.

Once established, however, the seventeenth-century congregations found that other factors besides diversity of origin restricted their ability to bring solidarity to the neighborhood or security to family life. One was that the churches, like the villages whose corporate life they helped to sustain, were subject to constant attrition from the removal of their members to new lands nearby. The larger number of these migrants were poor men, chiefly latecomers or servants who had completed their terms of indenture. Such persons needed even more than others the anchor of faith and communal discipline. In each colony they helped create a second tier of towns whose organic life was as unstable as the first. Charles Francis Adams's description of the origin of the Braintree congregation and Ola Winslow's account of the long search for seven worthy "pillars" for the church in Dedham make this fact clear. An equally troublesome hindrance was the divisive nature of the Christian faith itself, especially those radical versions of it which took root in the New World. Congregations preoccupied with fencing the Lord's table were not creating a community so much as playing odd man out. When the odd men proved to be citizens whose political and financial privileges were restricted, or who differed from the majority in language or national origin, control of the congregation by a clan of first settlers could undermine the unity of a neighborhood.

The religious congregation, therefore, like the family, suffered profound shock from the fragmentation and uprooting which migration to the New World involved. Yet its responsibility for the welfare of its members had greatly increased. Here, again, the tasks were many but the hands to perform them were few.

The seventeenth-century settlers turned instinctively to the political authorities for aid, regardless of the theory of church-state relationships they had held in Europe. The earliest American tradition became, therefore, not religious liberty, but state control. The difficulties which beset the first attempts of congregations to establish community life on a religious basis largely explain this development. The actions of provincial governments and county courts in ecclesiastical, moral, and educational matters aimed not at displacing the family and the congregation by a "secular" authority but at supporting their efforts to stabilize behavior in a mobile and remarkably pluralistic setting. Nor was the establishment of democracy or aristocracy the primary issue, for the experience of the first settlers was limited to a hierarchical status system, and they expected nothing different here. To them, as Bernard Bailyn has pointed out, the larger problem was the threat of social disorder, of barbarization, which hung over their common enterprise. They believed the creation of a Christian community was the only reliable protection from this threat.

At its initial meeting in 1619, for example, the Virginia House of Burgesses gave attention first to legislation requiring church attendance, forbidding idleness, gaming, drunkenness, and "excesse" of apparel, and laying heavy penalties upon adulterers, gossipers, and sowers of dissension. Succeeding sessions extended such godly watch-care to other matters as well. Here, as later in New England, the full power of the law supported a weakened church in the task of cementing neighborhoods together. Soon, however, tobacco planting encouraged a scattering of families which made the development of cohesive congregations virtually impossible. Thereafter, Virginia's illness, as contemporaries saw clearly, was the "scattered planting" which tobacco culture and bound labor made profitable. *Virginia's Cure*, as the title of a tract of 1662 put it, was the recovery of community by a forced-birth process. The author proposed that the generosity of Londoners be tapped for funds to build a town in every county of the colony, where planters might be directed to gather with their families and servants on weekends for worship and the instruction of the young. The idea seems absurd, until we reflect that this is exactly what intensive agriculture, communal settlement, and the Puritan instinct for organization made possible in New England during these years.

In the Middle Colonies, the diversity of religious traditions was from the outset a barrier to effective state action. In 1649, Johannes Megapolensis, having ended his tour of duty as pastor at Killiaen Van Rensselaer's settlement on the Hudson River, agreed to take charge of the struggling Dutch church in New Amsterdam. Megapolensis spent the remainder of his life there trying with Peter Stuyvesant's help to create a religious basis for communal solidarity. He urged the Classis of Amsterdam to request that the trading company close New Netherland to Jews and Quakers, and prohibit Lutheran ministers from exercising their office there. He also proposed that the company underwrite the salaries of both English and Dutch Calvinist clergymen. Governor Stuyvesant and the burgomasters supported these proposals heartily. But if the Classis acted upon the pastor's recommendations, it had no effect at all upon the West India Company. Instead, the directors admonished the governor sharply that the religious toleration which had drawn so many useful citizens to old Amsterdam would be their policy for the new.

When the English captured New Netherland in 1664, the Duke of York proclaimed a religious establishment which was similar in aim to the plan which Megapolensis had urged upon the Dutch authorities a decade before, but which took fully into account the fact of religious diversity. The freeholders of each village were to choose their faith and elect a pastor, but the public treasury would support him. Whenever a dissenting group in any community became numerous enough, they were to be free to organize their own congregation, and have their minister also placed on state support. Though Anglicanism gained a foothold through the operation of this system, it was neither in form nor in purpose an outgrowth of English tradition, but a new departure designed to deal practically with the problem of social order in a pioneer society. The Duke's Laws in fact paved the way for the development of several denominations in the colony during the succeeding century.

Pennsylvania passed through the same cycle somewhat more rapidly. William Penn was as troubled as any man of the time by the disintegration of family life which poverty and the increasing instability of village social life had produced. Yet he was opposed on principle to any effort by the state to impose a uniformity of faith. To be sure, Penn had no fears for the survival in America of his own sect. The Society of Friends had learned in England and elsewhere to rely upon the traveling ministry, the circulation of letters

57

from George Fox and other leaders, and the system of monthly, quarterly, and yearly meetings to maintain congregational discipline and family order among a mobile and minority people. But what of the other wanderers who, he hoped, would find their way from Britain and Germany to the colony which bore his name?

Penn concluded that a commonwealth founded on the principle of brotherly love must provide by law a framework of community which would stand above the differences in religion that every settlement was bound to display. He announced in 1681 that his lands in the New World would be sold in such a way as to require people to settle in hamlets of at least ten families, situated in the midst of townships containing 5,000 acres. Of this requirement, Penn wrote four years later, "I had in my view Society, Assistance, Busy Commerce, Instruction of Youth, Government of Peoples manners, Conveniency of Religious Assembling, Encouragement of Mechanicks, distinct and beaten Roads, and it has answered in all those respects, I think, to an Universall Content." Penn appealed to neither English tradition nor Quaker theory in justifying this close regulation of community life. He simply feared that without it, a dissolution of social bonds would occur, giving rise to conditions that would "tempt the people to frivolity." Enforcement of the requirement, however, did not outlast the first generation. Like subsequent efforts to establish community by decree in South Carolina and Georgia, Penn's framework succumbed to the confusion of economic with idealistic motives, the rivalry of religious and national traditions, the reluctance of Englishmen to transfer control of communal matters from local to central authorities, and the democratic tendencies of popular political sentiment.

Behind these factors lay also a larger obstruction: laws and decrees, however reasoned, could not reach the men of Penn's generation at the deeper emotional levels where the problem of community had to be worked out. Nor did the cultivation of a distinctive language or national culture, as at Germantown, prove an adequate substitute; for the Germans were themselves sharply divided in their religious loyalties. A sense of spiritual and moral kinship, rooted in voluntary adherence to a congregation, was to remain throughout the eighteenth century and long beyond the key to neighborhood stability, ordered family life, and the education of children. Legislation having proved inadequate, pastors and lay leaders of each persuasion united to form an intercolonial association to counter the weaknesses stemming from the diversity and mobility of the membership of congregations. These associations, later called denominations, became in the eighteenth century the mainstay of beleaguered local brotherhoods. Not until the end of the War for Independence, however, did Americans realize fully what had happened. The actions which they took then in ecclesiastical and constitutional conventions, and the debates which attended those actions, ratified in both law and ideology the system of denominationalism that had been for decades a central fact of their social experience.

A farsighted Englishman, Thomas Bray, was the first clergyman in the state-church tradition to grasp fully the new situation. He organized the Society for Promoting Christian Knowledge in 1699, to give permanence to his earlier program of raising funds for parish schools and libraries in Britain and America. Then, after a tour of duty in Maryland as commissary for the Bishop of London, he founded in 1701 the Society for the Propagation of the Gospel in Foreign Parts. The aim of this second organization was to raise money in the homeland to support clergymen and schoolmasters in colonial parishes. Some of Bray's disingenuous successors, and many of the clergymen whom the society subsidized, used the resources of both organizations in vain efforts to promote an establishment of religion in America. But the main thrust of Anglican activity in the eighteenth-century colonies was consistent with the emerging denominational principle that education and evangelism, in which different communions would both cooperate and compete, must propagate the Christian faith independently of civil power.

The impetus to centralized order in other churches that had enjoyed legal establishment in Europe came not from the homeland but from the colonies. As early as 1709, the Presbytery of Philadelphia began sending annual appeals for aid to the dissenting clergymen of London, the Synod of Glasgow, and the Presbytery of Dublin. The Pennsylvania preachers recounted "the desolate condition of sundry vacant places" and pointedly reminded the Presbyterians in Scotland of the generosity and zeal of the Anglican society. In 1719, having had little success, they set out to collect money from their stronger congregations in America, thus initiating the Presbyterian Ministers Fund. The pattern of native denominationalism took shape rapidly thereafter in declarations of doctrinal uniformity, in concern for the proper preparation of ministers, and in the establishment of a synod for the New World. In 1734, at the behest of Gilbert Tennent, the synod resolved, in order "to revive the declining power of godliness," to inquire carefully of each pastor whether and how he discharged his duty toward the young people of his congregation, "in a way of catechizing and familiar instruction," and whether and in what manner he visited his flock and instructed them from house to house. The spiritual awakening which followed these and other measures as Tennent and his log-college preachers sought out the Scotch-Irish on rural as well as urban frontiers is a familiar story. The emotions which they discovered in themselves and in their hearers signified more than simply a resurrection of Old World faith and discipline. As in the earliest colonial congregations, a reconstruction of family and community life was in progress; now, however, denominational order, rather than the decrees of a godly commonwealth, was helping to make it possible.

Precisely the same thing happened earlier when the Classis of Amsterdam sent Theodore J. Frelinghuysen to New Jersey, in response to an appeal from Dutch Reformed congregations struggling to establish themselves in Raritan Valley. Pastors of the wealthy Dutch churches in New York City protested Frelinghuysen's direct and earnest evangelism. Looking to the past instead of the future, they sought to have him recalled. Although the fathers in Amsterdam deferred action for a time, they at last concluded that voluntary structure and revival fervor must go hand in hand, and supported Frelinghuysen heartily.

The story of the Baptists, who were everywhere a minority

group, without a formally educated clergy, and in principle opposed to centralized direction, illustrates nascent denominationalism at the opposite ecclesiastical pole. The social and spiritual conditions of their progress in America made each Baptist congregation the center of a familial community. Closed communion, the kiss of charity, the rite of immersion, and, in some places, the admission to membership of "devoted children" explicitly affirmed the individual believer's identity with his spiritual kin. Yet associations slowly became the rule, following the early example of Rhode Island and Philadelphia.

A contemporary description of the ritual by which new congregations were formed in eighteenth-century North Carolina illustrates how the interdependence of Baptist churches emerged. The ritual echoed the marriage ceremony in the *Book of Common Prayer*. A group of members either living or planning to move a distance from the meetinghouse first requested permission to establish a new church. This voted, the entire parent congregation assembled on a day appointed for fasting and prayer, during which the prospective members presented their names and their individual certificates of dismissal. The minister then solemnly inquired whether they desired to become "a church," whether their habitations were "near enough to each other, conveniently to attend church conferences," whether they were "so well acquainted with each other's life and conversation as to coalesce into one body, and walk together in love and fellowship," and whether it was "their intention to *keep up a regular discipline* agreeably to the scriptures." These questions having been answered in the affirmative, the members of the new group repeated and signed a covenant, pledging themselves not only to observe the usual religious duties but "in brotherly love to pray for each other, to watch over one another, and if need be, in the most tender and affectionate manner to reprove one another." The minister then said, mentioning each person individually, "In the name of our Lord Jesus Christ, and by the authority of our office, we pronounce you . . . a true *gospel church*."

Obviously, the farmer-preachers had not found this ritual in the New Testament; it represented, rather, a folk accommodation to geographic mobility which was by then an established Baptist tradition. On all the American frontiers, "mother" congregations exercised spiritual discipline over their "daughter" churches during the years when regional associations were weak or nonexistent. Traveling Baptist evangelists, as in the case of the Society of Friends, provided additional direction, as did the circulation of approved books and tracts. None of these measures, however, violated the principle of congregational autonomy. Thus emerged out of necessity and experience a denomination whose cohesion has ever since belied the apparent lack of formal ties.

Congregations of the German "sects"—Mennonite, Dunker, Amish, and Moravian—had learned by long experience in Europe similar ways of protecting their members from the perils of the wilderness errand. As with the Baptists, initiation to their circles of familial fellowship came by way of both birth and the new birth. Love feasts, foot washings, the holy kiss, and rigid rules of dress and behavior separated the true believers from the unordered and hence "sinful" world outside.

Moravian history illustrates the connection between such intimate congregational practices and the development of a denominational consciousness. In 1722, Count Zinzendorf invited Brethren who were suffering persecution to settle on his estate near Berthelsdorf, in Moravia. The refugees soon discovered that the parish church nearby must continue to serve the needs of the local peasantry, rather than the gathered community. They began meeting separately, therefore, first for "love feasts," then in intimate groups called "bands" or "classes." Households of unmarried men and unmarried women soon appeared, testifying to the disintegration of family life which their migration had involved. Shortly, also, an elaborate program of missions to the world outside signaled their recognition that the spiritual community had a function, a peculiar calling, in an age when men at all social levels suffered from the dissolution of custom and kinship. Once created, such a community was itself exportable, mobile; its roots were not in the soil of Bohemia but in the souls of troubled men. In the 1730's Peter Bohler drew together a company of such migrants in London. A few years later, on board a vessel bound for Pennsylvania—a moving frontier if ever there was one—Bohler organized the "First Sea Congregation" to maintain discipline and cultivate brotherly love until the group reached the wilderness Zion which Zinzendorf was preparing for them at Bethlehem.

By contrast, a few ministers of the Lutheran or German Reformed churches accompanied redemptioners of their faith as they passed through what Oscar Handlin has called the "brutal filter" of migration to the New World. In small groups at best, sometimes singly or by individual families, they departed on foot from their villages for the ports of embarkation. Then followed anxiety and often illness aboard the immigrant ships, and the pathetic but what they hoped would be temporary separation of families by the sale of their labor under articles of indenture at dockside in Philadelphia or Charleston. The reunion of these fragmented families after their years of service were over, their journey a short distance into the wilderness, and the discovery of their fellows in the newly joyous emotions of congregational life all took place without the help of the clergymen they had relied upon in Europe. They often built schoolhouses before they erected chapels, pressing into service teachers of varying degrees of worthiness, not infrequently indentured servants as they had themselves recently been. The school-masters taught the children to read, write, and sing and, in time-honored German fashion, led the hymns at worship, cleaned and warmed the church, and in the absence of a clergyman read the liturgy as well. John Philip Boehm, one of the most able of these schoolmasters, later told how, being unordained, he had for five years resisted the pleas of three Pennsylvania settlements of Reformed Germans to become their pastor, only to see the people become "much scattered," like "wandering sheep having no shepherd." He relented finally, in a tearful scene when, as he said,

"With humbleness of heart I addressed myself to the Lord's work, and drew up with my brethren, as well as we could, a Constitution of the church, so that all things might be done in good order. . . . When the Constitution had been presented to and accepted by the whole people I was regularly elected by each one of the congregations, and a formal call was extended to me by the elders. Whereupon I began the ministry of the Lord in his name."

Clearly, in such a body, pietistic sentiments would prevail whatever the beliefs of the members had been before they left Europe. And democratic church government was a natural corollary of the brotherly emotions at work.

Boehm wrote repeatedly to the Classis of Amsterdam during these years, imploring them to send ministers and schoolmasters to Pennsylvania. A young Swiss clergyman, Michael Schlatter, finally arrived in response to these pleas in 1747. Meanwhile, Lutheran congregations in Pennsylvania, Virginia, and the Carolinas sent representatives to Germany seeking similar aid. The result was the establishment of another missionary center, at the University of Halle; from there Henry Melchior Muhlenberg came to Philadelphia in 1742. Both Schlatter and Muhlenberg arrived armed with funds to subsidize the salaries of pastors and teachers. Both sent back immediate and urgent appeals for much greater assistance. As a result of their labors, churches from Pennsylvania to Georgia pledged themselves by families to the support of the ministers they hoped to receive, revised both their doctrines and their practices to harmonize with denominational objectives, and willingly placed themselves under the supervision of authorities three thousand miles away.

The emotions with which isolated Lutheran and Reformed congregations received the ministry of these missionaries from their homeland produced scenes like those which in other communions have been ascribed to the Great Awakening. At Frederick, Maryland, for example, on his first tour of the Potomac region, Schlatter found a Reformed group worshiping in their schoolhouse and erecting a church building, though they had never had a pastor. He returned a few weeks later to preside at the dedication of the sanctuary. "When I was preparing myself for the first prayer," he wrote his sponsors in Amsterdam, "and saw the tears of the spiritually hungry souls roll down over their cheeks, my heart was singularly moved and enkindled with love, so that

I fell upon my knees . . . the whole congregation followed me, and with much love and holy desire I . . . wrestled for a blessing from the Lord upon them." After the sermon, he administered communion to ninety-seven members, baptized several children and older persons, married three betrothed couples, and installed new elders and deacons. This congregation owed much of its health to the schoolmaster, he declared, the best one he had met in America. By 1751, Schlatter had taken forty-six congregations under his care, all of them having been born of lay initiative, and many of them served previously by ministers whom neither God nor man, seemingly, had ordained. Through the years, their people had clung to one another steadily, finding fellowship and identity through a familiar tongue and ritual in a world where all else was strange.

Schlatter made important departures from European customs of church government in the process of creating the German Reformed denomination in America. He invariably dealt first with whole congregations, rather than with a board of deacons or elders. Like the pastors whom he placed elsewhere, he was himself called to his Philadelphia charge by vote of all the adult male members. He defended this procedure, in a letter to the Classis in Amsterdam, by reference to the "custom of taking a vote prevalent in Switzerland in great state assemblies, in which a majority of raised hands decides the question at issue." Such a statement might pass at face value among advocates of the germ theory of history. But democratically-governed congregations were implicit in the American religious situation from the beginning. That denominational structures eventually arose in response to the demands of such congregations strengthened the democratic tendency in all communions. And the emotional scenes which accompanied these developments seemed to participants to sanctify the whole.

Viewing in retrospect the entire history of colonial Protestantism, I think the use of the term "Great Awakening" to describe the wide-spread effort to solve the problems of evangelism, of education, and of congregational order which took place in the eighteenth century serves more to confuse than to clarify our understanding of what was happening.

Denominationalism

What we have called the "Awakening" certainly occurred at widely separated times and places. It began, perhaps we may say, with Frelinghuysen's labors in New Jersey, and it burned out (or, possibly simply took off across the mountains) on the Carolina frontier in the 1790's. With a little more imagination, one might say it began with John Cotton's arrival in Boston and continued, but did not stop, with Daddy Grace.

Another and less mysterious way of looking at these events would be to say simply that revivalism in American history has generally served communal purposes. Its major achievement has been to forge the links which bound together the two kinds of new voluntary associations that have provided for the people's religious needs: first congregations, and then, denominations. What was called an "effusion of the Holy Spirit" signified to participants a divine sanction upon their new arrangements, and meanwhile convinced onlooking members of other evangelical sects that the new organization should be recognized as a member of the family of Christian communions. The result, in the long succession of events, was to nurture the American Protestant consensus, the community of feeling and aspiration which in the nineteenth century helped give the nation itself a sense of oneness.

In summary, then, it seems to me that the colonists' departure from the society of village and kin-group they had known in Europe, and the establishment and repeated disruption of new patterns of family and neighborhood life in the wilderness, made the quest of community a central feature of early American experience. For large numbers of settlers, that quest was essentially religious. The worshiping brotherhood became the pivot upon which both tradition and innovation turned. Congregations, new and fragile, could not stand alone, however. They first looked to the colonial governments to strengthen and support them, thus reaffirming the interdependence of state and church which many of them professed to have sought by migration to escape. By the end of the first century of colonization, however, increasing diversity of belief made legislation in matters of religion impractical, while political and theological conviction made it unacceptable. Early in the eighteenth century, therefore, voluntary national associations of congregations recognizing a similar European background took over from the provincial governments the task of providing support and discipline for local religious communities. This happened at the prompting of the congregations themselves, and without regard to the doctrines of church government they had espoused before. The emotional fervor of religious revivals, whether regarded hitherto as a part of the so-called "Great Awakening" or not, cemented these new unions, making organizations organisms, denominations, "communions."

Neither revivalism nor denominationalism was an exclusively New World plant, to be sure. Both simply flowered earlier and more luxuriantly in America. The new institutional forms that they sustained—missionary funds and boards, charity schools, publishing societies, denominational academies and colleges, and techniques of supervising congregational life—were in fact the inventions of European churchmen who were concerned for the welfare of their uprooted brethren, in the homeland as well as overseas. By the nineteenth century, the quickening pace of urbanization made it clear that the migrations which had begun in the sixteenth and seventeenth centuries had prompted in both the Old World and the New an extensive reorganization of Protestant religious life. Its basis was consent. Persuading men to make and keep the commitments necessary to voluntary association was now the churches' central task.

3

Introduction

In his essays over the years Sidney E. Mead has shown a remarkable facility for grasping the inner principle, what the Germans might term the "spirit" of historical topics. Nowhere is the gift more evident than in the following essay. Here Mead deftly sketches the distinctive features or traits of American denominationalism. Mead is not concerned with morphology, with structural characteristics, with constitution or polity, with the theological or confessional facial features—the factors often treated as definitive of denominations. Nor is his discussion one which honors what seems most troubling to theologians and critics—the fact of divisions, the distinctiveness of each denomination, the schismatic character of denominationalism. Rather Mead, while dealing with such issues, cuts through the tissue of the denomination to disclose the vital forces which give life. The surgery reveals a number of energies—six major ones and numerous subsidiary energies—which animate the American denomination, making it at once a distinctive expression of the church and—like the American corporation—a common reality individualized in a variety of ways. In contrast to H. Richard Niebuhr's *Social Sources of Denominationalism*, which characterizes the denomination and denominationalism in terms of the social factors of class, caste, race, and section which divide, Mead characterizes the denomination and denominationalism by traits which unite.

Several other observations follow. First, Mead's portrait of his subject as an abstraction or generalization from the concrete possesses both the strengths and weaknesses of such an approach. Certain qualifications are necessary, many of which Mead notes. The reader, for example, may wish to reflect on the appropriateness of Mead's discussion to particular denominations. The strength of his approach is that it provides for the historian what the sociologist gains through the looking glass "ideal types." Other historians and Mead himself have tended to ignore the church-denomination-sect ideal typology and prefer Mead's portrayal as a more faithful idealization than that of the sociologists. The preference is clearly a perspectival one.

The historian desires a characterization that for a certain time and place aptly captures a movement. The sociologist, concerned for instance with the nature of authority, will doubtless find the Weber-Troeltsch typology and the continuing refinements of it more satisfying. The reader should use this as an occasion for judging what are the merits and weaknesses of the historical approach found in this essay and this volume.

Second, Mead suggests that the years 1787–1850 constitute the formative period for American denominationalism. Then, under conditions of religious freedom, the opportunity and challenge of an expanding population and religious pluralism, the distinctive form and defining traits of the denomination were forged. The denomination emerged as a purposive form. The reader should compare the depiction of the denomination in "Congregation, State, and Denomination"; Timothy Smith ranges in time but seems to take earlier and settlement periods as formative. Are the two treatments of the denomination compatible? Are different and successive expressions of the denomination brought under discussion?

Third, Mead's choice of period is closely related to what his critics regard as a restricted or limited treatment, an analysis of evangelical denominations and denominationalism defined in their own terms. Mead's traits emerge during this period of evangelical ascendency. They are, perhaps, less appropriate for ethnic denominations (Lutheran), for black denominations, for non-Evangelical denominations (Unitarians), and for the mainstream denominations after this evangelical period. The issues can be seen by contrasting Mead's discussion with that of E. Franklin Frazier, Martin E. Marty, or Timothy Smith. After comparing the conception of denominationalism in these essays, the reader may want to consider whether with certain modifications Mead's traits define a dominant or mainstream type of denominationalism, a model of the denomination toward which black, ethnic, or non-Evangelical denominations tend as they become more middle-class, mainstream, or acculturated.

Finally, the reader should explore Mead's suggestion that sectarian voluntaristic, missionary, revivalistic, pietistic, competitive denominations are bonded to the distinctive traits. Denominations experience crisis—for instance, when the missionary purpose which defines them is lost or displaced. To what extent have new traits replaced those described by Mead? What are the effects of commitment to new purposes by important segments of these purposive organizations?

3

Denominationalism: The Shape of Protestantism in America

Sidney E. Mead

The Christianity which developed in the United States [after 1800] was unique. It displayed features which marked it as distinct from previous Christianity in any other land. In the nineteenth and twentieth centuries the Christianity of Canada most nearly resembled it, but even that was not precisely like it.

Professor Latourette's generalization applies primarily to the institutional forms rather than to the theology of Christianity in the United States, which latter has been surprisingly derivative—lacking in originality, uniqueness, and distinctiveness.

The basis of this institutional uniqueness has been the "free church" idea. The phrase "free churches" is used in various and confusing ways—sometimes to designate those churches of congregational polity, sometimes those peculiarly distinguished by their "liberal" views. But most properly the phrase designates those churches under the system of separation of Church and State. Here the qualifyng word "free" is used in the basic sense of independent and autonomous, and in the context of long tradition thus designates those churches that are independent of the State and autonomous in relation to it.

The denomination is the organizational form which the "free churches" have accepted and assumed. It was evolved in the United States under the complex and peculiar situation that there existed between the Revolution and the Civil War.

The denomination, unlike the traditional forms of the

Reprinted, footnotes omitted, with the permission of *Church History* and the author. Footnotes available in *Church History*, 23 (1954), 291-320. Previously reprinted in *The Lively Experiment* by Harper & Row, Publishers, in 1963.

Church, is not primarily confessional, and it is certainly not territorial. Rather it is purposive. And unlike any previous "church" in Christendom, it has no official connection with a civil power whatsoever. A "church" as "church" has no legal existence in the United States, but is represented legally by a civil corporation in whose name the property is held and the necessary business transacted. Neither is the denomination a "sect" in any traditional sense, and certainly not in the most common sense of a dissenting body in relationship to an Established Church. It is, rather, a voluntary association of like-hearted and like-minded individuals, who are united on the basis of common beliefs for the purpose of accomplishing tangible and defined objectives. One of the primary objectives is the propagation of its point of view, which it in some sense holds to be "true." Hence to try to divide the many religious bodies in the United States under the categories of "church" and "sect" is usually more confusing than helpful, especially since by long custom "church" is commonly used in a way that implies approbation, and "sect" in a way that implies derogation.

Keeping these considerations in mind, however, I have for the sake of variety followed the practice common in America when discussing the Protestant bodies, of using the words "church," "sect," and "denomination" as synonymous.

It is the purpose of this paper to delineate some elements that were woven into the denominational structure during the formative years, and to suggest how these elements have conditioned the thought, life, and work of American Protestantism down to the present.

I

In Christendom from the fourth century to the end of the eighteenth Christianity was organized in an Established Church or Churches. The one Church reached its peak in expression and power during the twelfth and thirteenth centuries. At that time it actually possessed and wielded tremendous tangible, overt power in the affairs of men, and more subtly tremendous and formative cultural power in the souls of men. The heart of this Church was creedal or

71

confessional belief in supernatural power mediated to men through the sacraments. It claimed inclusiveness and universality as the one true Church of Christ on earth, but by the same token it was necessarily exclusive. Outside the Church and its sacraments there was no salvation, although this had to be asserted with humility because ultimately only God knew his own with certainty.

The Reformation broke up this tangible unity of the one Church in Christendom. On the one hand its claim to be, not a revolt *from* the Church but merely an attempt to reform the church within and on the true principles of the Church itself, was inherently valid. But on the other hand the true principles of the Church had become so inextricably mingled with the organizational forms and practices that honest re-formation meant revolt from the existing institution. This movement coincided with the emergence into self-consciousness of the modern nations, back of which were the complex economic, social, and political movements that ushered in and have shaped modern western civilization.

Inevitably the spiritual reformation and consequent institutional fragmentation of the Church developed affinities with the rising national consciousness—and found physical protective power in the new states to oppose the physical power controlled by Rome. Thus the one re-formation of the Church found diverse expressions in the nations— Lutheranism within the realms of the German princes and the Scandinavian countries, Anglicanism in England, Reformed in Geneva and Scotland, and so on.

The conflict culminated in the Thirty Years War that devastated Europe. The Westphalian settlements of 1648 marked a grudging recognition of the necessity to live-and-let-live within the several territorial areas. The basis for the churches that thus emerged was both confessional and territorial. And each of these churches in its own territory and in its own way continued to make the claims traditionally made by the one true Church. Each as a Church assumed the traditional responsibilities, and each clung to the long established principle of religious uniformity enforced by the civil power within a commonwealth. These were the churches of the "right-wing."

Meanwhile in the turmoil of re-formation had emerged certain "heretical" individuals and movements that, appealing to the commonly accepted authority of Scripture, began to claim freedom of religious belief and expression as a right. These were the "sects" of the "left-wing." They were voluntary groups without status or social responsibility and power. From the viewpoint of the official churches they were schismatic as well as heretical, and hence thought to be subversive of all order and government whether civil or ecclesiastical. And so almost universally strenuous repressive measures were invoked against them.

II

Representatives of practically all the religious groups of Europe, both "right" and "left" wing, were transplanted to that part of America that was to become the United States. There they learned in a relatively short time to live together in peace under the genial aegis of the Dutch and English combination of patriotic-religious fervor, toleration, cynicism, simple desire for profits, efficacious muddling through, and "salutary neglect" that made up the colonial policy of these nations. The eventual result was that by 1787, after independence was won, it was recognized that if there was to be a United States of America, then religious freedom had to be written into the new national constitution.

It was of course recognized that this was a departure from the prevailing tradition of almost fourteen hundred years standing in Christendom. But by this time many both within and without the religious groups were in a mood to agree with Thomas Jefferson:

As to tradition, if we are Protestants we reject all tradition, and rely on the scripture alone, for that is the essence and common principle of all the protestant churches.

Even so, the transplanted offshoots of Europe's State Churches—the "right-wing" groups—retained their position of prestige and dominance in the new land throughout the colonial period. At the close of the Revolution the four largest and most powerful religious groups were the Congregationalists, the Anglicans, the Baptists, and the Presbyterians. Of these four, the Baptist "sect" held nowhere near the position of power and respect accorded the other three. Fifth in size were the Lutherans, sixth the German Reformed, and seventh the Dutch Reformed. Meanwhile the Methodist body, still in swaddling clothes in the Anglican manger, was twelfth in size.

To be sure the dominant, powerful and respected "right-wing" churches had experienced considerable internal change during the vicissitudes of the colonial period, and especially during the upheavals growing out of the great revivals. But there was as yet little indication and less awareness that the church patterns of America would be markedly different from those of Europe. Hence Ezra Stiles' prediction in 1783 that no doubt the future of Christianity in America would lie about equally with Congregationalists, Presbyterians, and Episcopalians, seemed eminently plausible.

The radical change in the relative size of the religious bodies in America took place during the brief period between roughly 1787 and 1850. By the latter date the Roman Catholic church, which at the close of the Revolution was tenth in point of size and everywhere except in Pennsylvania laboring under some civil restrictions, was the largest. Second in size were the Methodists, followed by the Baptists, Presbyterians, Congregationalists, and Lutherans. Seventh in size were the Disciples—an upstart group less than twenty years old. The Protestant Episcopal church had fallen to eighth place, while perhaps most amazing of all, Joseph Smith's Mormons were ninth.

Since this configuration of relative size has persisted in the United States for about a century—with a few notable exceptions such as the Congregationalists' drop from fifth to ninth place—we may speak of this period as the "formative" years for the American denominations. The story of the numerical growth and geographical expansion of the several ecclesiastical institutions, while by no means complete in every detail is sufficiently well established for the immediate purposes of this paper.

III

Our concern is with the mind and spirit of these "free" churches—their genius which was woven from many diverse strands during this formative period and has continued largely to define their direction, life, and work down to the present.

Religious freedom and the "frontier" provided the broad ideological and geographical setting in which these developments took place. The first meant the removal of traditional civil and ecclesiastical restrictions on vocal and organizational expressions of the religious convictions and even the whimsies of all men. The "frontier" provided the necessary space and opportunities in which such expressions could thrive. It was this combination of freedom and opportunity in all areas that made this period what Whitehead called it, the "Epic Epoch of American life"—the period of "Freedom's Ferment" as Alice Felt Tyler most aptly dubbed it.

My general interpretation is based upon the view that what individuals and groups do when given freedom depends upon what they are (their character) when such freedom is offered. Hence an understanding of the development of what we note as characteristic traits of the denominations that took place during the formative period, hinges in large part upon a delineation of characteristic attitudes and practices that came to be accepted during the colonial period. In keeping with this suggestion I shall now take up in somewhat schematic fashion several important elements, ideas or practices, that went into the making of the denominations, and which together gave and still gives them their distinctive character.

A

The first to be noted is the "sectarian" tendency of each American denomination to seek to justify its peculiar interpretations and practices as more closely conforming to those of the early Church as pictured in the New Testament than the views and policies of its rivals. This tendency is closely related to a kind of historylessness exhibited as Professor Latourette has pointed out, in the "marked tendency" of American Protestantism during the nineteenth century "to ignore the developments which had taken place in Christianity in the Old World after the first century."

This anti-historical bias itself has long historical roots. Roman Catholicism developed the idea of the Bible as the Word of God within the context of the Church which through apostolic succession from Peter was the bearer of the tradition. The purity and authority of the Church in speaking out of the tradition, was in turn guarded by the sacraments of baptism and ordination. Thus the Church, as the continuing, tangible historical reality, always stood as interpreter of the Word to the individual, and in this sense spoke out of the tradition with authority equal to that of the Bible.

The Reformers, in revolt against the Church as it then existed, appealed over the practices of the Church to the Word as found in the Bible. But the Reformation which took shape in the "right-wing" Lutheran, Anglican, and Reformed versions, held the doctrine of the Word together with doctrines of the Church and Ministry in such fashion as to guard against individual "enthusiasm" and to preserve the sense of the unbroken historical continuity of Christianity.

The "left-wing" sects, in their fight for existence against almost universal opposition, sought a source of unquestioned authority that would undercut all the tradition-based claims of both Roman Catholics and "right-wing" Protestants over them. They found it in the Bible, which as the commonly recognized Word of God, they proposed to place directly in the hands of the Spirit-guided individual Christian as his only necessary guide to faith and practice. The common thrust of these groups was toward "no creed but the Bible" and the right of "private judgment," under grace, in its interpretation. In practice this meant appeal over the authority of all churches and historical traditions subsequently developed to the authority of the beliefs and practices of primitive Christianity as pictured in the New Testament.

Denominationalism: The Shape of Protestantism

In America, although the churches of the "right-wing" were everywhere dominant during the colonial period, the situation in the long run played into the hands of the "left-wing" view. For there, under the necessity to live side by side with those from other lands and different backgrounds, the angularities of the transplanted national and religious traditions tended to cancel each other out. Crevecoeur clearly delineated this tendency, and attributed it to the fact that

zeal in Europe is confined; here it evaporates in the great distance it has to travel; there it is a grain of power inclosed, here it burns in the open air, and consumes without effect.

Nevertheless as Christians, whether Lutheran, Anglican, Congregational, Presbyterian, Baptist, Quaker, or what not, all shared the Bible—the center and symbol of a common Christian beginning and heritage, and for all the highest authority. Hence each in defense of its peculiar way against the others, was increasingly pressed to fall back on this one commonly recognized authority and to argue that its denominational teaching and way most closely conformed to the Biblical patterns. Thus in America where, unlike their European parents, the transplanted "right-wing" churches never possessed or were soon shorn of effective coercive power to suppress dissent and enforce uniformity, their leaders were almost forced to enter the argument if at all pretty much on the terms originally set by the "left-wing" groups.

Meanwhile the common sense of opportunity to begin all over again in the new land, which was so characteristic a feature of the mind of the early planters, also worked to erase the sense of continuity with the historic Church and to accentuate appeal to the teachings of Jesus and the practices of primitive Christianity. For even to nominal or cultural Christians of the 17th century, this opportunity was bound to be interpreted as an occasion ordained by God to begin again at the point where mankind had first gone astray—at Eden, the paradise of man before the fall. Here is deeply rooted the commonly observed and usually irritating assumption of innocence on the part of many Americans.

But to ardent churchmen and Biblicists the opportunity was bound to be seen as a providential chance to begin over again at a selected point in history where it was thought the Christian Church had gone astray. John Cotton was not unusual in speaking of the churches formed by the Puritans in New England as exceptionally close to what would be set up "if the Lord Jesus were here himself in person."

Both the Pietistic and Rationalistic movements of the eighteenth century, each in its own way, worked to the same general end. The personal religious experience emphasized by the Pietists was assumed to be a duplication of the experience of New Testament Christians. And rationalistic social and political leaders and reformers, in their battle against existing ecclesiastical institutions, soon learned to appeal to the pure moral teachings of Jesus (whom they saw as the first great Deist) as the norm by which these could be judged and found wanton. In essence the views of Pietists and Rationalists were so close together that both could agree with the Unitarian Joseph Priestley that the story of the Christian Church was largely a sordid history of the "corruptions" of pure Christianity through the inventions and contrivances of clever men. Thus both reached the same conclusion, namely that the forms, practices and traditions of the historic church were neither binding nor of particular interest to the present.

Hence, in summary, in the constellation of ideas prevailing during the Revolutionary epoch in which the denominations began to take shape were: the idea of pure and hence normative beginnings to which return was possible; the idea that the intervening history was largely that of aberrations and corruptions which was better ignored; and the idea of the opportunity to begin building anew in the new land on the true and ancient foundations. It is notable that the most successful of the definitely Christian indigenous denominations in America, the Disciples of Christ, grew out of the idea of a "new reformation" to be based, not on new insights, but on a "restoration" of the practices of the New Testament church—on which platform, it was thought, all the diverse groups of modern Christendom could unite insofar as they could shed the accumulated corruptions of the Church through the centuries. Typically American, this beginning over again was not conceived as a new beginning, but as a picking up of the lost threads of primitive Christianity.

But the common view of the normative nature of the pure moral teachings of Jesus or New Testament religious experience and organizational forms, which undercut appeal to all intervening traditions, actually provided few restrictions on the ardent men and women who were busily engaged in building new churches in the new land.

For the actual content of the Rationalists' pure religion and morals of Jesus, although Jefferson happily thought it was "as easily distinguished" from other matters in the Gospels "as diamonds in a dunghill," turned out to be surprisingly like current Deistic Views. The Pietist as easily found his kind of emphasis on religious experience indigenous in the New Testament. And both found their versions of "the church" to be identical with the Church of the Bible. Hence those in both camps were free to move with the tides of history, pragmatically, experimentally—incorporating as much of the traditional and the new in their structures as to each seemed valid and desirable. Here is part of the explanation of the often puzzling combination of Biblical authoritarianism with experimental and pragmatic activism in American religious life.

Men of some historical learning and consciousness, like the doughty John W. Nevin of the German Reformed Church's Mercersburg Seminary, protested that the "sectarian" appeal to

private judgment and the Bible involves, of necessity, a protest against the authority of all previous history, except so far as it may seem to agree with what is thus found to be true; in which case, of course, the only real measure of truth is taken to be, not this authority of history at all, but the mind, simply, of the particular sect itself. . . . A genuine sect will not suffer itself to be embarrassed for a moment, either at its start or afterwards, by the consideration that it has no proper root in past history. Its ambition is rather to appear in this respect autochthonic, aboriginal, self sprung from the Bible, or through the Bible from the skies.

But by 1849 when this was published, such were passing voices crying in the lush wilderness of the American free church, sectarian system that had no mind to be bound by the past, and little thought that wisdom might be found even by American churchmen between the first and the nineteenth centuries.

Thus in spite of almost universal appeal to the authority of the Bible, and a tendency to literalistic interpretation of it, the architects of the American denominations appear to have been surprisingly unbound by the past, by tradition. But it must be added that their freedom in this respect was largely the appearance or feeling of freedom possible only to those ignorant of their rich history. Hence in a sense the very freedom which they felt and acted upon, freedom without historical perspective, served many times to bind them to the tendencies of the moment that appeared to be obvious. Hence in all innocence they built into the life of the denominations what time and tide happened to bring to their shores. And each tended to sanctify indiscriminately all the various elements of doctrine and practice that it for whatever reason adopted, under the supposition that it but followed a blueprint revealed in the Word of God.

B

The second element to be noted is the voluntary principle. Voluntaryism is the necessary corollary of religious freedom which, resting on the principle of free, uncoerced consent made the several religious groups voluntary associations, equal before but independent of the civil power and of each other. What the churches actually gave up with religious freedom was coercive power—the revolution in Christian thinking which they accepted was dependence upon persuasion alone.

The religious groups were somewhat prepared to accept such dependence by their experiences during the great colonial revivals that swept the country from the 1720's to the Revolution. The revivals in every area led to a head-on clash between the defenders of the forms and practices of "right-wing" Protestantism and revivalists, and in every case the revivalists triumphed, insofar as the acceptance of revivalism, however reluctantly, was concerned. Meanwhile the revivals had demonstrated the possibilities of and had taught confidence in dependence upon persuasion alone. Once this battle was won in the churches, the principle of voluntaryism became a leaven in the mind and practices of the religious groups, conditioning their development.

Conceiving the church as a voluntary association tends to push tangible, practical considerations to the fore, by placing primary emphasis on the free uncoerced consent of the individual. Thus a recent history of Congregationalism published by that denomination's press, declares that

a Congregational church is a group of Christians, associated together for a definite purpose, not because of peculiarities of belief

and the members of local churches

are not asked to renounce their previous denominational teachings but are asked to join in a simple covenant pledging cooperation and fellowship.

Hence the center of a denomination, as of any other voluntary association, is a tangible defined objective to which consent can be given. During the actual struggles for religious freedom, the common objective was recognition of the right to worship God in public as each saw fit and without civil restraints or disabilities. Once this was achieved, each group was free to define its own peculiar objectives.

In relation to the voluntary principle Christianity itself tends to be conceived primarily as an activity, a movement, which the group is engaged in promoting. If the group has a confessional basis, its attitude toward it is likely to become promotional and propagandistic, as for example, witness Missouri Synod Lutheranism. Anything that seems to stand in the way of or to hinder the effectiveness of such promotion is likely to be considered divisive and a threat to the internal unity and general effectiveness of the group. For example, insofar as theology is an attempt to define and clarify intellectual positions it is apt to lead to discussion, differences of opinion, even to controversy, and hence to be divisive. And this has had a strong tendency to dampen serious discussion of theological issues in most groups, and hence to strengthen the general anti-intellectual bias inherent in much of revivalistic Pietism. This in turn helps to account for the surprising lack of inter-denominational theological discussion, or even consciousness of theological distinctiveness among the many groups. "Fundamentalism" in America, among other things, was a movement that tried to recall these denominations to theological and confessional self-consciousness. But it was defeated in every major denomination, not so much by theological discussion and debate as by effective political manipulations directed by denominational leaders to the sterilizing of this "divisive" element.

Voluntaryism further means that a powerful selective factor is at work in the choice of denominational leaders, since such leaders finally gain and hold support and power through persuasion and popular appeal to the constituency. This means that whatever else top denominational leaders *may be*, they *must be* denominational politicians. Tocqueville was surprised to find that everywhere in America "you meet with a politician where you expected to find a priest." Similar factors are of course at work in the American Republic at large and all the factors that Lord Bryce pointed out as militating against the great man's chances of becoming President of the United States operate in the same fashion in the selection of a President of the American Baptist Convention.

Voluntaryism also means that each group has a kind of massive and stubborn stability, inertia, and momentum of its own, deeply rooted in and broadly based on the voluntary consent and commitment of the individuals composing it. Here is the real basis for the tremendous vitality of these denominations. This is likely to become evident in periods of internal stress or of threat to the existence of the group from the outside—as some proponents of mergers have learned to their consternation.

The acceptance of religious freedom by the churches had one important implication that has seldom been noticed. Written into the fundamental laws of the land at a time when rationalism permeated the intellectual world, it embodied the typically rationalist view that only what all the religious "sects" held and taught in common (the "essentials of every religion") was really relevant for the well being of the society and the state. Obversely this meant that the churches implicitly accepted the view that whatever any religious group held *peculiarly* as a tenet of its faith, must be irrelevant for the public welfare. Thus in effect the churches accepted the responsibility to teach that the peculiar views or tenets or doctrines that divided them one from another and gave each its only reason for separate and independent existence, were either irrelevant for the general welfare or at most possessed only a kind of instrumental value for it. It is little wonder that a sense of irrelevance has haunted many religious leaders in America ever since.

C

The third element to be noted is the place of the mission enterprise in the life of the denominations.

Since the free churches of America are voluntaryistic and purposive the defined objectives of a group are peculiarly definitive and formative.

It is a commonplace that Pietism became dominant in the American churches at the beginning of the nineteenth century. Pietism as a movement in the churches stressed personal religious experience and commitment, expressed in Christian works of evangelization and charity. Hence a concomitant of Pietism wherever it appeared—in German Lutheranism, in English Methodism, in American colonial revivals—was always a renewed interest in missions. Thus the tendency of Pietism as a voluntaryism, is to place the central emphasis on the objectives of the group, which is to make the missionary program of a denomination, both home and foreign, definitive for it.

Missions of course, are an aspect of the broad work of evangelization—the winning of converts through persuasion leading to conversion. But since conversion always takes place in the context of a group, it necessarily has two aspects, the conversion of the individual to God, and the individual's commitment to what the particular group is doing, which defines for him the nature of the Christian life in practice. The two aspects are separable, and the second may come to outweigh the first, placing the denomination under pressures to accept as members all who will cooperate in furthering the work of the local church or denomination—as witness the above quoted Congregationalists' conception of their church. For this reason the originally very exclusive sectarian denominations in America have tended always to move in the direction of loosely inclusive membership.

Further, the fact that the denomination is a voluntary association, has an effect upon the conduct of the over-all evangelistic or mission program it envisages. Since all depends upon persuasion, various aspects of the program, for example, home and foreign missions, necessarily compete for attention and funds within the denomination. Similarly, the several areas of the foreign field compete, with the result noted by H. W. Schneider, that

in the twentieth century, as well as in the nineteenth, the most popular missionfields were still those areas in which "heathenism" was most spectacular—India, China, and "darkest Africa."

Just as voluntaryism and sense of mission forms the center of a denomination's self-conscious life, so they provide the basis for the interdenominational or superdenominational consciousness and cooperation which has been such an outstanding aspect of the American religious life. This is seen in the host of inter- or super-denominational societies—the American Board of Commissioners for Foreign Missions, the American Home Mission Society, the Bible Society, the Tract Society, the American Sunday School Union, the Temperance Society, the Colonization and Anti-Slavery Societies, the Y.M.C.A., and the Federal and National Councils. Very typical is the statement of the Interchurch World Movement launched in 1919 as a

cooperative effort of the missionary, educational, and other benevolent agencies of the evangelical churches of the United States and of Canada to survey unitedly their present common tasks and simultaneously and together to secure the necessary resources of men and money and power required for these tasks.

The genius of these movements is the same as that of the individual denominations, namely, to instrument certain-defined objectives, in this case of such nature and extent as to enlist the support of individuals in many different denominations. It should be noted that most of these societies were not formed by the cooperative activity of denominations as such, but rather as voluntary associations of individuals from various denominations. In this sense they have been superdenominations, many times in recognized competition with the denominations, as witness for example the Old School Presbyterian attitude toward the A.H.M.S. and the Baptist attitude toward some of the work of the Bible Society.

There have been of course, outstanding examples of genuine cooperation of denominations as such, as for example the Congregational-Presbyterian Plan of Union of 1801 and the later Accommodation Plan, and more recently the Federal and National Councils. But the basic genius is the same, in this case cooperative work for the accomplishment of tasks too large for one group to do alone.

Here is the basis for the persistent American view that an ecumenical movement must begin with working together rather than with agreement on fundamental theological propositions; on "life and work" rather than "faith and order." This is the way to which American churchmen tend to be committed because of the nature of their long and successful experience in interdenominational cooperation.

Since the missionary enterprise plays such a central and definitive role in an American denomination's self-conscious conception of itself, even slight changes in the basic conception of it work subtle changes in the character of the denomination itself. Hence an understanding of the changing motifs of missions in America contributes greatly to an understanding of many denominational developments and reactions thereto.

During the formative period of 1783 to 1850, the most prevalent conception of the missionary enterprise in all the evangelical denominations was that of individualistic winning of converts one by one to the cause of Christ. To be sure it was assumed by most that, as Rufus Anderson, Secretary of the A.B.C.F.M. put it in 1845

that point being gained, and the principle of obedience implanted, and a highly spiritual religion introduced, social renovation will be sure to follow.

And he went on specifically to reject as a direct objective of missions the "reorganizing, by various direct means, of the structure of that social system of which the converts form a part."

Similarly, as Wade C. Barclay's second volume of his *History of Methodist Missions* makes clear, the Methodists commonly accepted Wesley's injunctions to his preachers which was written into the first discipline—"You have nothing to do but save Souls." And Bishop McKendree in 1816 had anticipated Rufus Anderson's general position in his answer to the question "What may we reasonably believe to be God's design in raising up the Preachers called Methodists?" which was, "to reform the continent by spreading scriptural holiness over these lands." One cannot say, therefore, that these leaders gave no thought to "social renovation"—but believing as they did that it was not of the essence of the work of the free churches but would automatically follow upon the dissemination of "scriptural holiness," one can say that they took a great deal for granted that time did not bear out.

This general conception of the mission enterprise largely defined the objectives of all the evangelical denominations during the first three quarters of the nineteenth century. In a real sense each became a great missionary organization devoted to pressing the claims of the Gospel as it saw them wherever and however opportunity offered. By the same token, every member was a missionary, either actively and directly as a consecrated worker in the field, or through his enlistment in and support of the common enterprise. Thus the General Assembly declared in 1847, that

the Presbyterian Church [U.S.A.] is a missionary society, the object of which is to aid in the conversion of the world, and every member of this church is a member of the said society and bound to do all in his power for the accomplishment of this object.

It was this that shaped and gave direction to each budding denomination.

But during the last quarter of the nineteenth century and the opening years of the twentieth, real belief in the all-sufficiency of this kind of missions declined, at least among those of the top leadership in most of the large denominations. During this period enlightened theological Professors hand in hand with "Princes of the Pulpit" responding to the impact of scientific thinking in the garb of evolution and to the deplorable economic and social conditions in the burgeoning industrial society shaped the "new theology" and the "social gospel." Inevitably as their views came to prevail the conception of the work of the Church underwent changes, and missions were metamorphosed from the simple task of winning converts to which, it was assumed, all else would be added, to the complex task of participating actively in social betterment and reconstruction. Foreign missions, from being simple outposts of Christian evangelization, became outposts of the latest technological, medical, agricultural and educational knowledge and practice being developed in the United States. This view of missions received most frank expressions in the "layman's inquiry" published in 1932 as *Re-Thinking Missions*. "We believe," the inquiry states,

that the time has come to set the educational and other philanthropic aspects of mission work free from organized responsibility to the work of conscious and direct evangelism. We must . . . be willing to give largely without preaching, to cooperate wholeheartedly with non-Christian agencies for social improvement. . . .

This of course was conceived as "Christian" work—but by what standards? Why should the devoted young medical missionary in Japan, China, or India be closely examined regarding his views of the Trinity or the Virgin Birth, or on any other "merely" theological views for that matter? Meanwhile as Professor Winthrop Hudson has made clear, in the United States itself Christianity was so amalgamated and identified with the American way of life that it was difficult for denominational leaders to distinguish what was peculiarly "Christian" in the work from the general culture. In this situation Christian missions were easily metamorphosed into attempts at intercultural penetration. "The Christian" said the laymen's inquiry

will therefore regard himself as a co-worker with the forces within each such religious system which are working for righteousness.

In the long run the results were somewhat embarrassing since while the younger churches throve in every mission land, yet in general it was easy for the East, for example, to accept the technology while in reaction rejecting the Christianity which had been assumed to be inseparable from it. In brief, the revolt of the "colonial" missionary countries of the East, armed with the latest "Christian" know-how of the West, somewhat undercut belief in this kind of missions, which meant the undercutting of the denominations' conception of their life and work at home.

Here is one root of much of the present confusion and distress in the American denominations. No longer really believing either in the sole efficacy of a simple Christian evangelization, or in the salutary effects of cultural interpenetration under Christian auspices, their purposive core and sense of direction is destroyed and they are set adrift. The one helpful element in the picture is that this, among other things, is pressing even American churchmen to re-examine the meaning of the Church not only as "life and works" but also as "faith and order."

The same principle applies to such outstanding interdenominational movements within the country as the Y.M.C.A. and the Federal Council. The "Y," a product of the revivalism of the second quarter of the nineteenth century, had as its original objective the evangelization of uprooted men in the traditional fashion. Beginning with this primary purpose it added libraries, reading rooms, inexpensive hotels, and recreational and other facilities as a means thereto. But as belief in simple evangelization declined the facilities themselves tended to take the leading role in the program, until today the primary appeal of the "Y" is likely to be as a community welfare organization which is somewhat embarrassed by its earlier evangelistic emphasis.

The Federal Council originating in 1908, was described by one of its historians as, in effect a marriage of American church unity or cooperative movements with the concern for social service. Thus it reflects the changed conception of the primary work of the Church at the time of its origin as Walter Rauschenbusch clearly stated. It was conceived by such leaders as Graham Taylor as a cooperative movement among the churches in the interests of social justice, and C. Howard Hopkins referred to it as "the climax of official recognition of social Christianity. . . . " Its first outstanding pronouncement was its "Social Creed of the Churches" adopted in the meeting in Chicago in 1912.

On the one hand then, the Council can be seen as an expression of the basic genius of the American religious organizations—cooperation in the interests of effective evangelization. But on the other hand it reflects the changed conception of "evangelization" from the traditional winning of individual souls to Christ coupled with charitable amelioration of distress to the winning of people to concern for social justice based if necessary upon radical social reconstruction. Inherent in the change was the tendency to substitute social-action for the Christian Gospel of redemption which Visser't Hooft pointed out in his study of The Background of the Social Gospel in America in 1928.

This tendency was vigorously combatted in the denominations by the Fundamentalist movement which insofar was right in conception, but which protested on the basis of a theological position generally so archaic and bankrupt that it had no prospect of widespread appeal to intelligent people. It succeeded merely in helping to identify Christianity with stubborn, recalcitrant reactionism in wide areas of America, and in making "Bible belt" a phrase for ultrasophisticated Menckenites to conjure with.

More recently a much more profound and truly sophisticated theological movement, commonly associated with the names of Reinhold Niebuhr and Henry Nelson Wieman has risen in the denominations, which bids fair to do justice both to the Christian tradition and the American activistic genius.

But meanwhile, under the stress of continuing social and political crisis, a genuinely reactionary movement has arisen both inside and from without the denominations which would limit the churches' work to the earlier conception of individualistic soul-winning. This explains the causes and nature of recent attacks on the denominations and the Council as exemplified in John T. Flynn's *The Road Ahead*, which accuses the churches of furthering "creeping socialism" instead of confining themselves to saving souls.

D

The fourth element to be noted is revivalism.

In the English colonies as uniformity enforced by the civil power broke down (e.g., in New England and Virginia) or where it was not, or not for long, attempted (e.g., in Rhode Island, New Amsterdam-New York, and Pennsylvania), and hence where the religious groups were, or were increasingly dependent upon persuasion and popular appeal for recruitment and support, revivalism soon emerged as the accepted technique of the voluntary churches. Not without protest of course, as witness the long and bitter opposition in all the old line churches, but notably in Congregationalism, Presbyterianism and Anglicanism, where doughty Protestant traditionalists correctly sensed that the revivalists "stressed evangelism more than creed," and attempted like King Canute and about as effectively to exercise a measure of control over the incoming tides.

Early revival leaders in the colonies like the Tennents among the Presbyterians and Jonathan Edwards of the Congregationalists, who were long accustomed to sober but effective periods of spiritual refreshing in their parishes, apparently stumbled upon the practice, as witness, for example, Edwards' narrative of "surprising" conversions. But they and especially their followers of lesser stature and more tenuous traditional roots, became apt and even enthusiastic pupils and imitators of the glamorous free-wheeling Anglican revivalist, George Whitfield, whose career, like the Sorcerer's great broom in the hands of a less skillful manipulator, was multiplied in innumerable splinters.

But if the situation in the colonies tended to work for the acceptance of revivalism in all the churches, the situation under religious freedom in the new nation tended to make it imperative. As Professor Garrison has succinctly put it,

With 90 per cent of the population outside the churches, the task of organizing religion could not be limited to encouraging "Christian nurture" . . . in Christian families, or to ministering to old members as they moved to new places farther west. It had to be directed toward that 90 per cent. What they needed first was not nurture or edification, but radical conversion, . . . [and since they followed] no chiefs, . . . they had to be brought in one by one.

"It is small wonder," he correctly continues, "that the revivalists put on all the heat they could and with some notable exceptions, appealed to the emotions more than to the intelligence." There is the heart of the matter. Revivalism in one form or another became the accepted technique of practically all the voluntary churches, the instrument for accomplishing the denominations' objective of evangelism and missions.

Now a commonly accepted practice, whatever the reason originally given for it, eventually reveals implications of a systematic nature—and revivalism tended strongly to influence the patterns of thought and organization of the groups affected. The "revival system" came to be much more than just a recruiting technique. Some colonial churchmen correctly sensed this, and many of their predictions regarding the effects of revivalism on the churches were fulfilled in the years following independence. What they saw was that revivalism tends to undercut and to wash out all the traditional churchly standards of doctrine and practice.

There are several reasons why this is so. First, revivalism tends to produce an oversimplification of all theological problems, both because the effective revivalist must appeal to the common people in terms they can understand, and because he must reduce all the complex of issues to a simple choice between two clear and contrasting alternatives. Said one convert of "Priest [John] Ingersoll," as the father of the famous agnostic was called, "He made salvation seem so plain, so easy, I wanted to take it to my heart without delay." How simple it could be made is indicated by "Billy" Sunday's proclamation:

You are going to live forever in heaven, or you are going to live forever in hell. There's no other place—just the two. It is for you to decide. It's up to you, and you must decide now.

Second, the revivalist gravitates almost inevitably toward the idea that "whosoever will may come," and this tendency coupled with the necessarily concomitant stress on personal religious experience in "conversion," tends to make man's initiative primary. Revivalism thus tends to lean theologically in an Arminian or even Pelagian direction with the implicit suggestion that man saves himself through choice. As John W. Nevin complained in *The Anxious Bench,* published in 1843, under revivalism it is the sinner who "gets religion," not religion that gets the sinner.

Thus in the hands of New England revivalists in the line of Timothy Dwight, Lyman Beecher and Nathaniel W. Taylor, Calvinism was "modified" almost beyond recognition by the emphasis placed on their interpretation of "free-will." The foundation of their theological system, said Beecher, was that even God exerts only persuasive power over men. This general emphasis in turn bolsters the voluntaryistic notion that converted men by choice create the church—an idea paralleled in the political realm by the notion that people create the government. And finally an extremely ardent revivalist may take as condescending an attitude toward God as he takes toward the President of the Republic, as when Charles G. Finney declared that "the devil has no right to rule this world" and the people ought "to give themselves to God, and vote in the Lord Jesus Christ, as governor of the Universe."

Third, revivalists are strongly tempted (and have commonly yielded) to stress results and to justify whatever means will produce them. Even Edwards defended the preaching of terrifying "hell-fire" sermons with the comment that he thought it not amiss to try to frighten men out of hell. And Finney and his friends justfied their "new measures" largely on the ground that they got results, namely conversions. Lyman Beecher and his alter-ego, Nathaniel W. Taylor, almost made "preachableness" in revivals normative for doctrines, and D. D. Williams has pointed out that for some of their revivalistic heirs in New England

the ultimate standard for judging every doctrine and every practice of Christianity was thus first, Will it help or hinder the salvation of men?

This pragmatic emphasis on results reached a peak in the eminently persuasive albeit muddled thinking (when judged by any rigorous standards) of Dwight L. Moody who reputedly said he was an Arminian up to the cross but Calvinist beyond—and who declared forthrightly that "It makes no difference how you get a man to God, provided you get him there." This emphasis culminated in the spectacular career of "Billy" Sunday and his professional imitators with their elaborate techniques for assessing their contribution to the Kingdom of Heaven and the Church of Christ on earth by counting the number of their converts. It is probably small wonder that the outstanding historian of Christianity in America, a Methodist, rather easily equated the numerical size of the several denominations with their significance and influence in the American culture.

Fourth, revivalism as voluntaryism, tended to bring a particular type of leader to the fore—men close to the people who could speak their language and rouse their emotions. During this formative period it is notable that educated, cultured, dignified religious leaders and ecclesiastical statesmen, men like Timothy Dwight, John Witherspoon, William White—tend to be replaced in the denominations by demogogic preachers and revivalists—men like Peter Cartwright, C. G. Finney, Henry Ward Beecher, Joseph Smith.

This tendency should be seen in the context of the general leveling or equalitarian trend of the times. The parallel development in the political sphere is striking. With the passing of the older revolutionary leaders, the removal of restrictions on popular suffrage, the removal of the barriers between the people and the government, the shift from Federalism and Jeffersonianism to Jacksonian democracy, the "orator" able to appeal in Congress to his peers declined in importance and the popular leaders of the masses increased in influence. Lord Bryce in commenting on the Presidency contrasts the "intellectual pigmies" who followed Jackson with the men of education, administrative experience, largeness of view, and dignity of character who had preceded.

Finally, as revivalism came to pervade the denominations with its implication that the Christian life was a struggle across dull plateaus between peaks of spiritual refreshing, not only was "Christian nurture" in the churches slighted, it was given a reverse twist. Bushnell pointed this out in his complaint that far from encouraging the child to grow up in the Church as a Christian, never knowing himself to be otherwise, the revival system encouraged him to grow up in flagrant sin in order that by contrast he would better know himself as a Christian through the crisis experience of conversion. Thus the revivalists' emphasis that Christ came to save sinners, had the effect of encouraging the Church to nurture flagrant sinners in its bosom in order that they might be "gloriously saved."

Not only did revivalism thus tend to a neglect of the Christian nurture of children in the Church, it tended also to have an adverse effect on the minister as a shepherd of his flock. For inevitably the sober local pastor tended increasingly to be judged by his ability to create the proper build-up and setting for the periodic revival campaign in his church. And naturally ardent members of the congregation were quick to compare him unfavorably with the more colorful, albeit less responsible, roving evangelists. Many a church prayed the prayer, "Lord, send us a man like Finney!" And the stock answer to decline and apathy in a local church was to import a forceful revivalist to "revive us again!" just as the stock answer to troubles in the country was the importation of a morally impeccable plumed knight in shining armor to lead a great crusade for spiritual renovation and to throw the rascals out.

Fifth, it is perhaps somewhat anti-climactical to suggest

here that revivalism tended to foster an anti-intellectual bias in American Protestantism. The over-simplification of issues, plus the primary emphasis on a personal religious experience, and on tangible numerical results, left little room or encouragement for the traditional role of the Church and its ministers in intellectual leadership.

Revivalism with these tendencies was a central element in the structure of the Protestantism that gained religious freedom and was an important factor in shaping the exercise of that freedom in subsequent years and in forming the denominations. There were those in the formative years who, from the viewpoint of "classical" Protestantism, regarded the sweep of the "revival system" with alarm and voiced a strong and cogent protest. Most notable perhaps was John W. Nevin of the Mercersburg Seminary who in 1843 published his *The Anxious Bench* as an attack on the whole "new measure" revival system which he contrasted with the "system of the Catechism." Similarly Horace Bushnell, a Connecticut Congregationalist, voiced a milder protest in his work on *Christian Nurture* published in 1847. But by and large revivalism made a clean sweep in practically all the denominations. Lyman Beecher noted with some amazement that even Emerson's "corpse cold" Unitarians in Boston attempted to hold revivals, but was inclined to agree with Theodore Parker that they lacked the essential piety and warmth for the work and hence succeeded only in making themselves a bit ridiculous. Among the denominations the Presbyterians probably made the most consistent and determined stand against the more radical effects of the system, and suffered fragmentation, ridicule and abuse for their defense of traditional standards of doctrine and polity. Even Lutheranism, its confessionalism undercut by rationalism and pietism, was swept by revivalism, as the replies to Nevin's work indicate and despite the efforts of confessionally minded men from within was probably saved from becoming just another typical American denomination by the great influx of new Lutheran immigrants.

Surveying the scene as a whole, the historian of Presbyterianism in America was not far wrong when he said that

"The Great Awakening ... terminated the Puritan and inaugurated the Pietist or Methodist age of American Church History."

E

The fifth element to be noted is the churches' general flight from "Reason" in reaction against the Enlightenment during the Revolutionary Epoch, and the concomitant triumph of Pietism in most of them.

The two live movements affecting Christianity during the eighteenth century were Rationalism (Deism in religion) and Pietism. During that century the foremost politico-ecclesiastical issue in America was religious freedom. Confronting this practical issue, Rationalists and Pietists could combine forces against the defenders of the right wing or traditional position of Establishment, in spite of basic theological differences. This they did, bringing the issue to successful culmination in the provisions for religious freedom written into the new constitutions of the States and the Federal Government. In brief, it is not too far wrong to say that rationalists conceived and shaped the form of the new government, while pietistic sentiments were riding to dominance in the churches.

But once religious freedom was accomplished and a popular interpretation of the French Revolution in America brought the theological issue of "Reason" versus Revelation to the fore, pietism rapidly realigned itself with classical right-wing, scholastic orthodoxy in opposition to rationalists and all their works—now included under the blanket term "infidelity." By and large, except perhaps for Unitarianism, the bulk of American Protestantism turned against the ethos of the Enlightenment, and thereafter found itself either indifferent to or in active opposition to the general spirit and intellectual currents of modern western civilization. Thereafter the bulk of American Protestantism was moulded primarily by pietistic revivalism and scholastic orthodoxy. The former made personal subjective religious experience basic, while scholastic orthodoxy defined the professed interest and content of theology. This provides a fair definition of evangelical Protestantism in America.

Denominationalism: The Shape of Protestantism

This triumph of pietistic revivalism in the American denominations, associated as it was with the strong reaction against the ideas and spirit of the Enlightenment which were to inform modern civilization, has had far reaching effects on their thought and life. Pietism as a movement has been peculiarly amorphous in character and intellectually naive. The early leaders intent on cultivating individual Christian piety in the churches—whether Spener and Francke in German Lutheranism, or the Wesleys in English Anglicanism—never conceived their work except as a movement within the saving forms of a church in the interest of revitalizing its Christian life. Only so does Wesley's use of the text, "Is Thine heart . . . as my heart? . . . If it be, give me thine hand" make sense. And if the context of a church is absent this can and has led to strange bedfellows for Christians. For Pietism, cut off from the forms of a traditional church and itself the guiding genius of a denomination, has successively loaned itself to whatever live movement seemed to give structure to current problems and their solutions.

Thus, as suggested, it loaned itself to the battle for religious freedom as structured by the Rationalists in the eighteenth century. During the Revolutionary Epoch when the issue seemed to be "reason" *versus* revelation, it as easily loaned its warm heart to hard headed reactionary scholastic orthodoxy and its structuring of that issue. However this alignment was largely on the theological question, and at the same time on the side of "moral and social ideals and attitudes" the emerging modern age was accepted. Here is the real basis for that strangely divided or schizophrenic character of American Protestantism that has baffled so many historians and observers. The two Randalls, John Herman Senior and Junior, stated the situation clearly in their *Religion and the Modern World* of 1929:

> Western society confronted the disruptive forces of science and the machine age with a religious life strangely divided. On the side of moral and social ideals and attitudes, of the whole way of living which it approved and consecrated, Christianity had already come to terms with the forces of the modern age. . . .

97

Denominationalism

On the side of beliefs, however, Christianity in the early 19th century had not come to terms with the intellectual currents of Western society. It found itself, in fact, involved in a profound intellectual reaction against just such an attempt at modernism. . . .

Thus it was that Christianity entered the 19th century with its values belonging to the early modern period, to the age of commerce and individualism, and its beliefs thoroughly medieval and pre-scientific.

This schizophrenia has affected every area of the American denominational life and work. It helps to explain why during the course of the nineteenth century the denominations so easily came to sanctify the ideals and spirit of the rising industrial, acquisitive bourgeois society until by the end of the century there was almost complete identification of Christianity with "the American way of life" until, as Henry May put it, "In 1876 Protestantism presented a massive, almost unbroken front in its defense of the social status quo."

It also helps to explain why Protestants could accept the "democratic way" with passionate fervor in practice, but fail to develop a critical Protestant theory of the Christian individual as a ruler. Yet in the democracy every man as a citizen, even though a Christian, is by definition a responsible ruler and cannot be set over against the magistrate and the State as under some other forms. The extent of this failure on the part of American Protestantism is indicated by the fact that when, following the Civil War, some churchmen, motivated at least by humanitarian concerns addressed themselves to pressing social problems they soon found as did Walter Rauschenbusch for example, that if they were to embark upon "Christianizing the Social Order" they had to find or create "A Theology For the Social Gospel." And if they be criticized, as they often are, for being more creative than Christian in this respect, it should also be remembered that there was little in the then current theology of the pietistic orthodoxy of the denominations upon which to build such a theology.

But again, when it was widely accepted that, as Francis Greenwood Peabody put it in 1900, the social question of the present age is not a question of mitigating the evils of the existing order, but a question whether the existing order itself shall last. It is not so much a problem of social amelioration which occupies the modern mind, as a problem of social transformation and reconstruction

then wide areas of the predominantly pietistic churches easily loaned themselves to identification of the Christian Gospel with this endeavor. Men like George D. Herron, and even Walter Rauschenbusch, came close to blurring the line between Christianity and Socialism, as their heirs sometimes tended to equate it with "New Deals," with "Fair Deals," and "Crusades."

More recently we have seen a clash between the earlier evangelical pietistic view that separation of Church and State means that the churches shall confine themselves to "saving souls" and say nothing about social, economic, and political problems, and the later identification of the Christian message with concern for social betterment and reconstruction. Thus Stanley High professed to speak for those who were shocked by what took place at Amsterdam—

But the most disturbing fact in this listing of alleged capitalist evils [by the Amsterdam Conference] is the revelation of how far the church—at least in the persons of its ecclesiastical leadership at Amsterdam—has transferred its concern from the spiritual business of converting man to the secular business of converting man's institutions.

The nature of the reaction against the eighteenth century during the Revolutionary Epoch, also meant that the "free churches" accepted religious freedom in practice but rejected the rationalists' rationale for it. And finding within the right-wing scholastic orthodox tradition that they fell back upon little theological basis for the practice, the denominations have never really worked out a Protestant theological orientation for it. Here is the basis for a widespread psychosomatic indigestion in American Protestantism, since it can neither digest the Enlightenments' theory nor regurgitate its practice.

A. N. Whitehead noted that "the great Methodist

movement"—roughly equivalent to my "pietistic-revivalism"—marks the point at which "the clergy of the western races began to waver in their appeal to constructive reason." In comments above on voluntaryism and revivalism it was suggested how and why these tended to foster a general anti-intellectualism in the denominations. The present comments on the reaction against the eighteenth century suggest how and why such anti-intellectualism was made official. In brief, at this point evangelical Protestantism, as defined above, parted company with the intellectual currents of the modern world. Thereafter the former defined "religion," while the latter defined "intelligence." Hence since around 1800 Americans have in effect been given the hard choice between being intelligent according to the standards prevailing in their intellectual centers, and being religious according to the standards prevailing in their denominations.

This is really no secret. In fact, one of the most commonly accepted generalizations is that the churches during the nineteenth century largely lost the intellectuals. In America as early as 1836, Orestes A. Brownson noted, that

Everybody knows, that our religion and our philosophy are at war. We are religious only at the expense of our logic [or knowledge].

At about the same time, a more orthodox brother expressed approximately the same sentiment in more euphemistic fashion. "There is," he said

an impression somewhat general—that a vigorous and highly cultivated intellect is not consistent with distinguished holiness: and that those who would live in the cleanest sunshine of communion with God must withdraw from the bleak atmosphere of human science.

Or, as he finally put it more bluntly toward the end of the same article, "It is an impression, somewhat general, that an intellectual clergyman is deficient in piety, and that an eminently pious minister is deficient in intellect." His article, contrary to his purpose, leaves one with the feeling that the impression was not unfounded.

And only yesterday Hugh Hartshorne upon his retirement after many years spent as a Professor of Psychology of Religion in the Yale Divinity School, stated as his mature conclusion that what is called "theological education" in America "is neither theological [according to theological standards] nor education [according to accepted educational standards]." Not unnaturally many, unable to achieve such clarity or accept the situation with such candor, became schizophrenic trying to be intelligent in the schools and religious in the churches. They could be whole in neither. A student entering our theological schools recently, said to me, "In college all my basic interests were religious, but I couldn't seem to find a place to express them in any denomination." Exactly so.

This situation helps to explain why educational leaders in our great Universities, the centers of our burgeoning intellectual life, have never quite known what to do with theological schools in their midst which pretended to train ministers for local parishes. Meanwhile, "practical" churchmen in the United States have by and large been suspicious of nothing more than University education for ministers, unless at every point it could be made obviously applicable to the immediate practical concerns of the churches.

Hence it might be said that the real patron of administrators in University related Seminaries is Janus—who aside from his exceptional physical and mental equipment which enabled him always to face in two directions at once and to speak from either of two mouths, is described as the "guardian of portals and patron of beginnings and endings." Indeed, such Seminaries have been possible largely because men so gifted have been willing to engage in a kind of consecrated duplicity which has permitted the long-range intellectual task of theological reconstruction required by the Universities to be carried on under the guise of ministering directly to the practical needs of local parishes. Whether or not the work of these men abstractly considered is "good" or "evil" is a question purely "academic." It is a necessary work, and I am willing to leave the question of their ultimate salvation with the pronouncement of highest

101

authority that "with God all things are possible." But we ought to be aware that the very success of their necessary work is apt to lure some into the supposition that a kind of subterfuge is of the essence of the religious life in the modern world. Here is the knotty problem that our tradition poses for us.

F

The sixth and final formative element to be noted is the situation of competition between the denominations. In good rationalistic theory, which was basic, competition among the several religious sects, each contending for the truth as it saw it, was of the essence of the free-church idea under the system of separation of Church and State—and was, indeed, the true guarantee of the preservation of "religious rights," as James Madison suggested in the 51st Federalist Paper.

The free-churches were not reluctant to accept this view, and situation, since "in the existence of any Christian sect" the

presumption is of course implied, if not asserted . . . that it is holding the absolute right and truth, or at least more nearly that than other sects; and the inference to a religious mind, is that right and truth must, in the long run, prevail.

If theoretical considerations made competition between the religious sects acceptable, the practical situation made it inevitable and intensified it. At the time the declarations for religious freedom were written into the fundamental laws of the land there was a large number of religious bodies, each absolutistic in its own eyes. To them such freedom meant the removal of traditional civil and ecclesiastical restraints on free expression and propaganda. These free-churches were confronted with a rapidly growing and westward moving population, around 90 per cent of which was unchurched. This offered virgin territory for evangelization. The accepted technique was revivalism, a way of reaching and appealing to individuals gathered in groups for their individual decision and consent.

These factors combined, worked to intensify the sense of

competition between the free, absolutistic groups in the vast free market of souls—a competition that helped to generate the tremendous energies, heroic sacrifices, great devotion to the cause, and a kind of stubborn, plodding work under great handicaps that transformed the religious complexion of the nation. But it cannot be denied that, as L. W. Bacon said of a specific situation during the colonial period that many times

the fear that the work of the gospel might not be done seemed a less effective incitement to activity than the fear that it might be done by others.

This of course was competition between Christian groups sharing a common Christian tradition and heritage, and indeed, really in agreement upon much more than they disagreed on. It was not competition between those of rival faiths, but competition between those holding divergent forms of the same faith—and probably not the less bitter for being thus a family quarrel. This fact meant that ever changing patterns of antagonism and competition were developed, and, by the same token, ever changing patterns of alignments and cooperation.

Robert Baird in his *Religion in America*, first published in America in 1844 at the time when the competition was most keen, divided all the denominations into the "Evangelical" and the "Unevangelical." The former

when viewed in relation to the great doctrines which are universally conceded by Protestants to be fundamental and necessary to salvation . . . all form but one body, recognizing Christ as their common head.

The latter "either renounce, or fail faithfully to exhibit the fundamental and saving truths of the Gospel."

Roman Catholics belong to the latter classification for although "as a Church [they] hold those doctrines on which true believers in all ages have placed their hopes for eternal life" yet they "have been so buried amid the rubbish of multiplied human traditions and inventions, as to remain hid from the great mass of the people." According to Baird, then, Roman Catholics stood in a special category. The great unbridgeable division was between those who "recognize Christ as their head" and those who did not. Notable among the latter were Unitarians, but Universalists, Swedenborgians, Jews, Deists, Atheists, and Socialists were also included. This commonly accepted schematic categorization set the patterns of competition and cooperation among and between the groups.

A Roman Catholic threat could unite all the other groups—even the Evangelical and Unevangelical—in a common front of opposition, especially when as in the west attention was directed to the supposed social and political threat of the Catholic Church to "free institutions." On the other hand, evangelicals might upon occasion borrow a weapon or accept aid and comfort from Roman Catholics in opposition to Unevangelicals. Evangelicals would of course unite against Unitarians and Universalists. Conservative Unitarians might in the stress of conflict with "the latest form of infidelity," seek substantial aid from the staunchest of the orthodox, as when Andrews Norton of Harvard had the Princeton Presbyterian attacks on Transcendentalism reprinted in Boston. Baptists and Methodists, although the outstanding antagonists on the frontier, might easily combine against Presbyterians and Episcopalians. But finally each sect stood by itself against all others, a law unto itself in defense of its peculiar tenets which it inherently held as absolute.

The general effect of such competition was an accentuation of minor as well as substantial differences—the subjects of baptism and its proper mode, ecclesiastical polity, the way of conducting missionary work, pre and post millennialism, "Vater unser" versus "Unser Vater" in the Lord's prayer—and a submergence of the consciousness of a common Christian tradition. Further, such competition helped sometimes to make sheer stubborn perpetuation of peculiarities a chief objective of a group long after real understanding of and hence belief in them had faded into limbo. And lastly, it many times produced a somewhat less than charitable attitude toward other Christian groups, and even the kind of sardonic jealousy reflected in the reputed remark of the Baptist revivalist who in commenting on his meetings said, "We won only two last night, but thank God the Methodists across the street did not win any!" In the long run these more questionable results of the competition have been most obvious and most generally lamented.

Nevertheless, it must be recognized that such competition and conflict is inherent in the system of free churches, and as Talcott Parsons had observed, it would exist "even if there were no prejudice at all, . . . a fact of which some religious liberals do not seem to be adequately aware." In contemporary terms, this is "a struggle for power among [the] religious denominations," as each tries to extend itself. So long as the total membership of the denominations was but a fraction of the total population, this aspect of the competition was largely obscured. But as the percentage of total church membership rises higher and higher, it becomes increasingly clear that each may be seeking to extend itself at the expense of others, as for example, when Southern Baptists "invade" Northern (now American) Baptist territory, and Roman Catholics "invade" traditionally Protestant rural areas.

Meanwhile, however, other factors noted in this paper have tended to a general erosion of interest in the distinct and definable theological differences between the religious sects that historically divided them until increasingly the competition between them seems to be related to such non-theological concerns as nationality or racial background, social status, and convenient accessibility of a local church. Finally what appears to be emerging as of primary distinctive importance in the pluralistic culture is the general traditional ethos of the large families, Protestant, Roman Catholic, and Jewish. Thus so far as Protestants are concerned, in the long run the competition between groups inherent in the system of separation of church and state, which served to divide them, may work to their greater unity.

4
Introduction

Denominationalism has ironic qualities, a fact often missed by its detractors. Much of this irony derives from the tension between a passion for the vision of unity that animated the denominations and the realities of division and competition that resulted. The selections by Winthrop Hudson and Sidney Mead analyze the theoretical and general dimensions of this irony. The following essays by Elwyn A. Smith, Fred J. Hood, and Russell E. Richey explore its presence in the emergence of particular denominations.

The ironic qualities of the denominational system were not apparent to its architects. They were fired by the fears and aspirations inherent in the assumption of responsibility for the religious and moral nurture of the new nation. The zeal for civil and religious liberty that fueled the Revolution and was embodied in the Constitution and amendments singled out no religious bodies or leadership to entrust with the collective religious life. This was reserved to the states and to the various sects. The implications of religious liberty dawned slowly during the National period as the un-churched frontier, the spread of Unitarianism and Deism, the specter of irreligion and barbarism, and paranoias unleashed by the French Revolution and Jeffersonianism were impressed on the minds of the Calvinist clergy, many of whom shared the New England heritage. Congregationalists "established" in Connecticut and Massachusetts and entrusted with the religious life of the citizenry (and by the Great Awakening imbued with a more inclusive sense of that trust) sought with like-minded Presbyterians and others to exercise that trust nationally by creating national and denominational voluntary societies.

Ironies abound. The most obvious irony is that the basic structures of the denominational system—the purposive missionary boards, departments, and agencies—were not derived from the Christian theological heritage, not taken out of confessional experience, not even elaborated within a specific denomination. They were interdenominational structures by intention and design and were devoted to assuming the trust of national religious nurture. It is ironic that prominent among the architects of these structures were Congregationalists who by heritage lodged authority in the congregation, not in such supracongregational organizations. One of the legacies of this origin, rather more of a dilemma now than an irony, is that in most denominations the national structures have not been adequately integrated with the formal polity and comprehended in the formal ecclesiology. The dilemma is most acute within the denominations which share the congregational heritage, as Paul M. Harrison shows in *Authority and Power in the Free Church Tradition* (1959). But denominations with other polities also face the problem of providing legitimacy for boards and agencies (now bureaucratic in character) whose operations are needed but whose status and power lie outside the traditional theory of polity with which the denomination still functions. The origin of the dilemma can be seen in the appropriation and internalization by denominations of the conception and functions of these interdenominational voluntary societies. The Presbyterian experience ably analyzed by Smith is unique in its details (and in the Presbyterian involvement in the interdenominational societies), but the overall pattern was a common one. Denominations appreciated (and feared) the power and influence of the societies, their ability to function as a quasi-establishment of Protestant religion, their threat to the denominations. The response was to create such structures within each denomination. In a real and ironic sense the external threat was made an internal one. Denominations have often found the boards and agencies once interdenominational (which strive to carry on the efforts in missions, Sunday school, church publication, and theological education) as difficult to domesticate within as to fight without.

The structures of the denomination betray their origins. Created by individuals challenged by national responsibilities, interdenominational and national in character, imbued with the purpose of Christianizing the nation and the world, and expansive and missionary in style, the structures were (in terms of context, clientele, purpose, and style) ecumenical, visionary, expansive, and independent. Even when tethered within denominations and domesticated for denominational use, the denominational structures retain much of the independent and unitive spirit. Structurally as well as by the denominational theory (examined in Hudson's article) the denominations possessed potentialities for unitive or ecumenical action. Denominations are, by this reading, much more than organizations to serve themselves. They are institutions of and instruments for the kingdom.

4

The Forming
of a Modern American
Denomination

Elwyn A. Smith

Among the reasons for the emergence of American denominationalism, the impact of the separation of church and state has never been under-rated by scholars. The same is true of the religious pluralism of the nation. Other environmental conditions of comparable importance have been listed but those who recognize the toughness and adaptability of the modern American denominational structure have reason to ask whether historians have done full justice to its internal dynamic. The reaction against denominational history in the grand style is, of course, well warranted. Over against "denominational historians who can recount the achievements of the several denominations as separate bodies, the reasons for their separateness, and the grounds of their greatness and glory," W. E. Garrison wrote, "we must concern ourselves chiefly with the movements of the common Christian mind, the issues which drive planes of cleavage through all denominations transverse to those which divide them from each other...." Some of these unitive issues are American-made; others are rooted in Europe. But the denomination, as Garrison recognized, is the mode in which American church history manifests itself, a vehicle whose continuities must be grasped if modern American churchmanship is to be understood.

It is especially to be regretted that so many writers, whether or not they consider themselves church historians, exhibit an astonishing lack of concern with American religious thought. . . .

Illustrations of ineptitude in American religious thought might be multiplied. What is more important is to find its

Reprinted, footnotes omitted, with the permission of Church History and the author. Footnotes available in Church History, 31 (1962), 74-99.

cause. The difficulty is that in cross-sectional study of American religion, theology can appear as little more than a set of identifying tags. The significance of American theology can be discovered only when it is grasped as an element in the development of a total tradition. Perry Miller is one of the few who writes American cultural history in both perspectives. He treats theology, both written and presupposed, as a voice which must be heard in its own right if the conduct of American Christians is to be understood.

Our complaint is not new, but it may be novel to suggest that the denomination, for all its hostility to vigorous theological inquiry in certain eras, must be studied in relation to changes that occurred within the major American church traditions; changes, moreover, motivated by the understanding of value and reality preserved at their heart and not simply forced on them by changing times. The difficulty is to know precisely what is meant by such a claim. The specific purpose of this paper, therefore, is to identify and recount certain sequences of events within the American Calvinist churches that were set in motion not only by environmental pressures, the importance of which is granted, but also by the inner imperatives of the tradition itself. These sequences of events created new structures in order to conserve and perpetuate established values. It is not in its failings, which are reasonably obvious now, but in its relation to the continuum of church history, both European and American, that the significance of the denomination is to be sought.

I

In an article in *Church History*, Winthrop Hudson has articulated the modern conception of denominationalism. "Denominationalism is the opposite of sectarianism. . . . The basic intention of the denominational theory of the church is that the true church is not to be identified in any exclusive sense with any particular ecclesiastical organization." The established meaning of "denomination" until the nineteenth century equated it with any religious grouping; but between 1790 and 1840 it acquired a more specialized modern definition. To its general use as synonym for a religious group, both Hudson and Sidney Mead adhere in very illuminating articles on the development of American church patterns. Samuel Davies, for example, a Presbyterian evangelist of Virginia, wrote to Joseph Bellamy of Bethlehem, Connecticut in 1751 that he was concerned not to erect a rival to the Establishment in Virginia but to serve "the serious of all denominations among us." In 1791 Samuel Langdon of Hampton Falls, New Hampshire spoke of "the peculiarities which distinguish one denomination of Christians . . . from another . . ." and deprecated the differences. In 1809 Jedediah Morse referred to "Old Calvinists" and "Hopkinsians" in New England as "those two denominations"; the difference was partisan rather than formally ecclesiastical. Early American documents granting religious liberty spoke of individual "persuasion, opinion, and profession" but at the end of the eighteenth century the word "denomination" was appearing regularly in civil codes. "Every denomination of Christians . . . shall be equally under the protection of the Law," affirmed the Constitution of Massachusetts of 1780, "and no subordination of any one sect or denomination to another shall ever be established by Law." Quakers were included as one of the denominations of Christianity in several state constitutions. The Constitutions of Maryland (1775), North Carolina (1776) and South Carolina (1778), the last of which spoke of "all denominations of Christian Protestants," and others, used the word in the general modern sense. Only the distinction sometimes encountered in our own time between "main-line denominations" and sects is lacking. This mutation of meaning became appropriate only after 1830 when early "sect-type" religious bodies outstripped the Congregationalists and Presbyterians and entered the new category of "denominations" by their new relation to the culture, type of organization, and outright size.

The terminology of the new churchmanship was furnished by the eighteenth century but the denominations that emerged in the nineteenth were much more specific in form and character than anything indicated by the loose synonyms of the eighteenth. The "denominations of Christian Protestants" in the newly founded nation entered that century as groups adhering to a variety of traditions of belief, conduct, and church government. Before the mission movement created societies for raising money and recruiting, these traditions lacked "management personnel." Not all were without general officers—bishops, clerks, superintendents, or presidents—but none were so organized as to create typical managerial problems: promotion, budget management, and the direction of staffs and educational programs.

The modern American denomination emerged in a series of steps between 1790 and the breaking up of the great cooperative benevolent societies sponsored by Congregationalists and Presbyterians. The first step was the founding of the executive and promotional missionary societies. Conversion of the Indians lay heavily on the consciences of the founders of Plymouth and for two centuries resolute men undertook the unrewarding task of mastering strange tongues and preaching the gospel in the wilderness but not until the founding in England of the Society for Promoting Christian Knowledge (1698) and the Society for the Propagation of the Gospel in Foreign Parts (1701) did a distinct mission movement get under way. Scots and Moravians also organized societies for mission work in the eighteenth century but it was late in that century before the action society for missions and church extension developed on a general scale in the United States among Baptists, Congregationalists and Presbyterians. It was the founders of the voluntary societies for missions who took a first long step in the direction of modern American denominationalism.

The second stage in denominational development was the integration of the myriad independent societies for missions and other worthy purposes into a single system which sustained and ramified the motivation injected into American church life by the Second Awakening. Local mission groups first began to cooperate regionally; Baptist congregations, for example, joined in support of such societies as the Massachusetts Baptist Missionary Society in 1802. Among Baptists, the movement toward more comprehensive missionary action continued; the Baptist General Tract Society was established in 1824 and the American Baptist Home Mission Society in 1832. Around the mission impulse there occurred a "nationalization" of Baptist action.

By 1814, Lyman Beecher's vision of Christian action had leaped beyond the uniting of separate mission societies. He recognized that a total system of voluntary groups for missions, education, publication, and moral reform could wield great power and he set forth a theory of church-culture relations that eventually became one pole of the denominational mentality of Congregationalists and Presbyterians. The scattered mission societies of the eastern seaboard took on a very different social significance when united as auxiliaries of a fully staffed national society, the American Home Mission Society. Furthermore, this Society functioned as a part of a larger system of organizations fully equipped to evangelize, to recruit and educate a ministry, and to transport graduates to western settlements and subsidize new parish beginnings. With its coordinate societies, the American Home Mission Society formed and administered cooperative arrangements with other religious traditions as a means of implementing the vision of the New England leadership. The New England "engine" ran smoothly not only because its member bodies were directed by a group of capable men who knew and agreed with one another on policy but also because many of them sat on the executive committees of a number of constituent organizations.

But the American denomination had not yet appeared. Sidney Mead has argued that the touchstone of the denomination lies in its purposive character. "It is a voluntary association of like-hearted and like-minded individuals who are united on the basis of common beliefs for the purpose of accomplishing tangible and defined objectives." But this holds true of the voluntary societies of the post-revolutionary era and they are clearly not identical with the "churches" of their time. A third ingredient was needed before the denomination in its essentially modern form could appear: the amalgamation of the comprehensive and systematic method of Christian action with particular American religious traditions.

The order in which these steps were taken and the rate of

progress in the development of the modern denomination varied among the main American religious traditions. The Great Awakening produced many new Baptist churches in New England and registers of mission societies published by the *Panoplist* indicate that specifically Baptist missionary societies were multiplying swiftly by 1800. Here the union of action groups with a single tradition appeared early, by contrast with the inter-denominational ventures sponsored by Congregational and Presbyterian leaders. Methodist action also was specifically Methodist from the beginning; the Methodist book concern, for example, was founded in 1789 and the Methodist Missionary Society emerged from the Methodist movement itself rather than from an earlier cooperative enterprise. Yet a fundamental characteristic of modern denominationalism can be verified: the gathering of local and regional efforts into comprehensive organizational unity specifically joined with an early tradition of American Christianity.

Presbyterian and Congregational denominationalism passed through a stage of cooperation into separation. During the period of cooperation the machinery of denominationalism was perfected; when separation occurred, both groups, but specifically the Old School Presbyterians, to whom autonomy was particularly dear, became denominations in the modern sense.

The American denomination, like all living things, went far beyond the rudiments it had developed by 1840. New concerns swept over the churches in the industrial era, for example, but denominational executive structures proved immensely flexible. They adapted swiftly to the new interests of the churches. The independent societies withered or were converted to denominational organs, as with the American Board of Commissioners, which became the Congregational Church's mission body when Presbyterian support failed. Vestiges of the old system remained in the American Bible Society, the American Sunday School Union, the Lord's Day Alliance, and a few others. But the idea of the early voluntary society lived on in the boards of the denominational churches.

II

The process that produced modern denominations began with an upsurge after the Revolution of new groupings of local churches in which the missionary impulse was inherent or dominant. In 1787 the newly nationalized Episcopal Church founded the Society for Propagating the Gospel among the Indians and Others in North America, an American counterpart of the earlier English mission effort. By 1808 this body was controlled by Boston's Old Calvinists. The first missionary society under joint auspices was the New York Missionary Society, founded in 1796 by Presbyterians, Associated Reformed (Scottish), Dutch Reformed, and Baptists. Congregational associations soon were acting as missionary societies in the valley of Connecticut where consociational congregationalism dated back to Solomon Stoddard. Massachusetts congregationalism was much slower to "presbyterianize" but formed an association in 1802, declaring it one of its purposes to "cooperate with one another and similar institutions in the most eligible manner for building up the cause of truth and holiness."

As early as 1774 the Congregational Association of Connecticut attempted to meet the need for itinerant ministers on the frontier but the demand was too great and in 1797 the task was assumed by a special arm of the associated churches, the Missionary Society of Connecticut. It included a Presbyterian, Samuel Miller of New York, later a professor at Princeton Seminary. The Massachusetts Missionary Society's accounts, regularly published in the *Panoplist*, exhibited the tributary bonds of the local societies to the state-wide body. The groundwork of a powerful national society was well laid before 1800, not only in the abundance of local societies for domestic mission work but in the modelling of a type of organization which became national through the merger of strong local and state-wide societies.

The mission impulse was greatly stimulated by events in Great Britain, notably the dramatic work of men like William Carey, the moving spirit of the Baptist Missionary Society of 1792, and the union of English Independents, Presbyterians, and Episcopalians in the London Missionary Society in 1795. Full accounts of the early missionary societies and their intimate association with the revival may be found in Oliver W. Elsbree, *The Rise of the Missionary Spirit in America, 1790–1815* (1928) and Charles R. Keller, *The Second Great Awakening in Connecticut* (1942).

While the roles of revival and missions in the first stage of the process that was to issue in modern denominationalism must not be underestimated, comparably important were the "moral societies" for it was in the course of their establishment that Lyman Beecher enunciated his conception of the social function of a highly organized voluntary Protestantism. American Puritans had always deplored the decay of godliness incident upon New England's prosperity and shortness of memory, and Timothy Dwight and Lyman Beecher were the preachers of jeremiad for their generation. Before disestablishment, Beecher looked to the state, with the full support of the churches, to regenerate society. "The Kingdom of God is a kingdom of means," he declared in 1814, "and though the excellency of power belongs to him, exclusively human instrumentality is indispensable." The clergy were to expose social evil and persuade as best they might, but "in a free government, moral suasion and coercion must be united." Furthermore, the magistrate could not perform his task without a friendly public opinion. "Local voluntary associations of the wise and good to aid the civil magistrate" were the answer: "a sort of disciplined moral militia prepared to . . . repel every encroachment upon the liberty and morals of the State." Beecher argued that civil order could not be established in the "waste places" of Connecticut without the moral groundwork of Christianity.

Beecher's thinking was not superficially practical. He deplored the separatist and parochial spirit of the divisions a half-century earlier and blamed "enthusiasm" for many social ills. Against it he argued that "the gospel recognizes no independent churches. All are the subjects of one Kingdom . . . members of one body united in one common head. . . . There is a fellowship of Churches which Jesus Christ has constituted. . . . It is not a matter of discretion whether the churches of Connecticut shall help feeble churches. They are bound to do it."

How could orthodox Congregationalists perpetuate the

revival and regenerate society? First, said Beecher, never vote for candidates who tolerate social evils such as duelling. Christian citizens have a right to demand that their governors adhere to a generally Christian moral system. This did not mean that "churches are bound in point of duty . . . to confine their suffrages exclusively to persons of their own denomination" or even necessarily to professing Christians. But there must be "such belief in the being of God and of accountability and future punishment as lays a foundation for the practical influence of an oath; such exemption from immorality as will render the elevated example of rulers safe to the interest of public morals; such general approbation of the Christian religion and its institutions as will dispose them to afford to religion the proper protection and influence of government. . . . " "It is both the duty and policy of legislators to countenance the Christian religion and its institutions."

The moral societies should neglect no corner of the country, believed Beecher. The public stood in constant need to be reminded of the gravity of apparently minor misdemeanors such as drunkenness, blasphemous speech, profanation of the Sabbath. "A society . . . is calculated to do good from the influence it may have in the formation of public opinion." Furthermore, it was needed to educate the young in sound morals.

To his general conception of church and society Beecher brought the support of a specific interpretation of the Bible. *The Bible a Code of Laws* . . . presented the charter of a comprehensive social order. "The Scriptures are to be regarded as containing a system of moral laws revealed to illustrate the glory of God . . . [and] the salvation of man," he said at the ordination of Elisha Swift, later to become a leader of Old School Presbyterianism in Pittsburgh. Man is so constituted as to be fully responsible to the law of the Bible. "The faculties of understanding, conscience, and choice constitute an accountable agent. Their existence is as decisive evidence of free agency as the five senses are of the existence of the body. . . . " The fundamental doctrines of the Bible are those "which are essential to the influence of law as means of moral government and without which God does not ordinarily renew and sanctify the soul." The minister is an agent of God to inform and remind man of the divine requirement. The good magistrate, irrespective of church affiliation and apart from any establishment of religion, allies himself with the church in this effort.

The driving power behind moral societies, colportage, and missions is "real, experimental religion" to which any man, by his very constitution, may be challenged, argued Beecher. Summarizing the fundamentals of the Christian religion, he placed first the doctrine "that men are free agents; in the possession of such faculties and placed in such circumstances as render it practicable for them to do whatever God requires; reasonable that he should require it; and fit that he should inflict, literally, the entire penalty of disobedience. . . ." Beecher deprecated the half-way covenant. His words bespeak the Matherian ideal of congregationalism: "a careful maintenance of the apostolic tenure of membership in the visible church . . . a credible profession of repentance towards God and faith in our Lord Jesus Christ. . . ."

The integral relation between Beecher's anthropology, his "theocratic" view of state-church relations, his adherence to the revival, and his conception of social control through voluntary church-based societies placed him in the forefront of the theorists who created the genius of denominational church life: a view of the church as a Christianizing agent, neither dependent on state favor nor yielding to the heresy and secularism that menaced New England after 1790. Winthrop Hudson remarks on Charles Beecher's astonishment that his father should shift from advocacy of established religion to vigorous effort in behalf of the voluntary system of Christian action. There is, of course, no inconsistency at all. Beecher's aim was a Christian society. If it could not be had by means of an established church, it must be produced by equally systematic social action on a voluntary basis. Beecher simply seized a new instrument.

III

To the decline of morals in New England was added the threat to orthodoxy posed by the French philosophy and its ecclesiastical kin, Arminianism and Unitarianism. The counter-attack of orthodoxy brought the scattered Calvinist action societies of the East into effective cooperation and assembled the engine later resented by Old School Presbyterians.

Timothy Dwight became president of Yale in 1795 and soon began to lecture on the danger of infidelity to soul and society. In 1797 the Moral Society of Yale College was founded. Its members swore to live by the moral law of the Bible and "by all prudent measures to suppress vice and promote the interest of morality. . . ." In 1802 there was revival and the horde of ideas spawned in "that suburb to the world of perdition," France, began to retreat. The campaign of Morse in Boston was no less a Connecticut affair than Dwight's work at Yale, for he was a product of the non-urban orthodoxy of Connecticut.

As pastor of the First Congregational Church of Charlestown Jedediah Morse sat on the Board of Overseers of Harvard College. At the death of David Tappan, Hollis Professor of Divinity at Harvard, the lines were drawn between the friends of orthodoxy on the Board and in the Harvard corporation and the ethical "Calvinism" of men like John Clark of Boston, who had opposed Tappan's election in 1793. Tappan had not been a formidable apologist for orthodoxy "his friends rather loved than admired him," wrote William Bentley. Bentley's characterization of his own religion summarizes the view that appalled Morse: "the only evidence I wish to have of my integrity is a good life, and as to faith, his can't be wrong whose life is in the right."

Morse had made his devotion to orthodoxy altogether plain in an early jeremiad, prepared jointly with Tappan, deploring the decadence of New England; in an alarmist attack on the "Bavarian Illuminati," in which he was supported by Dwight; and by his efforts to found a General Association of Massachusetts which would provide machinery for common action with Presbyterians such as Ashbel Green, who in 1802 was not more radical than most of his colleagues in Philadelphia. Morse's assault on the Illuminati, an all but imaginary plot against Christianity and liberty, and his diffuse criticism of French thought came to little, and his association was composed of orthodox clergy alone. The defeat of his candidate for the Hollis Chair of Divinity, Jesse Appleton, and the election of Henry Ware, widely believed by orthodox congregationalists to be unitarian, convinced Morse that the cause was lost at Harvard—as in fact it was. Morse now published an attack on his conquerors that brought a sympathetic response from Connecticut and the Philadelphia Presbyterians but exacerbated the division in Boston. Reconciliation now impossible, Morse turned his mind to the establishment of a seminary to prepare an orthodox clergy.

The *Panoplist*, founded in June 1805, and Andover Theological Seminary, opened in September 1808, were the first results. "Times of peace and outward prosperity," wrote Morse in the first issue of the *Panoplist*,

have always been fruitful in errours. Carnal security is ever the offspring of worldly ease and affluence. . . . Prosperity corrupts the heart and warps the understanding and thus prepares the way for a dislike, hatred, and rejection of the pure and humbling doctrines of the gospel. . . . At a period like this, when through various channels and under various forms principles are disseminated subversive of Christian piety and morality and hostile to revealed religion and general happiness, the Editors of the *Panoplist* feel it incumbent on them to cooperate with the conductors of similar periodical works . . . in detecting the corruptions of modern literature, in opposing the progress of dangerous principles, in stripping skepticism and imposture of their artful disguise and in exposing libertinism and impiety in all their deformity to deserved contempt and abhorrence. . . ."

In the first issue of the *Panoplist* appeared the constitution of Phillips Academy, of which Morse had been a trustee since 1795. Here the doctrinally minded Calvinist moderates of Massachusetts—as distinguished from the Harvard school on the one hand and Samuel Hopkins' "consistent Calvinism" on the other—had long intended to erect a theological school. But the Hopkinsians were already self-consciously partisan and were planning a school of their own at Newbury. Morse quickly saw that the contest with Harvard's liberal moralism could not be waged by a divided group and undertook the arduous task of reconciling the parties.

While Morse was counted a "moderate" or "old" Calvinist rather than a Hopkinsian, he did not consider complete precision in doctrine essential. "The Editors [of the *Panoplist*] explicitly avow their firm adherence *generally* and for *substance* to what has been called the doctrines of the Reformation. These doctrines with modifications and retrenchments, which affect not their essence, are recognized in the articles of the Church of England, in the Confessions of the Presbyterian Churches of Scotland and in the United States of America and in the great body of New England churches." The doctrines of the Trinity and the divinity of Christ and confidence in the reliability of the Bible were the stake in battle with Harvard as numerous articles in the *Panoplist* testified. Morse lent himself to maneuvers that now aligned him with the Hopkinsians and again made it possible to hold the old Calvinist group. The delicate negotiations that made Andover possible on a united basis are reviewed by J. K. Morse.

Morse presented the case for the Seminary to the public in a series of articles in the *Panoplist* between December 1807 and the spring of 1808, having already discussed the "state of the churches of New England" at length. Seminary trained men will be "better qualified to combat infidelity and error in every form" and would compose a "solid phalanx, well armed for the defence of divine truth. . . ." The Bible would be the great foundation of the curriculum which would include natural and Christian theology, biblical criticism, church history, and "pulpit eloquence."

In 1808 the Seminary opened with a sermon by Timothy Dwight and financial backing that had been built up in behalf of a theological department of Phillips Academy. It was supported by Hopkinsians and old Calvinists and enjoyed strong sympathy from Presbyterians. Its constitution provided that its five professors must be either Congregationalist or Presbyterian in affiliation. Edward B. Griffin, pastor of the Presbyterian Church at Newark, New Jersey, was inducted into the Professorship of Pulpit Eloquence in June 1809. Morse unsuccessfully approached

Samuel Miller of New York and Henry Kollock of Georgia, two of the ablest Presbyterians, and solicited Presbyterian students in the Middle States. But in 1808 Archibald Alexander had formally proposed a denominational seminary system and in 1811 Princeton was authorized by the Assembly. In 1816 the Presbytery of Philadelphia issued a pastoral letter warning its members against the insidious errors of the time, lumping Arianism, Arminianism, and Hopkinsianism. From that time forward, Morse's ambition to unite the two wings of Calvinism in both New England and Pennsylvania was foredoomed.

The founding of Andover catalyzed the process by which a system of independent agencies, coordinated through interlocking directorates and congenial executive leadership, was given form. Although Andover owed its existence to the contest with Harvard, it was no less a center of mission propaganda than apologetic teaching and writing. From the beginning the *Panoplist* carried regular news of American and foreign mission bodies, such as the London Missionary Society.

In publishing and mission sponsorship as well as in planning a seminary, Hopkinsians had been in competition with Old Calvinists and Morse set his heart on uniting the parties at these points also. *The Massachusetts Missionary Magazine* was edited by Samuel Spring and Leonard Wood, Professor of Theology at the seminary, who had led the Hopkinsian party into support of Andover. The delicacy of the negotiation for Andover necessitated a postponement of Morse's plan to absorb the Hopkinsian journal, which reached a number of pastors of Hopkinsian bent; but in 1808, coincident with the founding of the Seminary, the journals united in response to the "affectionate invitation" of the *Panoplist*. The title of the new journal reflected the harmony of the polemic, instructional, and missionary purposes: *The Panoplist and Missionary Magazine United ... under the Patronage of the Massachusetts, Hampshire, Berkshire, Maine and Rhode Island Missionary Societies*. The *Panoplist* worked in tandem with its counterpart in Connecticut, *The Connecticut Evangelical Magazine* (1800–1825).

A high proportion of New England's missionary societies

had well established Hopkinsian ties. Nathanael Emmons and Samuel Spring were officers of the Massachusetts Missionary Society and Samuel Hopkins himself was elected Vice-President of the Hampshire Missionary Society in 1807, along with Joseph Lyman and others prominent in the party as officers. The Calvinist front drew powerfully on revivalist missionary motivation, which reached new heights at the establishment of the American Board of Commissioners for Foreign Missions.

In 1810 Adoniram Judson and three young colleagues came before the Massachusetts General Association to ask, in effect, whether they might become missionaries to the heathen under American auspices. The Association appointed Commissioners for Foreign Missions and this "Prudential Committee" reported three months later to a meeting called in Connecticut, proposing a joint venture of orthodox Congregationalists, Presbyterians, and others. Their report was referred to the General Associations of both Massachusetts and Connecticut. The Prudential Committee included Samuel Spring, Joseph Lyman, and others identified with the Hopkinsian party and the Andover venture. Both identities are important in order to understand the conflict which was to divide the Presbyterians.

In this same year, Jedediah Morse invited a young attorney, Jeremiah Evarts, to become editor of the *Panoplist*. Evarts had been secretary of the Connecticut Religious Tract Society, led by Timothy Dwight and Isaac Mills. Evarts became treasurer of the American Board of Commissioners in 1811 and continued as editor of the *Panoplist* until 1821 when he was elected secretary of the American Board, an office which he held until his death in 1831. Evarts was also treasurer of the Massachusetts Missionary Society in 1812. The Society for Propagating Christian Knowledge among the Indians and Others in North America, originally an Anglican foundation, elected a slate of officers in 1808 which included William Phillips of the Phillips Academy Board and a founder of the Seminary; Morse, also a member of the Phillips Board; and Abiel Holmes, Minister of the First Congregational Church at Cambridge. This group was never Hopkinsian—William E. Channing is listed as assistant secretary of the Society in 1811—but accepted cooperation on both wings in order to repel infidelity, social decadence, disrespect for the Bible and doctrine, and the dampening of the zeal of the Second Awakening. The same group controlled the Massachusetts Society for Promotion of Christian Knowledge.

With party differences repressed, a strong polemic and missionary journal, a well-financed theological school, and organizations for home and foreign missions, there remained the question of recruiting and supporting orthodox candidates for the ministry. The situation was serious. Yale's average annual output between 1775 and 1815 was only nine; Beecher showed that in order to sustain a proportion of one clergyman to a thousand people, which did not then exist, it would have to be eighty per year. Furthermore, for lack of money, candidates able to do the work were being turned away by Yale. "From 16 to 20 applications of this kind have been made [each year to Yale] and refused," said Beecher. "Our college constitutes the broken link" between the power of the revival to recruit clergy and a church staffed to implement the social vision of New England orthodoxy.

The minutes of the Evangelical Society of western Vermont typify the Yankee attack on this problem. Revival had then produced a number of "pious and ingenious young men in indigent circumstances" ready to become ministers and in March 1804 this little group organized to help the "hopefully pious of orthodox faith and members of some regular Congregational or Presbyterian Church. . . ."

In the year 1810 in Maine was formed "The Society for Theological Education . . . to assist pious, promising, though indigent young men in preparing for the gospel ministry." Another such action was taken by the "Religious Charitable Society in the County of Worcester, Mass." whose "combined objects" were "to aid indigent young men of piety and talents in the acquisition of a suitable education, with a view to the Christian ministry . . . to afford pecuniary aid to the ABCFM . . . and to assist feeble churches and societies in maintaining among them the preaching and institutions of the Gospel." Innumerable small groups of this kind especially the "Female Cent Societies," had no means of making appointments or disbursements, so they remitted their collections to competent agencies. The full maturing of such bonds produced the astonishing financial strength of the national societies.

During 1814 Beecher entered the field of ministerial education and put the case for a united effort to increase the number of orthodox clergymen. "The Charitable Society, formed in Connecticut, for the Education of Indigent Pious Young Men for the Ministry of the Gospel" (September 1814) and the "American Society for Educating Pious Youth for the Gospel Ministry" (October 1814), a Massachusetts organization, were founded. The former brought together Timothy Dwight, Nathaniel Taylor, Lyman Beecher, Jedediah Morse, Jeremiah Evarts, Calvin Chapin and others on the orthodox team. In December 1815 the American Society elected William Phillips president and chose Eliphalet Pearson, Abiel Holmes, Ebenezer Porter, a professor at Andover, among others, as directors. Evarts had been temporary treasurer of the latter organization and as editor of the *Panoplist* pushed the cause vigorously. "A large part of our nation is destitute of competent religious instructors," wrote Evarts, "and the ordinary supply from our colleges is utterly insufficient to meet these wants. . . . An extraordinary and vigorous effort, therefore, is demanded. . . ." Beecher had spoken eloquently to the Connecticut "Charitable Society" of the "energy, alertness, and piety that adorn so many in the poorer classes of society . . ." and presented at length his argument that "the civil welfare of the nation demands imperiously the universal cooperation of religious institutions. . . . A more effectual and all-pervading system of religious and moral instruction [must] be provided." Republicanism had put the right to vote in the hands of "an ignorant and vicious population" which only the Gospel can "restrain and civilize." Furthermore, the "integrity of the Union" was in his view menaced by sectionalism. The cure for "this vital defect in our national organization" was not the abolition of the states' rights but "the prevalence of pious, intelligent, enterprising ministers through the nation, at the ratio of one for a thousand." They would furnish not only moral strength but an educational system capable of meeting the national need.

Beecher established a direct connection between charitable theological education and revival. Indigent youth would be selected primarily for their piety and among them revival would constantly glow. "What a security to our sons to have in the College ... a select band of pious companions to watch over and pray for them and lead them in the right way." But the poor were being refused for lack of money. Beecher termed the charitable support of theological students the only alternative to a national "relapse into heathenism."

Evidence that Beecher's wide-ranging social theory was accepted by the American Education Society may be found in its "Address" to the public of August 1817. "While it is the grand aim of Christianity to train man to future blessedness, it sheds the most benign influence on his present condition. It is ... the support of government, the cement of society. ... To preserve, then, and to perpetuate the Christian ministry is the first dictate of patriotism and philanthropy as well as of piety. ..."

The Massachusetts Society grew into the American Education Society and by 1826 Moses Stuart, defending it against Presbyterian criticism, stated that 70 per cent of the money raised in the first ten years of the New England education movement had been in that state. In 1826 the Society determined to engage a full-time secretary and asked Elias Cornelius, who had assisted Samuel Worcester, corresponding secretary of the American Board of Commissioners until the appointment of Jeremiah Evarts, to assume the task. Immediately it expanded beyond New England and within five years had aided 1300 students, as against about 550 in the period 1815–1826. About 20 per cent of all theological students in the country, distributed in five denominations and twenty states, were being assisted by the Society in 1832.

Cornelius' career was closely intertwined with the leadership that had founded the orthodox machine and furnished it with an ideology. He graduated from Yale in 1813 and studied theology two years with Dwight and one year with

Beecher at Litchfield, Connecticut. He greatly respected Evarts, who frequently pled the cause of the Education Society during his service to the American Board of Commissioners. Upon Evarts' death in 1831 Cornelius was elected to the corresponding secretariat of that body but died before fairly launching his new task. Cornelius never held a full-time pastorate; he and Evarts were the first career executives to appear in the American churches. Cornelius was expert in promotion, raising an estimated 130 to 150,000 dollars in his lifetime. In the management of the American Education Society the executive staff was primary, since its electing body before 1826 consisted of all donors; after that, of 350 directors, 111 of them Presbyterian. Directors served for only one year. These included such familiar figures as Leonard Woods and others of the orthodox-Hopkinsian alliance.

Under the impetus furnished by Cornelius, the American Education Society founded its own journal in 1827. A survey made that year showed that of 422 men educated at Andover, 320 had been "charity" students; at Princeton the figure was 200 of a total 375; at Auburn (founded 1818), 35 of 75. By 1830 Yankee energy had given Calvinism the means to cope with the West.

The home mission movement, one of the earliest products of the revival, never lost ground to the new foundations by which the New England leadership strengthened its program of church extension and social reconstruction. The separate mission societies were the last to be combined in a national organization. The American Home Mission Society was formed in 1826 by the merger of the New York Young Men's Missionary Society and the United Domestic Missionary Society, the first highly successful, the latter nearly bankrupt. Under the executive leadership of Absalom Peters it developed into an instrument of considerable power, much resented by the Old School Presbyterians because it enjoyed the advantage of the Association Plan, a cooperative arrangement that admitted New England recruited and trained candidates to western pulpits, both Presbyterian and Congregational.

Thus was completed the "New England engine," as the

Old School partisans called it. While societies for a myriad of other purposes abounded—for publication of tracts, Bibles, and educational literature; seamen's aid; education of the poor; temperance; Sabbath observance—the driving wheels were the Seminary at Andover, the periodical press, the education societies, and the foreign and domestic mission societies. All this was erected upon an alliance of doctrinally-minded Calvinists, both Hopkinsians and moderates, against the enemies that Jedediah Morse identified in 1804. A back-handed tribute to its effectiveness was paid by Calvin Colton in his angry book *Protestant Jesuitism*. Beginning with well-intentioned reforming plans, he argued, the societies for the repression of vice, mainly drunkenness, had grown until a new power elite had subtly come to rule American opinion. Colton wrote,

"If the clergy of this land and the Christian public will open their eyes they will see that the interests of moral and religious reform in this country are, almost entirely, in the hands and under the control of a few combinations of individuals who . . . devised and put in operation a system of measures which by their own supervision and that of their sub-agents, force the wide community in, socially and individually, into their schemes. . . . No man can openly oppose them without the risk of being crushed by their influence. Their eyes are everywhere; they see and understand all movements; and not a whisper of discontent can be breathed. . . ."

There should be a "Society-reforming Society" established "to correct the morals of these institutions." Colton believed that Christ had commissioned only his church to effect "the reformation of morals and manners in the world and for the gradual and ultimate subjection of all mankind to the laws and principles of the Bible."

IV

The *Panoplist* noted the publication of Ezra Stiles Ely's attack on Hopkinsian theology in 1811 without review; but it could not be ignored indefinitely. The strife which ensued within Presbyterianism was interwoven with doctrinal differences and personal frictions but its heart lay in the struggle of the Old School party to establish a system of action societies and seminaries under the control of the General Assembly—under the circumstances, this implied control by the Old School leadership—which would command the giving and personnel of Presbyterians and extend their characteristic doctrine and churchmanship through the West unmixed with New England elements.

Before 1816, Presbyterians possessed no organs of action comparable to the New England societies. Their courts were qualified to do judicial and legislative businsss but these met periodically and in the case of the General Assembly the highest, only annually. Before the forming of the Assembly's Board of Missions in 1816 no person or committee of the Assembly possessed the authority to conduct even incidental business on behalf of the church. The Board established in 1816 differed from an Assembly committee in being authorized to conduct the "missionary business" on behalf of the Assembly: recruitment, disbursement of funds, and the interpretation of Assembly directives. It reported to its controlling body only once each year. By this step, the Presbyterians brought the idea of the voluntary society into the exclusive service of their own church order. A Presbyterian "board" was a creature of the Assembly and its membership was selected by the Assembly, but it was not responsible to the lower church courts and in practice enjoyed great freedom. While the authorizing of one such board by no means converted Presbyterianism into a denomination, the establishment of other permanent boards and their progressive integration into a single executive system authorized to transact the church's business did effect that conversion.

The strife which produced denominationalism among Calvinists did not break out until 1818, but the friendships later to cement the nuclei of the two parties were established as early as 1800. The core of the conservative faction that subsequently led the way to the denominationalizing of the Presbyterians was formed when in 1800 Ashbel Green, then pastor of the Second Presbyterian Church of Philadelphia, brought together for discussions of religion several personalities who later look leading roles in the Old School party. Its senior member was John Ewing, a survivor of the

Old Side party of Presbyterianism that had opposed revival and advocated subscription to the Westminster Confession in the eighteenth century. Green's assistant, Jacob J. Janeway, was later Green's first choice for Professor at Western Seminary in Alleghenytown, Pennsylvania, by which the Old School party hoped in 1827 to possess the West. George Potts and Phillip Milledoler were both prominent in the debates between 1830 and 1837, the latter being elected a moderator of the General Assembly. Nothing is known of Archibald Alexander's contacts with this group while he was a pastor in Philadelphia between 1807 and 1812. Samuel Miller, the second professor elected at Princeton, had studied at the University of Pennsylvania under Ewing, then its provost, and was a parishioner of Ashbel Green while a student. During his pastorate in New York, Miller worked with men of many theological bents: Dutch Reformed, Hopkinsian, and Presbyterians of the Scottish tradition. He was persistently friendly toward such Andover men as Moses Stuart. He stood so firmly for moderation throughout the great Presbyterian debate that Green suspended correspondence with him entirely after 1830, when Miller advised against opposing Barnes' installation as pastor of Philadelphia's First Presbyterian Church, the action that led to Barnes' trial in 1831. When the Old School party captured the Assembly of 1837, however, Miller was obliged to conform. From 1818 his preference for denominational rather than independent action had been clear.

Ashbel Green established early bonds with the family of Charles Hodge. He married Hodge's parents, catechized young Charles, and was president of the College of New Jersey while the future Princeton professor was an undergraduate. Hodge read Witherspoon under Green's direction and heard his lectures on Logic, Bible, and Moral Philosophy.

Jedediah Morse had brought Hopkinsians and old Calvinists together in New England by 1808; and there was no active theological dispute among Presbyterians when Archibald Alexander first proposed that Presbyterian seminaries be established to meet the pressing demand for clergymen. In 1806 Ashbel Green had overtured the

Assembly to act more decisively on recruitment for the ministry and Miller was awake to the problem even earlier. After Alexander's sermon Green was appointed chairman of a committee and wrote a seminary plan that became a model of several later Presbyterian schools. The Plan was adopted in 1811 and the Board of Directors of the Seminary elected Green its president in June 1812, an office which he held until 1848. In 1810 Green, Alexander, and Miller considered Assembly control not a device to keep Presbyterianism in the hands of old Calvinists but an inference from the Presbyterian form of government they had learned from Scotland.

Ashbel Green had been wholly friendly to New England well into the second decade of the century and was fully persuaded of the potency of its method of action. In 1799, for example, Green and Janeway, his associate, had explicitly encouraged Morse. Green participated in the founding of New England-type societies for enforcing community morals; he wrote the constitution of a New Jersey Society for the Suppression of Vice. He heartily favored the establishment of Andover, against which he later fulminated.

The break came in 1818 when a group of Presbyterians friendly to the New England theology and method met in Brick Church in New York City to form "The Education Society of the Presbyterian Church in the United States of America" for the support of indigent ministerial candidates. Its chairman was Elias Boudinot, Director of the Mint and venerated for his role in the Revolution. By November 10 he had drafted a constitution for the new foundation and he served as its president until his death, being succeeded by Arthur Tappan. Associated with Boudinot in this venture was the nucleus of the coming New School party: Presbyterians opposed to Assembly control of missions and education, sympathetic to voluntarism in both thought and action, and piqued by the attack on Hopkinsianism mounted by Ely in 1816 in Philadelphia. The directorate of the new society was a roster of the New School. N. S. S. Beman, George Duffield, and Thomas McAuley were vice-presidents; Gardiner Spring (a Hopkinsian who opted for the Old School), Samuel Fisher, and Samuel H. Cox were among its directors by 1831. None of these men had been members of the New

England orthodox core but all were friendly to its method and the theology.

Archibald Alexander and Samuel Miller had attended the constitutive meeting of the New York group but did not share its preference for independent action. On December 17, 1818, seven weeks later, with Green and others they founded a rival society to be called "The Education Society of the Presbyterian Church under the care of the General Assembly." Its constitution provided for Assembly control; its annual meetings were to be held in Philadelphia. Immediate efforts to unite the two groups failed and the denominational society overtured the General Assembly to establish a controlled agency. This was done, but without enabling action, so that Assembly's Board of Education existed without promotion or funds until 1831, the year in which Albert Barnes, a Philadelphia New School pastor and apologist, was brought to trial. At that time the Old School obtained control of the Board, and appointed John Breckinridge, later a professor at Princeton, as secretary. Thereafter the Board became an effective arm of the Old School party. Its constitution provided that "no appropriation shall be made to any whose attachment to the standards of the Presbyterian Church is questionable and who may be unwilling to receive their theological education in a Presbyterian seminary."

For lack of executive leadership, the independent New York Society did not prosper until 1826 when it became auxiliary to the American Education Society and was served by Cornelius. It accepted New York, New Jersey, and Pennsylvania for its field of promotion and recruitment but left granting of funds to the parent group. Hoping to offset criticism in the crisis year of 1831, the New York group became fully autonomous, extended its field of operations to all areas where Presbyterians lived, and by agreement absorbed the established work of the American Education Society wherever it encountered it. When Cornelius died, William Patton, a Presbyterian, became its executive. By 1833 quarterly reports showed contributions and grants almost as large as those of the American Education Society itself.

While organizational activity among Presbyterians was stimulated by conservative fears of New England influence, their church had been trying to adapt its traditional machinery to the frontier challenge since 1790. Like congregational associations, presbyteries had sent resident ministers on brief tours; but when the inadequacy of such methods became apparent, the Assembly established first a committee (1802), then a board (1816) to take charge of mission work. Between these dates, Philadelphia interests obtained a special hold on Assembly's mission activity by sponsoring a regulation in 1805 that ten of the seventeen members of the Assembly committee must be from Philadelphia or its environs. A similar geographical regulation was proposed in 1828 in a further revision of the constitution of the Board: "every ordained minister of the Presbyterian Church in the city and liberties of Philadelphia shall be a member of the Board, together with one ruling elder. . . ." This was calculated in part to put Philadelphia New School Presbyterians under obligation to the Assembly controlled mission board, but there were numerous commissioners friendly to independent missions in the Assembly and the proposal was refused.

Ashbel Green had stood at the nerve-center of churchwide action since 1802 when he was appointed chairman of Assembly's committee on missions. The trigger of the Presbyterian schism was the realization of these early organization men that unless real patronage could be built up, the Assembly's committee structure would remain a house of straw. The principal obstacle was the generous patronage that the independent societies enjoyed among Presbyterians. At this point a struggle for power developed: power to command Presbyterian giving, to recruit and aid students of assured orthodoxy, to control theological education and to establish new churches in conventional Presbyterian relationships. Only such an apparatus of promotion, education and extension as New England had devised could accomplish the task; but only if such an apparatus could be organized, controlled, and financed by the Presbyterian Church alone could the goal of the Philadelphia-Princeton leadership be realized. This logic, operating from the founding of Princeton Seminary in 1811 to the schism of 1837–38, gave form to the modern American Presbyterian denomination.

In the intellectual and ecclesiastical climate of the twentieth century, it is difficult to feel any great sympathy for the Old School Presbyterians. Their ethic of Christian life was throughly legalistic; their "intellectualism" was rigid without being either comprehensive, consistent, or penetrating. Yet the great majority of Old School men would have preferred compromise to division had the schism not been forced by such radicals as Ashbel Green, George Junkin, and Robert J. Breckinridge. When that had been accomplished, the Princetonians took over, notably Miller and Hodge. From one point of view, the Old School reaction against the New England swing to the left, itself a betrayal of the Northampton prophet, must be regarded as the assertion of an impulse in American Presbyterianism deriving from both its eighteenth century New England and Scottish sources. It is very remote from the facts to understand the schism of 1837–38 as no more than a fresh outbreak of the Old Side-New Side schism of 1741–1758, or a raw imposition of Scottish churchmanship. Had Jonathan Dickinson confronted the decision forced on Archibald Alexander, he might very well have made Alexander's choice for the older Swiss and Dutch orthodoxy as against the semi-Pelagianism and permissive churchmanship of the Congregational-New School wing. Dickinson spent four years seeking reunion before joining Tennent's theologically orthodox revival movement; he would have had as much reason as Alexander, a monument of loyalty to the revival, to prefer the Old School to the New England philosophy of religion and its pragmatic revivalism.

Schism in Presbyterianism was an extreme consequence of a struggle which under other circumstances might not have been pressed so far. The transformation of Presbyterianism into a denomination did not itself produce the division. That was an effect of the great power within the General Assembly of Presbyterians who believed that strong Assembly agencies could only harm already successful independent enterprises in missions and education. The New School denied the Assembly Boards of Missions and Education any material strength until 1830; it frustrated the establishment of a Presbyterian Board of Foreign Missions; it refused to condemn the views of Albert Barnes in 1831 and 1836 and of Lyman Beecher in 1835; and it permitted only minor modifications of the Plan of Union of 1801, which actually did open the courts of the Presbyterian Church to the influence of New England doctrine and churchmanship. The process was not only forcing back the doctrinal rigidities of Green and his men but dissolving the older theological substructure that the Presbyterian revivalists of the 1830s considered fundamental to their preaching. Whether these problems should have been dealt with as they were may be questioned; there can be little doubt that in 1836 distinctive Presbyterian churchmanship was swiftly giving way to protean organization of post-Calvinist moralism.

Acutely exasperated and already prone to seek solutions by law, trial, and expulsion, the Old School party seized control of the Assemblies of 1837 and 1838 and expelled four synods in New York and the Western Reserve. It then established a Board of Foreign Missions, abrogated the plan of Union and redirected Presbyterian giving to its own agencies. Foster [in *An Errand of Mercy* (1960)] sees in this the definitive breakdown of the "United Front." So it was; but it was also a transition to the denominational system, its successor.

V

The new type of American denomination could not have existed in the state church era or before the development of executive structures. "Sects" did exist in protest against both state churches and the inclusive denominationalism that developed later, and were themselves seeds of denominations; but the denomination as such succeeded the established church and was neither a sect nor simply an *ad hoc* action group. It possessed fundamental forms that proved capable of adapting themselves to modern social and political conditions.

American denominationalism possesses three constitutive elements: a purposive system of executive and promotional agencies, as indicated by Mead; the association of this structure with a particular American religious tradition; and a conservative, sometimes legalistic, determination to maintain a distinctive identity in the face of change.

In the final stage of Presbyterian denominational development here discussed a sociological change of considerable significance occurred. New England Calvinism, both before and after disestablishment, had aimed to penetrate, even dominate American society for Christian morals. The forming of the Old School General Assembly marked a withdrawal. Although adapted to a free society, the New England crusade was of the "church-type" in its comprehensive concern for the national life; the removal of the system of executive agencies from its early association with general Christian moral opinion into a formal tie with a conservative Presbyterian tradition necessarily involved the abandonment of the ideal of social comprehensiveness. This was precisely the purpose of the Old School Presbyterians. Between 1800, when more optimism about the national future prevailed among Presbyterians than orthodox Congregationalists, and 1830 there occurred an important shift of sentiment. The New England theology had moved steadily leftward from the positions of Bellamy and Hopkins toward Taylor and Finney; the republicanism of Jefferson had become the radicalism of the Jacksonian age; the development of the popular churches had reduced the Presbyterians to one among many churches and sects. Fear for the nation had replaced hope in the hearts of those who saw the rising cloud of slavery controversy.

The early Presbyterian denominational conception aimed to provide a total life of a specific sort for the faithful. It was sectarian in that it built a fortress within which the true Christian was protected from the assault of the world. By determinate rules all who threatened the integrity of the community could be identified and ferreted out. The Presbyterian denomination was not originally designed for thrust into the world, as Beecher would have had it. It invited a decadent America to turn from infidelity and immorality and submit to the discipline of a holier company.

The necessity for withdrawal was confirmed in the minds of the denominationalists by the inpouring of Roman Catholics in the 1830s.

The denomination, however, even at its most conservative was not a sect. Its genius lay in its flexibility and less than a generation elapsed before it was moving in the direction of a "church-type" mentality. The true church-type of Ernst Troeltsch, expressed in Europe by the state church, could find no exact parallel in a pluralistic American society. But the shift of the denomination from its early sectarian bent toward social inclusiveness approximated it. Old and New School Presbyterians reunited in 1870, measurably inhibiting although not dispersing, the sectarian mood. As the denominations expanded they began to understand themselves in terms of their common form; they found that they composed a reasonably homogeneous federal entity, American Protestantism. With the coming of the social gospel and its major institutional achievements, the founding of the Federal Council of Churches and the Home Missions Council of 1908, the denominational system recovered the concern of the voluntary movement for social reconstruction on a national scale. At last even the theological enterprise, left in virtual ruins by the apologetic service forced on it by the divisive era of denominational development, began to recover. By nature it could not live without free mutual exchange between the historic traditions. The abandonment of the separatist mood opened the way and the theological recovery now makes its own reconciling contribution.

Nevertheless, the point of reference for these highly significant changes was the specific type of ecclesiastical body formed between 1787 and 1837. As the bearer of both the separatist and the unitive spirit of American Christianity, the denomination remains the fundamental church structure of this country.

5
Introduction

Both the preceding essay by Elwyn A. Smith and this one by Fred J. Hood treat denominationalism within the context of Presbyterianism. By focus and emphasis the essays differ and complement one another. Smith, concerned to illustrate the theological issues at stake, examines the developments and tensions in Congregational and Presbyterian cooperation in the Plan of Union and the voluntary societies. Hood treats the several Reformed denominations of the middle and southern states, focuses upon constitutional issues, and examines these issues in light of the goals of the Reformed denominations to Christianize the nation (these goals being articulated in their doctrines of Providence and the millennium). Both see the internalization of the society principle as vital to the emergence of mature denominationalism. Their divergent discussions of that development should be reflected upon by the reader.

An important feature of Hood's argument is his recognition of two conceptions of denominationalism. The Reformed denominations initially understood their structures as "means for the internal government of the church." Such a self-conception, inadequate for their own professed aspirations for a Christian nation, led them into a groping embrace of voluntary societies. While dominated by Congregationalists and the Reformed, these autonomous, extra-ecclesiastical, and interdenominational associations struggled towards a national style of activity. As the character of such national Christian endeavor and the implications for particular denominations became clear, the smaller Reformed denominations and a large segment of Presbyterianism withdrew their consent. Their retreat was to a new understanding of denominations as missionary societies—that is, as structures properly incorporating the variety of voluntary activities previously carried on interdenominationally.

The two conceptions of the denomination—as a "means for the internal government of the church" and "as a great missionary society, instituted for the conversion of the world"—have frequently been confused. The confusion is understandable. As Hood indicates, the effect of acceptance of the Reformed and the Old School conception (accepted also by Methodists, Baptists, Disciples, and other evangelical denominations) was to fragment the attempt to Christianize the nation. Thus the providential and millennial goals that produced the voluntary associations and in the name of which Reformed and Old School espoused the new conception of denominationalism were undermined. Thereafter the missionary conception of the denomination was particularly susceptible to the various forms of confessionalism which in a sense again reduced denominations to a means of internal church government. That capitulation was not inevitable, as George M. Marsden shows, for the New School Presbyterians. Despite its position on the issues of theology, voluntary societies, revivalism, slavery, and sectionalism that divided the Presbyterians, the New School eventually followed the Old School pattern. It is interesting, however, that during the Civil War the New School arrested its confessionalism and reaffirmed its activistic commitment to the providential and millennial views that gave the missionary conception of the denomination particular force.[1]

The irony that Hood points out and the implications of this irony for denominations today represent one fruitful line of inquiry. The reader might also examine the degree to which essays in this volume utilize the two conceptions of denominations just delineated. Hudson, Mead, Elwyn Smith, Richey, and Hood apparently view the denominations as missionary societies. Does Timothy Smith see them as means for the internal government of the church? Does Niebuhr? Is the choice between conceptions a perspectival one, or do the particular ethnic and social factors to be examined, the period under discussion, and the denominations in question dictate the conception adopted? To what extent do the two conceptions of the denomination apply today? Are there denominations that are content to understand their structures as means for the internal government of the church and others that conceive of themselves as great missionary societies, instituted for the conversion of the world? What leads a denomination to lean towards the one or the other? Are there forms of the missionary understanding particularly appropriate for the twentieth century?

1. See George M. Marsden, *The Evangelical Mind and the New School Presbyterian Experience* (New Haven: Yale University Press, 1970), particularly pp. 128-41 and 199-211.

5

Evolution of the Denomination Among the Reformed of the Middle and Southern States, 1780–1840

Fred J. Hood

The concept and character of the religious institution commonly designated the denomination underwent a marked evolution in the period from the American Revolution to the 1830s. Initially the term referred simply to Protestants called by different names, governed under a different form of church policy, and holding varying beliefs—all while considering each other a part of the Christian church however. In its institutional expression the denomination had come into being in the context of Erastianism and was designed primarily to regulate the religious life and promote the uniformity of doctrine and morals of its ministers and members. While the evolution of this concept could be observed within the framework of a number of American religious expressions, it was perhaps nowhere more clearly revealed than among the distinctly Reformed denominations of the middle and southern states. The Reformed way of thinking about the American nation demanded that its adherents take forceful and aggressive action to promote national prosperity. Initially they turned to voluntary associations as the most appropriate institutions by which to implement their national goals. By the 1820s, however, there were increasing pressures to include these functions within the denomination, and by 1840 the denomination as we know it had emerged. The denomination became a multifaceted institution that was not only concerned with its own membership but was oriented toward producing changes across the whole spectrum of national political and social life.

In the early years of national existence the Reformed developed an ideology which linked American prosperity with a national commitment to Protestant Christianity. This ideology had a profound impact on the development of Reformed institutions. The traditional doctrine of Providence, which was infused with eighteenth-century rationalism primarily through the influence of John Witherspoon and Samuel Stanhope Smith of the College of New Jersey, was altered so that it came to be understood that God controlled the prosperity or decline of nations through certain fixed laws. Religion, it was alleged, was the most powerful force contributing to national prosperity in all nations and at all times. It was argued that in America, however, adherence to the Protestant religion had produced the distinctive features of American political life—republican government, civil and religious liberty—and that these could therefore only be maintained through a continued national commitment. Thus, in the face of the states' disengagement from religion, the Reformed continued to insist on "the Association between Religion and Patriotism" as necessary to national prosperity.[1]

At the same time, the Reformed were also greatly influenced by their understanding that the millennium was imminent. The millennium represented an idealized and uniform society completely subservient to the will of the deity as understood by the Reformed leadership. It was believed that the existence of such a society was assured by the promise of God but that its realization required the cooperation and labor of man. While the millennial goal was ultimately universal, the belief that America had a special role in producing the millennium tended to make the vision intensely nationalistic. The millennial ideal became a prototype for an attempted reconstruction, or "renovation," of American society. These ideas complemented and reinforced the demands of the emerging doctrine of Providence and also influenced the evolution of the denominational structures.

Any analysis of the Reformed denominations in the middle and southern states must give major attention to the Presbyterian Church in the United States of America. That denomination was the largest and most influential, maintaining about 70 percent of the Reformed churches in the middle and southern states in 1820. The Reformed Church in the United States, or German Reformed, ranked second in number of churches; but many of these were without ministers, and the denomination was on the whole very weak. Most of its energies were consumed in internal affairs. The Reformed Church in America, or the Reformed Dutch, was second in influence, but in 1820 had only about one-tenth as many churches as the Presbyterians. The smaller Reformed denominations, while sharing the national goals, were in no position to exert widespread influence by themselves. In the evolution of denominational structures the smaller Reformed denominations usually followed, at some distance in time, the development of the larger groups. Because of these factors, it becomes essential to focus on the Presbyterian and Reformed Dutch denominations.

When the Reformed were organized in the wake of the American Revolution, they conceived of the denomination almost solely as a means for the internal government of the church. Each denomination was based on a presbyterial form of government with varying numbers of local or regional bodies occurring between the local church and the highest body in the denomination. Each denomination's constitution specified in great detail the duties and responsibilities at every level of church government. Only the Presbyterians provided for expansion—and that in a single page in an otherwise lengthy document. Even at this point, however, the Presbyterians were primarily concerned with supplying vacancies in already existing churches. The only provision for expansion was that "the general assembly may, on their own knowledge, send missions to any part to plant churches, or to supply vacancies."[2] In fact, the American Reformed church organizations differed little from that of the established Church of Scotland. Differences were of detail rather than basic design, function, or structure. As Professor Sidney E. Mead has observed of the 1780s, "There was as yet little indication and less awareness that the church patterns of America would be markedly different from those of Europe."[3]

There were several factors at work during the 1780s that promoted the survival of such a narrowly defined concept of the denomination. The first of these was the belief that the United States was a Christian nation whose policy and laws would conform to the standards of Christianity taught by the existing denominations. This presupposition was accepted as fact, and found explicit statement in the Presbyterian *Constitution*, which declared, "And if at any time the civil power should think it proper to appoint a fast or thanksgiving, it is the duty of the ministers and people of our communion, as we live under a christian government, to pay respect to the same."[4] The Reformed Dutch standards contained a similar provision.

Implicit in this thinking was the idea that in some way Protestant Christianity, as distinguished from any single denominational expression of that religion, was to be the established religion of America, at least informally. By continued use of the expression "nursing fathers" the Presbyterian revision of the Westminster Confession concerning civil magistrates expressed the idea of an informal establishment. Having affirmed that civil magistrates had no religious jurisdiction, the revision continued, "Yet as nursing fathers, it is the duty of civil magistrates to protect the church of our common Lord, without giving the preference to any denomination of Christians."[5] The Reformed Dutch assumed in 1790 that the United States Congress was the most logical body to secure copies of Bibles for Americans.

Since the rapidly developing historical situation soon belied these presuppositions, there was never a theoretical or practical demonstration of how the system was to function. A letter from the first Presbyterian General Assembly to the recently elected Washington, however, breathed this spirit. After reciting the providential formula "Public virtue is the most certain means of public felicity; and religion is the surest basis of virtue," the Presbyterians praised Washington as an "avowed friend of the Christian religion; who has commenced his administration in rational and exalted sentiments of piety; . . . and on the most public and solemn occasions, devoutly acknowledges the government of Divine Providence." While entertaining the hope that such an example would have the "most happy consequences," the Presbyterians promised "to add the wholesome instructions of religion . . . to render men sober, honest, and industrious citizens." But this important function was not to be the work of Presbyterians alone.

In these pious labours, we hope to imitate the most worthy of our brethren of other Christian denominations, and to be imitated by them; assured that if we can, by mutual and generous emulation, promote truth and virtue, we shall render a great and important service to the republic; shall receive encouragement from every wise and good citizen, and, above all, meet the approbation of our Divine Master.[6]

Thus, at the time of the reorganization, the Presbyterians envisioned themselves and "the most worthy of our brethren," meaning primarily those of the Reformed traditoin, as serving collectively in the capacity of a state church.

The Presbyterians of 1788 were of the opinion that they could do most to influence the nation by maintaining the doctrinal and moral integrity of their own denomination. This belief was reflected in a letter from the first General Assembly to the four newly created synods.

The dignity of our church, its weight and influence in the United States, and even the utility of its ordinances, to the great ends of religion, will depend much on the unity of our counsels; and on the order and efficiency of our government. While the interest of religion ought to be our first and ruling object, we ought not to forget how necessary it is, for that great purpose, to preserve our character as a body, and our consequence in the republic, in comparison with other denominations of Christians.[7]

A second factor which produced an intense concern with internal church government was the fact of religious liberty in America. As has been demonstrated, the significance of this for the Reformed was that religion, the church, was now free from the control of civil government and free to conform as nearly as possible to the scriptural ideal. In the Presbyterian revision of the Westminster Confession the sentence following the one designating magistrates as "nursing fathers" of the church, stated that "as Jesus Christ hath appointed a regular government and discipline in his church, no law of any commonwealth, should interfere with, let, or hinder, the due exercise thereof." [8]

That the Presbyterians recognized the uniqueness of the situation and determined to use it to best advantage was illustrated in the introduction to "The Form of Government and Discipline," which was written to "make the several parts of the system plain." After declaring in the first paragraph that "they consider the rights of private judgment, in all matters that respect religion, as universal and unalienable," the founding fathers of modern Presbyterianism indicated the implications of this for their task of structuring the denomination.

That, in perfect consistency with the above principle of common right, every Christian church, or union or association of particular churches, is entitled to declare the terms of admission into its *communion* and the qualifications of its ministers and members, as well as the whole system of its internal government which Christ hath appointed: That, in the exercise of this right, they may, notwithstanding, err, in making the terms of communion either too lax or too narrow: yet, even in this case, they do not infringe upon the liberty, or the rights of others, but only make an improper use of their own. [9]

The Reformed Dutch reflected the same attitude in the preface to their *Constitution* of 1792, which began, "In consequence of that liberty wherewith Christ hath made his people free, it becomes this duty as well as privilege, openly to confess and worship him according to the dictates of their own consciences." Since membership in the denomination was "wholly voluntary, and unattended with civil emoluments or penalties," they could "bear a proper testimony" without "infringements upon the equal liberties of others." [10]

Since the concept of the denomination was limited primarily to the internal government of the church, the national endeavors of the Reformed were primarily promoted through a number of voluntary associations. These were established in America with a frequency that heralded a new era in the history of this type of organization (which had actually originated in the era of the Reformation). The creation of these societies grew at an accelerated pace in the first quarter of the nineteenth century so that by 1826 the local societies numbered in the thousands, and seven societies claimed national status. Although any initial definition of these societies as institutions would require subsequent qualification, they were usually nonecclesiastical organizations of individuals sufficiently concerned with some given issue to come together, pay annual dues, and promote the designs of the society with their time and energy. The names of the national societies suggest in broad outline the nature of all the societies. They were the American Board of Commissioners for Foreign Missions (1810), the American Bible Society (1816), the American Education Society (1816), the American Colonization Society (1816), the American Sunday School Union (1824), the American Home Missionary Society (1826), and the American Temperance Society (1826).

The trend toward the preference of voluntary societies in areas of national concern was evident as early as the year 1800 when the trustees of the Presbyterian General Assembly presented to that body a comprehensive statement of the Reformed national goals. The trustees presented four areas for consideration. The first was the "gospelizing" of the Indians and a plan for their civilization "the want of which it is believed has been a great cause of the failure of former attempts to spread Christianity among them." The second object was the "instruction of the negroes, the poor, and those who are destitute of the means of grace." The third suggestion was for "the purchasing and disposing of Bibles, and also books and short essays on the great principles of religion and morality." The fourth called for "the provision of a fund for the more complete instruction of candidates for the gospel ministry, previously to their licensure." [11]

The General Assembly agreed with the report and added to the second recommendation. The Assembly suggested the possibility of instituting an "order of catechists" to instruct the poor and others. These men, who would not have the education necessary for the ministry, could offer private religious instruction and lead devotional exercises "with a view to prepare the way for a few regular and ordained ministers to follow them, to organize churches and administer ordinances." While not ministers, these functionaries would be examined and would work under their direction. This program was not to be viewed as replacing missionary work but "to be considered as additional to it." [12]

There was in this report the essence of the entire program that was launched to make the American nation conform to the requirements of the doctrine of Providence and the vision of the millennium. But this program was not to be implemented through the Presbyterian denomination or any of the other Reformed denominations. In ordering these statements published so that "the judicatories and people at large . . . may be acquainted with the views and wishes of their highest judicature," the Assembly made the following comment.

But the Assembly neither judge it expedient themselves to attempt to carry into immediate effect all that is here suggested, nor to urge on their judicatures and people to attempt it. Some things only that are here specified will be entered on by this Assembly; and the judicatures and people will judge for themselves what other objects it may be proper for them voluntarily to regard. [13]

What the Assembly meant by "voluntarily to regard" was not clear. What was clear, however, was that the program suggested was attempted primarily through the system of voluntary societies formed specifically to carry out a single phase of the program. In this report were clearly the germs of the missionary, Bible, tract, and education societies, with the Sunday school unions reflecting a revised version of the "order of catechists," and the "instruction for negroes" giving way to a scheme for their removal.

In addition to the positive advantages of the voluntary societies there were several considerations which made the denomination a secondary institution for action designed to affect the nation. The task of internal government for which the structures had been created occupied a large portion of the time and energy of the various judicatories, produced disharmony, and thereby made the denomination less efficient than the voluntary societies. The denominations attempted only missions and the education of ministers, and in these two areas they were constantly frustrated by inadequate accomplishment and the inability to stimulate greater exertion. There was a tendency for the denominations to mold their own organizations on the pattern of the voluntary societies. These maneuvers worked to destroy the coherence of the original hierarchical structures so that the judicatories functioned more like autonomous societies than links in the chain of a larger integrated organization. By the 1820s the strictly denominational efforts had become indistinguishable from those of the voluntary associations.

This tendency toward the society principle was most pronounced in the area of missions. The first step in that direction was the formation of standing committees of missions that was accomplished by the Presbyterians in 1802, the Reformed Dutch in 1806, the German Reformed in 1813, and the Associate Synod in 1822. With slight variations these committees had the power to solicit and distribute funds, appoint missionaries, and carry on all of the missionary business of the denomination. They were required to make annual reports to the denomination.

The standing committees proved to be largely ineffective, and the denominations went through a series of reorganizations which moved them further in the direction of the voluntary societies. Between 1802 and 1816 the Presbyterian committee was only able to supply the equivalent of four full-time missionaries per year. The Reformed Dutch committee was never able to raise more than four hundred dollars in any given year during the first decade of operations. The Standing Committee of Missions of the Associate Synod of North America employed only one missionary in 1822 and was attempting to get missionaries from Scotland or Ireland by offering a hundred dollars to any who would come and accept the principles of the synod. In 1816 the Presbyterians organized a Board of Missions which they believed would "be able to carry on the missionary business with all the vigour and unity of design that would be found in a society originated for that purpose." [14] This movement toward the society principle within the denomination in order to gain efficiency was followed by the

Reformed Dutch in 1822, the Associate Reformed in 1824, and the German Reformed in 1827.

The pattern developed in missions was transferred to the denominational efforts to educate ministers. After preliminary experimentation with "Cent societies," the Presbyterians in 1819 and the Reformed Dutch in 1828 formed boards of education on the society principle. This "new and more efficient measure" was fraught with difficulty that became significant in the development of a new concept of the denomination. These problems were illustrated by developments in the Presbyterian Board of Education. In the early years of its existence the Board of Education was completely overshadowed by its two largest auxiliaries, the Presbyterian Education Society, located in New York, and the Philadelphia Education Society. The New York branch functioned as an autonomous society with no denominational connection, while the Philadelphia society worked in close harmony with the Board of Education. The New York group believed that the denominational judicatories should do nothing other than manage the internal concerns of the denomination and that voluntary societies should attend to those things designed to convert the nation. From the Philadelphia group, which believed that all such concerns should come under the control of the denomination, emerged the new concept of the denomination as a "missionary society" that was ultimately to dominate in America. The fact remains that during the period before 1826 when the great national voluntary societies were being established, the Reformed denominational organizations did not appear to offer a viable alternative.

The voluntary societies definitely appeared to be the best means to promote the "association between Religion and Patriotism." In the wake of the fragmentation of Protestantism and the retreat of civil government from jurisdiction in matters of religion, the societies seemed to be the most efficient way to encourage religion and therefore promote the national welfare in light of a theory of the denomination that had relied on civil government to provide religious cohesion to the society. In the societies the Reformed could appear to be unsectarian and therefore could cooperate with the nation's patriots in a way that was impossible within the framework of the denomination. For the Reformed, it was the societies rather than the denomination which also seemed to foreshadow the unified millennial church which would reign in theocratic splendor.

Through the societies the Reformed could act in a way that was not possible in the denominations. They could associate in patriotic activities which might otherwise appear to be selfishly motivated or engaged in for sectarian advancement. In addition, they could work with statesmen who formerly would have supported religious affairs through the civil government but who would tend to shy away from denominational activities for political or other reasons. The societies not only provided a method for this kind of association but also performed tasks either considered too large or inappropriate for the denomination. The societies could promote those activities believed to be of national concern but found to have no appropriate place in the denomination as it was then conceived. They could instruct those groups in America which were beyond the influence of organized religion but whose presence seemed to endanger the national character and threaten the nation with providential ruin.

While after 1826 participation in the societies became a matter of dispute among the Reformed, the early societies elicited their united support. One indication of this was the numerous, constant, and unqualified statements of praise in the minutes of the Reformed denominations, especially of the Presbyterian General Assembly. The Assembly first took cognizance of voluntary societies in 1798 in response to a letter from the General Association of Connecticut, which had formed itself into a missionary society. The Assembly answered that while it had had "no convenient opportunity" to engage in this work, it was its "fixed resolution to undertake the same whenever the means shall be in our power." The Assembly noted "with great pleasure," however, that "institutions" for missionary purposes had been formed in New York and Albany and that one was planned in Philadelphia. This same year the Assembly gave its blessings to a society formed in Philadelphia "to aid the civil authority in the suppression of vice and immorality." [15]

Several years passed before the General Assembly again took notice of the voluntary societies. During that time a number of societies had been formed, and the Assembly demonstrated the unity of purpose in these societies by giving them a blanket approval rather than pointing to specific associations. In 1804 the summary of the state of religion noted briefly that "the Assembly have likewise heard with uncommon satisfaction, of the increasing number of societies for the purposes of prayer, and for the promotion of piety and good morals." On the same occasion in 1808 the Assembly declared that "among the visible fruits of an increased attention to the gospel, we recognize the establishment of benevolent institutions, as peculiarly characteristic of the religion of Jesus." In the following year, after listing the work of various societies, the Assembly made this significant statement:

These institutions, by calling into exercise the latent gifts and graces of the people of God, in an essential part of his worship, as well as in promoting zeal and brotherly love, have served as nurseries of the Church, and are producing, almost incredible effects upon the moral and religious state of the community. [16]

This recognition of the value of the societies in influencing the community beyond the organized life of the denominations was an important consideration in the pattern reflected for the next several years in the Assembly's commenting "with peculiar pleasure" on the activity of the societies.

Prior to 1812 the General Assembly confined its activities largely to this policy of recommendation and praise. Presbyterian ministers often formed the core of the local societies, and in 1812 the Assembly recognized the possibility of cooperating organically with societies. The Assembly "resolved, That the Committee of Missions be authorized to expend in support of a mission to the Cherokees, annually, $500; and that they be authorized to revive that mission, in conjunction with the New Jersey Missionary Society." Thus began, on a denominational level, a pattern of cooperation between ecclesiastical and extra-ecclesiastical institutions that was to continue for a number of years.

The usefulness of the societies led the General Assembly not only to recommend societies already established but also to recommend that new ones be created. As early as 1809 the Assembly's Committee of Overtures recommended the establishment of a "general religious tract society." The national society approach had not as yet received general acceptance, and the Assembly called for the formation of more local tract societies. Again in 1814 some of the commissioners to the General Assembly wished to use the influence of that body in the formation of a "general Bible Society." While there was by that time considerable support for such a society, most of the commissioners desired to relieve the prospective society of the charge of "sectarianism," and the subject was "indefinitely postponed." It was thought that the better approach to the formation of a national society would be for some state society to bring the measure forward. Elias Boudinot, president of the New Jersey Bible Society, was present at the meeting, and having been convinced of the utility of a national society, he used his influence toward that end.[17]

By 1815 the General Assembly was convinced that the societies could be powerful agents in the promotion of the "association between Religion and Patriotism." In reviewing the state of religion in America, the Assembly spoke of the "judgments of pestilence and war . . . [which] the alien from the commonwealth of Israel, the man of earth, the unbelieving servant of the corruption which is in the world through lust has regarded . . . with indifference," and wished for "a more general amelioration of manners and habits, that improvement of the dispensations of Almighty God, which he expects, and mankind are obligated to exhibit." In turning to the work of the societies the Assembly reflected:

The social principle is mighty in its operations. . . . When sanctified by religion, and consecrated to the immediate service of God, what results of high import and holy advantage may not be expected from it? . . . The practice of uniting the talents, influence, and resources of individuals, by these hallowed bonds, and for these religious, moral, and charitable purposes, is not novel. . . . But it seems, that at no former period has it been pursued with such vigour, extension, and success, as recently.[18]

The General Synod of the Reformed Dutch Church was less prone to statements on the societies in the early years of the century, but their support for the movement was not less enthusiastic. In 1823 the General Synod gave a favorable account of the societies and in 1826 gave over a considerable portion of the address on the state of religion to a discussion of the progress of the societies. The General Synod felt that the societies reflected the glorious situation, "which has been promised in the latter day glory of the Church." [19]

Increasingly during the 1820s, however, there were some who desired the denomination to incorporate the work of the societies. Perhaps the earliest major statement which encouraged greater denominational efforts to promote national goals was made by John Holt Rice in the opening sermon before the Presbyterian General Assembly of 1820. Rice made an elegant plea that the necessary ecclesiastical business of the judicatory be carried on with harmony and dispatch so that the General Assembly could focus primarily on those things that would "edify" the nation.

Although the Presbyterian church is now large, and growing, all know that the numbers of our ministers bear a very small proportion to the population, on which we might exert an influence. Of course our personal influence as a body of men is comparatively small. We are making great, and ought to make much greater exertions to remedy this evil. From the nature of the case however the process is slow: and the people whom we might edify, and ought to edify, are in the mean time exposed to many sinister and disastrous designs. It does seem to me then, that while convened in General Assembly, we ought to improve the opportunity afforded of bringing the talents and intelligence of the gifted geniuses and learned men among us, to bear on all our members, and exert a continual influence on society.

Rice wanted to see the ecclesiastical machinery of Presbyterianism brought to bear on the life of the nation. It was his conviction that anything not having that effect should be avoided. If such a change could be made in the General

Assembly, it would have repercussions throughout the organization, as that body gave to the whole denomination its "tone and colouring." Rice was convinced that, if properly directed, "Eight hundred Presbyterian ministers supported by their congregations, may produce mighty effects in such a nation as ours."[20]

This desire to see the denomination undertake greater responsibilities grew in intensity during the 1820s, when the tendency toward the formation of national societies threatened the hegemony of the Reformed in the middle and southern states in the societies which they supported. While all the societies claimed to be broadly ecumenical, most of them were in fact sectarian in nature. In spite of rhetoric to the contrary, most of the societies gave evidence of some sectarian bias in their organization; and, as has been demonstrated by Whitney R. Cross, most of them were sectarian in activity as well.[21]

The societies were not only sectarian in a theological sense but in a regional sense as well. Before the late 1820s the "national" societies were very largely regional and therefore were dominated by either the New England Congregationalists or the Reformed groups of the middle and southern states. The American Board of Commissioners for Foreign Missions was a New England society having only token representation from the rest of the nation. The American Education Society was likewise primarily Congregationalist, while the Presbyterian Education Society of New York and societies auxiliary to the General Assembly's Board of Education were supported by other Reformed bodies. The American Tract Society was located in Boston, and the New York Religious Tract Society, which was the larger of the two although without a national title, served the middle and southern states. On the other hand, the American Bible Society, the American Colonization Society and the American Sunday School Union were largely controlled by the Reformed bodies of the middle and southern states. Perhaps of even greater significance was the fact that the United Domestic Missionary Society was the creation of the Presbyterians, Reformed Dutch, and Associate Reformed. Thus, the early societies were in effect regional societies.

After 1826 this pattern of regional sectarianism began to break down, but the basic sectarianism was so great that this deterioration created problems in the society movement. In 1825 the older American Tract Society and the New York Religious Tract Society joined to form a new American Tract Society. In that same year the Presbyterian Education Society of New York united with the American Education Society. In 1826 the United Foreign Missionary Society, organized by the Presbyterian, Reformed Dutch, and the Associate Reformed denominations in 1817, united with the New England–based American Board of Commissioners for Foreign Missions. The American Home Missionary Society, organized in 1826, was a unification of the United Domestic Missionary Society with various New England societies. In 1829 the powerful Connecticut Bible Society became auxiliary to the American Bible Society. It was only after this series of mergers that various factions among the Reformed in the middle and southern states began to criticize the societies and propose that all activity carried on through the societies ought to be conducted under the responsible eye of the denominational judicatories.

The major problem was the clashing of theological traditions, one being associated with New England and the other taking its strength in the middle and southern states. The New Haven theology also penetrated Presbyterianism, especially in those areas where Presbyterians and Congregationalists cooperated under the 1801 Plan of Union. In the late 1820s this gave rise to New School Presbyterianism. Given the support of the New School, the New England tradition after 1826 began to dominate the societies. These came to reflect a form of revivalism and evangelicalism repugnant to both the smaller Reformed denominations of the middle and southern states and the Old School Presbyterians, and they were also unacceptable to many Presbyterian moderates. It was these latter groups that had been the originators and staunchest supporters of associated activity. They now became those responsible for a new definition of the denomination.

Evolution of the Denomination Among the Reformed

The smaller and theologically more conservative Reformed denominations withdrew from the societies quickly without too much internal turmoil. Several members of the Associate Synod of North America began a sustained attack on the societies in the columns of the *Religious Monitor* in 1829. The editor affirmed that while the Associate Church was not opposed to the "benevolent operations of the day," it was "bitterly . . . opposed to the unscriptural practices, and doctrines which the corrupters of God's word have introduced into these benevolent institutions."[22] At the meeting of the synod, committees were appointed to "consider and report on the propriety of forming a Bible Society with a view to distribute Bibles with Psalms in metre" and to suggest "measures for the circulation of Tracts on the peculiar principles of our witnessing profession." It was believed that the societies had become subversive of the denomination and that the church itself should be the Bible society, the tract society, and the missionary society. By 1834 the Associate Presbyterians "disapproved of all other mission plans" except those conducted through the denomination.[23]

The Associate Reformed Synod of New York followed a similar course. In 1831 the editor of the denomination's *Christian's Magazine* wrote "An Apology for the Associate Reformed Church." Some had objected that the denomination did "not approve of the 'great movements' and benevolent operations of the day." The Associate Reformed, according to the editor, only objected to some of the "acts and Measures."[24] In 1834 the Associate Reformed Synod formalized its withdrawal from the society movement with a resolution "that . . . we, as a denomination are imperiously called to arise in our strength."[25]

The Reformed Dutch also rapidly disengaged from the society movement as it became New England–oriented and revivalistic. The General Synod refused to cooperate when the United Foreign Missionary Society was merged with the American Board of Commissioners for Foreign Missions. William Craig Brownlee explained that they declined "entering into the Eastern policy" because they were "strongly opposed to Hopkinsianism, and Independency.

155

... We can never amalgamate with them." The Dutch had been second to none "in pecuniary contributions," but their generosity had been to their own detriment. As a result, Brownlee argued, "our hedges are being broken down, and the paths of the good old ways are being shut up."[26]

The Reformed Dutch involvement in the societies had been such that withdrawal was not easy, and there was considerable difference of opinion within the denomination. In 1827 Brownlee complained that not one in four of the communicating members supported the Missionary Society of the Reformed Dutch Church. By 1829, however, the General Synod's committee on missions reported optimistically that "whatever may be the difference of opinion with regard to objects, not immediately connected with our own denomination," everyone agreed to support the denominational efforts. The denomination was still divided between the supporters of the voluntary associations and those of denominational boards in 1833, as indicated by several close votes in the General Synod of that year.[27]

The trend, however, was clearly from associated to denominational activity. Early in 1828 the adherents of denominational boards formed the Sabbath School Union of the Reformed Dutch Church. The managers argued that many "baptized children of our churches" attended Sunday schools and ought to be taught the "truth" as contained in the catechisms of the church. They also objected to unconverted teachers. Immediately after its organization, the society applied to the General Synod to be taken under its care. Sentiment was still such at this time that the Synod believed it "inexpedient to legislate."[28] That same year a Board of Education for the Reformed Dutch Church was formed in New York. This move was supported by some of the more eminent members of the denomination. It was not an official denominational organization but indicated the strong desire of many of the Reformed Dutch to withdraw from the society movement. There was also strong support among the Reformed Dutch in 1828 to affiliate with the newly formed Presbyterian Foreign and Domestic Mission Board. Brownlee and Eli Baldwin met with that board to discuss the possibilities of cooperation.[29]

Evolution of the Denomination Among the Reformed

By 1831 a majority in the General Synod favored denominational activity over associated activity. The voluntary Education Board requested that the General Synod take charge of its activities. The Synod reappointed the existing officers as its own, and by 1833 the Board of Education was an integral part of the denomination. It was more difficult to bring the independent Missionary Society of the Reformed Dutch Church under the control of the General Synod. A thriving organization since 1822, the society came into conflict with the Synod of Albany, and in 1830 the Synod's committee on missions expressed a desire to bring "the missionary operations of our church . . . under the control of General Synod." The independent society resisted, and a second Board of Missions was established at Albany. In 1831 the General Synod proceeded to organize its own Board of Missions, and in 1834 the independent society became auxiliary to the Synod's board. In 1832 the General Synod worked out an arrangement with the American Board of Commissioners for Foreign Missions whereby the Synod could choose a missionary, the field of labor, and retain control of the churches formed. Thus they achieved effective denominational control without formally withdrawing from that society. By 1836 several denominations wished to discontinue this arrangement. Thus, by around 1834 the Reformed Dutch had effectively withdrawn from the society movement and had emerged as a denomination in the new sense of the term.[30]

It was even less easy for the Presbyterians to withdraw from the society movement because the denomination was more seriously divided. The New School was sympathetic to New England theology and vigorously supported the new revivalism. The Old School continued to adhere to the Reformed tradition of the middle and southern states. This conflict has been extensively discussed, and so there is no need to rehearse the events at length. Members of the Old School, along with their Reformed allies, had clearly been the initiators of the society movement. After 1826 and the merger of the societies, these same leaders became the most ardent advocates of denominational, as opposed to associated, activity.

In 1828 a number of Old School ministers, including Ashbel Green and Jacob Janeway, presented an "Overture to the General Assembly of the Presbyterian Church on the Subject of Missions" in an attempt to strengthen the denominational Board of Missions by making foreign missions an integral part of its operations. Green argued that voluntary associations were contrary to Scripture and that the church had made an error "through inattention." The "Overture" had repercussions beyond foreign missions, however, and the American Home Missionary Society sent a committee to confer with the Assembly. After extensive debate, the General Assembly decided that the board already had all the necessary powers, and the subject was "indefinitely postponed." In August the supporters of the denominational board sought a cooperative arrangement with the Missionary Society of the Reformed Dutch Church. This was a clear indication that the Old School was opposed on principle not to associated activity, but to the new theology and new revivalism. The denomination was so divided on the question that agreement was impossible, and in 1829 the General Assembly resolved "that the churches should be left entirely to their own unbiased and deliberate choice" between the voluntary associations and the denominational board.[31]

The result of the Old School dissatisfaction with the societies was a new concept of the denomination. The new theory was simple. In addition to its former functions the denomination was to be considered a "missionary society." The Old School Presbyterians generally credited this "discovery" to John Holt Rice. Rice held that the church ought to "consider herself as a great missionary society, instituted for the conversion of the world; and that henceforth she would make that her great object."[32]

Whether Rice was the first Presbyterian leader to make this distinction or not, by 1830 it was becoming commonplace among supporters of the Old School. By 1831 Joshua Wilson, best known for his prosecution of Lyman Beecher, had elevated this idea to the status of religious orthodoxy. In *Four Propositions Sustained Against the Claims of the American Home Missionary Society*, Wilson held that:

I. The management of Christian missions is committed by the Lord Jesus Christ to his church.

II. The Presbyterian church is, by her form of government, organized into a Christian Missionary Society.

III. The American Home Missionary Society is not an *ecclesiastical* but a *civil* Institution.

IV. The American Home Missionary Society ... disturbs the peace and injures the prosperity of the Presbyterian church.[33]

The new concept of the denomination actually was broad enough to include all functions of the societies, but since missions and ministerial education most affected the denomination, they received the initial attention. Wilson's *Four Propositions* actually appeared just previous to a convention (scheduled for November in Cincinnati) that was to decide whether missions in the West would be carried out by the General Assembly or the American Home Missionary Society. The convention resulted in a total stalemate between Old School supporters of the new theory of the denomination and New School proponents of the idea that the only proper function of the denomination was internal government.[34]

Growing divisions within the Presbyterian church resulted in a schism in 1837. After that, Presbyterianism in America was represented by two denominations, each with a different conception of what that meant. The New School continued to cooperate with voluntary societies in every function not related to its internal government. The Old School, operating on the idea that the denomination was a "missionary society," strengthened the Board of Home Missions and the Board of Education and in 1837 established a Board of Foreign Missions. But the new theory of the denomination went further. It included all those areas of labor previously attended to by the societies. In 1838 the Old School organized a Board of Publication, thus becoming a tract society in addition to being a missionary and education society.

It was the Old School concept of the denomination that reflected most clearly what a denomination was to mean in America. In 1852 the New School established its own church boards and left the Congregationalists with, in effect, the same structures. The denomination was no longer a religious group among many, concerned only with the regulation of its own members. Denomination in America came to signify a complex organization, with numerous boards, employees, and purposes. It is somewhat ironic that the major impetus in this development, the desire to promote a uniformly Christian nation, suffered as a result of the process.

6
Introduction

"Like the tribes of Israel, the American churches shared a special relation with God and a special destiny on earth which conferred on them a singularity eclipsing their disparate origins, histories, and confessions."[1] So observes J. F. Maclear in a discussion of the providential and millenial conceptual framework, the ideal of a Christian America, that was shaped by and in turn shaped American Protestantism. Maclear's essay, Robert T. Handy's *Christian America*,[2] Martin E. Marty's *Righteous Empire*, and other recent works on millennialism and the Protestant establishment describe a national millennial mythology—America the elect nation, the new Israel, the redeemer nation, providentially ordained to realize and spread liberty and piety, a nation in covenant with God, the nation within which the millennium would appear. Implicitly they analyze the conceptual framework, what students of organization term "the organizational goals," which contained and defined the denominations. It was this effort to build a Christian America, to inaugurate the millennium, which in the early decades of the nineteenth century knit the separated evangelical denominations into a common force and provided them with the sense of being a collective and divinely ordained united reality, the church. America was, as Sidney Mead has so cogently phrased it, "The Nation with the Soul of a Church."[3] What this meant in the early 1800s was that each denomination was not a church, but an instrument; it did not define its own goals so much as participate in the definition and realization of these larger millennial goals; its boundaries, structures, creeds, and ritual did not contain it; it was contained by the hurried providential pace toward the destiny of America as a whole. To be sure Methodists spread Methodism and Presbyterians Presbyterianism, but in this the denomina-

1. Maclear, "The Republic and the Millennium," *The Religion of the Republic*, ed. Elwyn A. Smith (Philadelphia: Fortress Press, 1971), pp. 183-216.
2. New York: Oxford University Press, 1971.
3. *Church History*, 36 (1967), 262-83.

tions' formative period, the purposes and goals of the (evangelical) denomination were set within the larger context of a Christian America.

The following selection by Russell E. Richey analyzes the development of one denomination, the Methodists, within this context. It also argues that the Methodists possessed a share of the responsibility for creating the denominational form of the church, that is a national, voluntary, purposive structure instrumental to the Christianizing of America. The essay shows that contrary to the sociological and Niebuhrian view, which portrays the denomination as a compromise of sectarian zeal and purity, the denomination was designed as a vessel or instrument for zeal. It was not society's kept creature but an agent of the kingdom.

The capitulation to caste and culture Niebuhr describes (see selection herein) did occur. It represented not so much the revelation of the denomination's true character as it did a state to which it could fall. To pursue Maclear's image, like the tribes of Israel, the denominations have the capacities both for participation in a larger destiny and for tribalism. What they are depends in large measure on what they feel called to be. In the 1840s a crisis in the millennial mythology, the fracturing of American society by slavery and the sectional crisis, the resurgence of confessionalism inspired in part by Romanticism, and competition itself led to the erosion of this unitive vision. With the loss of the higher purpose to which the denominations had bound themselves, the denominations forged tribal goals; they became ends in themselves. It may be that the denominations have never recovered from the loss of the millennial vision which gave them meaning.

The basic question to be asked of this essay touches several of the selections. To what extent did the ideal of a Christian America actually inform denominational development? Were the Methodists as disinterestedly dedicated to "spreading Scriptural holiness over the land" as they and this essay suggest? Did the commitment to the Christianizing of America sufficiently moderate Methodist attachment to their own forms and theological emphases to warrant the notion that the overriding purpose of the denomination (Methodism in this case) was of that unitive millennial sort?

6

The Social Sources of Denominationalism: Methodism

Russell E. Richey

The great iron wheel in the system is itinerancy, and truly it grinds some of us most tremendously; the brazen wheel, attached and kept in motion by the former, is the local ministry; the silver wheel, the class leaders; the golden wheel, the doctrine and discipline of the church, in full and successful operation. Now, sir, it is evident that the entire movement depends upon keeping the great iron wheel of itinerancy constantly and rapidly rolling round. But, to be more specific, and to make an application of this figure to American Methodism, let us carefully note the admirable and astounding movements of this wonderful machine. You will perceive there are "wheels within wheels." First, there is the great outer wheel of episcopacy, which accomplishes its entire revolution once in four years. To this there are attached twenty-eight smaller wheels, styled annual conferences, moving around once a year; to these are attached one hundred wheels, designated presiding elders, moving twelve hundred other wheels, termed quarterly conferences, every three months; to these are attached four thousand wheels, styled travelling preachers, moving round once a month, and communicating motion to thirty thousand wheels, called class leaders, moving round once a week, and who, in turn, being attached to between seven and eight hundred thousand wheels, called members, give a sufficient impulse to whirl them round every day. O, sir, what a machine is this! This is the machine of which Archimedes only dreamed; this is the machine destined, under God, to move the world, to turn it upside down.

The genius of Methodist organization has often been remarked. George Cookman in this passage from Speeches Delivered on Various Occasions (1840), employed the vision of Ezekiel as a figure to suggest the heavenly design of its operation. Abel Stevens, seeing the danger of barbarism in

Most footnotes are omitted. An adapted version of this article, inclusive of all footnotes, will appear in the April 1977 issue of Methodist History.

the spread of population beyond the reaches of religious influence, conceived of Methodism as a "religious system, energetic, migratory, 'itinerant,' extempore, like the population itself" necessary for and "providentially designed" for the United States. This theme, expanded and secularized, has received scholarly affirmation by William Warren Sweet in his works on Methodism and American religion. Methodist organization has been celebrated; it has also had its detractors—prophetic voices from within—some of whom exited in the name of republicanism or antislavery and critics from without. One such critic, the Baptist J. R. Graves, organized his reflections under Cookman's image of *The Great Iron Wheel*. Its machinelike characteristics impressed Graves as "a crushing military despotism," "The very system of the Jesuits of Rome," "Antichrist," "spiritual tyranny," "clerical despotism" a threat to free institutions.

It is not the purpose of this paper to review or resolve the debates over the character, efficiency, methods, leadership, and impact of the Methodist organization, which have ranged from the earliest days of British Methodism. Rather, the purpose of this paper is to pursue a point implicit in the fact and substance of the discussion about Methodist polity. The thesis expressed in the title is that the distinctive form of the church that we know as the American denomination and as described by the term "denominationalism" is deeply indebted to Methodism. The principle of organization in Methodism has become the principle of denominationalism. And Methodism was the religious movement which first fully, effectively, and nationally exemplified that principle. Methodism, to borrow (with alteration) H. Richard Niebuhr's phrase was a "significant social source of denominationalism." This thesis will have to be qualified in a number of important respects, that is, Methodism's borrowings acknowledged, the role of other denominations and religious movements admitted, and the place of denominationalism in larger societal and intellectual transformations noted. The qualifications should serve to suggest the complexity of the history of denominationalism and to raise questions about the ethical and sociological reductionism that has been allowed to stand as an explanation of denominationalism. The thesis when appropriately qualified should suggest that the form (as well as the idea) of denominationalism is rooted in vital religiosity. Denominationalism as a form of the church is not simply the resultant of the several divisive compromises of the Christian gospel.[1]

Denominationalism as a Problem

A contemporary of the maturity of American denominationalism, Robert Baird, celebrated its basic principle. The voluntary principle, he suggested, evoked Americans' "energy, self-reliance, and enterprise in the cause of religion." More than adequate to the challenge posed by disestablishment and an expanding population, it betrayed the real genius of free enterprise, the American (Anglo-Saxon) peoples and American religion, and bespoke the will (hence voluntarism) of Americans to make religious freedom work for the kingdom of God. That it produced separate denominations was not disturbing because the denominations, at least the evangelical denominations, were unified in a common mission.

Baird's treatment epitomizes a basic strength—but perhaps also a weakness—in analyses of denominationalism. Baird looked through the denominations and denominationalism to more fundamental realities—evangelicalism, mission, voluntarism, religious freedom. Many of the most penetrating discussions of American religious institutions have shared this trait; they have looked through or around denominationalism to what appeared most basic. Hence the best treatments of religious structures are to be found in works on evangelicalism, mission, voluntarism, religious freedom, toleration, religious pluralism, separation of church and state, religion and the nation. There is, of course, no want of studies of particular denominations and ample numbers of works treating the denominations together. But Americans have been strangely reluctant to look directly at what is celebrated frequently in passing, the denominational form of the church. This reluctance must be attributable, at least in part, to a Christian conscience uneasy about divisions in the body of Christ.

Denominationalism

This uneasiness, expressed eloquently in H. Richard Niebuhr's *Social Sources of Denominationalism*, has occasioned the search for unitive realities and an unwillingness to speak about what is experienced on a day-to-day basis. Denominationalism has been left to the sociologists, whose ideal types (suggestive as they are) do not exhaust what historians and members of denominations ought to know about it.

Denominationalism as a Form of the Church

The denomination and denominationalism are dynamic religious structures and processes which have altered considerably in the several centuries during which the term "denomination" was being employed to designate religious movements. For that reason it is important to specify that "denominationalism" will be used for the pattern of interinstitutional and intra-institutional structures, processes, and relations that existed among mainstream American Protestants in the nineteenth century. That delimitation, while arbitrary, provides the term with specific social meaning and is necessary for a discussion of the origins and character of denominationalism.

It must be acknowledged at the outset that to unravel the thread of denominationalism is to separate it from the fabric into which it was woven and thereby to remove it from that to which it belongs and by which it is given shape, purpose, and significance. To affirm this is to acknowledge the value of the treatments of denominationalism under the rubrics mentioned above. Denominationalism is a form of the church possible in a society characterized by toleration or at least the spirit of tolerance, by laws and customs supportive of religious liberty, and by *de facto* (if not legal) disestablishment. Denominationalism, then, has to be understood in relation to the sagas of religious liberty, the democratic state, and bourgeois society. Quite clearly, Baptists, Quakers, and other dissenting groups, in their advocacy and embodiment of religious freedom, were social sources of denominationalism. So, too, the struggle in this direction within other religious groups in the several colonies was part of the social origins of denominationalism. The appropriation of the voluntary church was an essential ingredient, perhaps a precondition, of denominationalism. The histories conceived under the several rubrics related to freedom do indeed describe important dimensions of the beginnings of denominationalism. They also point to denominationalism's place within the larger story of Western voluntarism, societal differentiation, organizational specialization, and secularization. The denomination belongs within the array of associations, among free and often competitive institutions (essential to bourgeois, democratic society) upon which de Tocqueville, Channing, Emerson, and others commented. Association seemed the principle of democracy. Association in political life and association in civil (and religious) life were mutually reinforcing.

Denominationalism, then, is to be seen as a form of the church adjusted to the realities of American society. It clearly is an adjustment to the realities of religious pluralism which characterized American society.

The most important descriptions of denominationalism have been sketched against this background. Among the most perceptive is Sidney Mead's depiction. It is worth quoting at some length:

> The denomination is the organizational form which the free churches have accepted and assumed. It evolved in the United States during the complex and peculiar period between the Revolution and the Civil War.
>
> The denomination, unlike the traditional forms of the church, is not primarily confessional, and it is certainly not territorial. Rather it is purposive. . . . A church as church has no legal existence in the United States. . . . Neither is the denomination a sect in a traditional sense and certainly not in the most common sense of a dissenting body in relationship to an established church. It is, rather, a voluntary association of like-hearted and like-minded individuals, who are united on the basis of common beliefs for the purpose of accomplishing tangible and defined objectives. One of the primary objectives is the propagation of its point of view.

Mead elaborates the meaning of this purposive form of the church by noting a number of traits characteristic of denominations. They are (1) sectarian, primitivistic, and antihistorical; (2) voluntaristic, self-promotional, and activistic; (3) missionary; (4) revivalistic (and therefore oversimplifying), Arminian, pragmatic, emotional, egalitarian, and anti-intellectual; (5) antirational (anti-Enlightenment); and (6) competitive.

Second to its purposiveness is another feature of denominationalism to which Winthrop Hudson as well as Mead draws attention. Denominationalism is predicated upon an understanding of the church as pluralistic yet united and in a sense ecumenical. "Denominationalism," Hudson suggests, "is the opposite of sectarianism."

The word "denomination" implies that the group referred to is but one member of a larger group, called or denominated by a particular name. The basic contention of the denominational theory of the church is that the true church is not to be identified in any exclusive sense with any particular ecclesiastical institution. The outward forms of worship and organization are at best but differing attempts to give visible expression to the life of the church in the life of the world. No denomination claims to represent the whole church of Christ. No denomination claims that all other churches are false churches. No denomination claims that all members of society should be incorporated within its own membership. No denomination claims that the whole of society and the state should submit to its ecclesiastical regulations. Yet all denominations recognize their responsibility for the whole of society and they expect to cooperate in freedom and mutual respect with other denominations in discharging that responsibility.

Never adequately articulated but implicit in the self-understanding of denominations was the recognition that there was a unity of the church which transcended the observable disunity. The disunity, an inevitable result of human diversity, did not undermine unity on essentials, on fundamentals. It did not mean that individual denominations were schisms (as Niebuhr's analysis would suggest). It did mean that unity was not to be achieved through coercion. And it meant, most importantly, that the true church and its unity were not to be fully manifested in human institutions. Denominationalism was a witness to the true church by its pointing beyond the divisions in human structurings of the church to the shared unity.

Social Sources of Denominationalism: Methodism

The denomination in the view of Mead and Hudson is a purposive structure and conception of the church implicitly unitive or ecumenical in character. A third feature of denominationalism related its purposive character to this wider vision. The denomination was instrumental to the Christianization of society—the Christianization of the new Republic and also of the world. The several denominations were united in building a Christian commonwealth in preparation for the coming of Christ's kingdom. In some instances this common task motivated and expressed itself in cooperative endeavor. The various voluntary societies—Bible, tract, Sunday school, reform societies—were the most obvious reflections of the common end. More frequently the common end was sought through competition, competition among the denominations and competition of denominations with the voluntary societies. The competitiveness has sometimes obscured the common end. But commentators on American religion from Robert Baird to H. Richard Niebuhr, James Maclear, Elwyn Smith, Martin Marty, and Robert Handy have described the common efforts to erect a Christian (Evangelical Protestant) society.[2] As Baird recognized in dividing American religion into Evangelical and non-Evangelical denominations, and as recent commentators have recognized in analyzing the building of a Christian empire (society, establishment, kingdom), this unitive end of the denominations permitted and elicited degrees of participation. Religious, ethnic, racial, and regional factors affected the level of participation. Roman Catholics, Jews, and Unitarians were by definition and hostility excluded; Lutheran and certain Reformed bodies allowed ethnic and theological factors to regulate the degree of their participation; Episcopalians, Presbyterians, Methodists, and Baptists struggled over the implications of participation for tradition, theology, and polity; black denominations, while animated by the passions of the Christianization of society, were by racial exigencies and racial prejudice excluded from full participation; Mormons, millennial groups, and utopians defined their Christian societies over against the dominant society; slavery and sectionalism finally wrought divisions within denominations and in the nation as a whole in the labor for a Christian empire. But when the spectrum of participation in the cause of building a Christian America is recognized, the fact remains that the dominant or normative conception of the denomination was this instrumental one. The denominations (Evangelical) singly and collectively were means, that is, instruments for the Christianization of society and the building of the kingdom of God.

H. Richard Niebuhr in *The Kingdom of God in America* recognized the dynamism, unity, and force in American religion. In emendation of his stance in *The Social Sources of Denominationalism* he analyzed the ideal of the kingdom of God on earth, showing it to have been a central preoccupation of American religious movements. But he continued to view the denominations as the halting places, the forms for preserving, the institutionalizations of these dynamic processes. Denominationalism marked the end of the dynamic movements in the church. It was the end in the sense that in attempting to conserve and preserve, leaders created institutions which killed the spirit of the movements. It was an end in the sense that the denomination became an end in itself, thus displacing with a static structure the dynamic ideal of the kingdom of God.

Niebuhr's conception is at variance with the view just set forth of the denominations as purposive voluntary associations, that is, as structures possessed of a vision of their place in a wider Christian unity and instrumental to the kingdom of God and the Christianization of society. Niebuhr is probably right in viewing the denominations as having eventually become ends in themselves. The question is whether intrinsically they were the death of Christian vitality; or more to the point perhaps, whether they were by definition static, conservative, and lifeless. Much depends upon the attitude held toward institutions and upon the point at which the several movements are to be defined as denominations. This in turn is related to the inevitability of the sect-to-denomination process which Niebuhr posits. These broad theoretical and historical questions cannot be addressed directly here. What can be investigated is the appropriateness of the view here set forth to the development of one denomination, the Methodist Episcopal Church. What can also be shown is how the vitality of institutional development within Methodism served as a model for the denomination-building process in other religious movements. Implicitly, then, Niebuhr is answered by showing Methodism in its dynamic phases to have been a social source of denominationalism.

Methodism as a Social Source of Denominationalism

The Evangelical denomination in early nineteenth-century America was a purposive voluntary association, possessed of a vision of its place in a wider Christian unity and structured as an instrument for bringing in the kingdom of God and Christianizing society. The denomination was then a missionary structure and by intention national in its aspirations. Where were its origins, its fabricators, its early manifestations? They were, as the second section above indicated, imbedded in the American and European experience, in the thrust of various religious movements, in the fact of pluralism, and in the conditions of religious freedom and disestablishment. To single out one religious movement as a social source of denominationalism is only to suggest a prevalence within it of influences from other religious movements and of trends affecting various facets of American and European society. To argue that Methodism was a social source of denominationalism is only to suggest that Methodism was representative, an early embodiment, an available model.

Methodism's role as exemplar of the purposive, ecumenical, and instrumental church structure derived from the genius of Wesley, from the ambiguous status of early Methodism, from the new meaning conferred on Methodist structures and activities by its transference to the American environment and consequent loss of Anglican context and ecclesiology, and from its very successes. These factors and certain strategic and ethnic ones were to make it, rather than Moravianism (also an embodiment of the denominational principles and also a forceful mediator of Pietism's practical [purposive], ecumenical [unitive], and reforming [instrumental] impulses), the effective transmitter of the denominational form of the church.

What was Methodism's genius? It was largely the genius of Wesley. By upbringing, education, inclination, and theology John Wesley was, as Frank Baker has argued, a High Church Anglican, an early bigot for the Church of England, whose later comprehensiveness represented an appropriation of that other spirit of the Anglican Church. Wesley's experientially and theologically derived eclecticism and his maturation as a folk theologian or catholic theologian did not dissolve Wesley's dedication to the Anglican Church or his resolve to maintain the evolving Methodist connection within it. By principle and prejudice averse to falling in with the Dissenters, Wesley, through the force of his own indomitable will and a richly textured Evangelical Anglicanism, kept his connection in a formally and legally anomalous position. Methodism was not a new church; nor was it to be during Wesley's lifetime one of the denominations within Nonconformity. Poised between theologically and legally constituted systems of ecclesiastical authority, the Methodist structures could, like the Pietist structures that preceded them, be governed by their purposes. Methodism was purposive, a leaven within the Anglican Church, a movement to spread scriptural holiness across the land. "The chief design of His providence in sending us out is, undoubtedly, to quicken our brethren." "We look upon the Methodists," Wesley affirmed, "not as any particular party . . . but as living witnesses, in and to every party, of that Christianity which we preach." Affirming Methodists are to be distinguished only in their commitment to "the common principles of Christianity" (not by opinions, emphasized phrases or parts of religion or "action, customs or usages, of an indifferent nature"). Wesley asserted:

By these marks, by these fruits of a living faith, do we labour to distinguish ourselves from the unbelieving world, from all those whose minds or lives are not according to the Gospel of Christ. But from real Christians, of whatsoever denomination they be, we earnestly desire not to be distinguished at all, not from any who sincerely follow after what they know they have not yet attained.

Social Sources of Denominationalism: Methodism

No: "Whosoever doeth the will of my Father which is in heaven, the same is my brother, and sister, and mother." And I beseech you, brethren, by the mercies of God, that we be in no wise divided among ourselves. Is thy heart right, as my heart is with thine? I ask no farther questions. If it be, give me thy hand.

Methodism was a purposive religious society, a people dedicated to the spread of scriptural holiness as a way of life; and it was, at least by its own intentions, unitive in character. Its structures and disciplines were instrumental to these ends. Wesley was candid on this point.

What is the end of all ecclesiastical order? Is it not to bring souls from the power of Satan to God, and to build them up in His fear and love? Order, then, is so far valuable as it answers these ends; and if it answers them not, it is nothing worth.

Wesley's understanding of the development of Methodism betrays this instrumental or pragmatic view of order. Methodists, he insisted,

had not the least expectation, at first, of any thing like what has since followed . . . no previous design or plan at all; but every thing arose just as the occasion offered. They saw or felt some impending or pressing evil, or some good end necessary to be pursued. And many times they fell unawares on the very thing which secured the good, or removed the evil. At other times, they consulted on the most probable means, following only common sense and Scripture: Though they generally found, in looking back, something in Christian antiquity likewise, very nearly parallel thereto.

Also reflective of Wesley's instrumental view of order or structure was his willingness to borrow what seemed to work—classes, bands, love feasts, covenant services, watchnights. The efforts to save souls produced a remarkable freedom over the structuring of the religious life. Expediency, "inspired practical improvisation," common sense, pragmatism, eclectic borrowing, the ability to recognize the general applicability of a successful local experiment, the willingness to be tutored or corrected by experience and the Holy Spirit became the Methodist way. This experimental approach to structure, appropriate to the experiential mood of the eighteenth century, was evident throughout the development and history of Methodism. Methodism's structures were instrumental to its unitive purposes. The bands, classes and societies, itinerancy, circuits and conferences, rules, directions, minutes, sermons, the *Notes upon the New Testament*, the preachers and leaders—the social network that comprised the Methodist connection—was, as the "Large Minutes" declared, intended "to reform the nation and to spread scriptural holiness over the land."

British Methodism was in its own estimation no denomination or church. Yet in its national aspirations and missionary style (since its structures were instrumental to its unitive purposes) Methodism embodied what was to become the denominational principle. Of course British Methodism's denominationalism was in the very real sense suspended. Wesley's churchmanship kept the connection from perceiving itself and from being perceived as a new form of the church, the denomination. By Wesley's death, when the connection was in the process of becoming independent, the organizational and missional principles constitutive of the denomination would be appropriated by the Dissenting denominations. These facts have obscured the development of denominationalism. It appears that Methodism's denominationalism consisted of its break with the Church of England and its reconstitution as an independent body. The survival of Methodism after the founder's death, the agonies over authority, ordination, licensing, sacraments, make this reading plausible and in one sense accurate. British Methodism could not be fully a denomination until the structural principles it embodied were allowed to become fully determinative of the connection. This could happen when the efforts to be part of the established church were stopped. But it was not the actual break that made Methodism a denomination; what made Methodism a denomination was its inner structure.

By the same token the Dissenting denominations may appear to have been denominations for the duration of the eighteenth century. They bore that name. Were they not denominations? By the criteria established here—purposive, unitive, instrumental, national, missionary in character—

they were in fact not. Until mid-century the primary institutions in Dissent were described as "Dissenting" (rather than "denominational"); and Presbyterian, Congregationalist, and General and Particular Baptist were specific names—denominations—applied to ministers and congregations loosely bound by history, belief, and practice. The primary self-identification was that of "Dissenter." The internal structuring of Congregationalism gathered momentum in response to the growth of rational and heterodox currents in Dissent in the 1730s. It was not until evangelicalism impacted itself upon both Congregationalists and Particular and General Baptists in the final third of the century that they developed structures or recast structures—ministerial associations and academies initially—for the purposes of self-propagation and mission. Their maturity as denominations was as evangelical denominations, purposive in character, whose unitive and missionary intentions manifested themselves in the work of Carey and others like him. Whether this denominational form is borrowed from Methodism is difficult to say. What can be said is that the evangelicalism that through the agency of Wesley informed the organization of Methodism, came by the end of the eighteenth century to inform Baptists and Congregationalists as well. The Presbyterian interest languished until revivified by Scottish missions in the South. The Unitarians who emerged out of Presbyterian, Congregationalist, Baptist, and Anglican ranks began the process of organization in the 1790s. In their own way— hardly evangelical—they developed structures for growth and elaborated a theology unitive in its own terms, which in turn provided them with the denominationalism necessary to stabilize their cause.

Methodism's contribution to denominationalism was ironical. Wesley's efforts prevented it from falling in with the Dissenters and becoming a Dissenting denomination. Yet the principles in the Methodist movement—what, among other factors, assured its growth and what Whitefield and company lacked—were to become essential to Dissenting denominationalism. For the bulk of the century critical of the Methodists, the Dissenters eventually came to emulate them. A movement which at all costs avoided becoming a denomination was, despite its best efforts, to become the quintessential one, not in the details of its polity or ecclesiology but in the principles which, in fact, underlay them. Methodism, which has probably not received its due as a preliminary phase of the missionary movement, has also lacked credit for its contribution to denominationalism. Priority has been given to those who possessed the name "denomination" rather than to the movement within which the denominational principles were elaborated.

Denominationalism and American Methodism

The Methodist contribution to American denominationalism is not totally unacknowledged. Martin Marty in *Righteous Empire* comes close to crediting Methodists with the most basic change "in the administrative side of Christian church life in fourteen hundred years."

William Warren Sweet argues that Methodists were the first to organize nationally. The overall importance and influence of Methodism has driven some, as for instance Winthrop S. Hudson, to speak of the nineteenth century as the "Methodist Age." The "stirrings" towards denominationalism within the Wesleyan movement noticed by Marty; the example of Methodist organization nationally cited by Sweet; and the Methodist mediation of revivalistic, Arminian, practical, and emotional lay Christianity analyzed by Hudson suggest a large but diffuse Methodist contribution to denominationalism. Here we are concerned with a more specific contribution by Methodism. It is the principle of denominationalism (of which the stirrings, organization, and religiosity are expressions) that Methodism witnessed to most effectively in America. The principle was that with respect to church order, church structure, and church polity, the church as a visible reality was purposive, instrumental, and missionary; moreover, though in aspiration national, it was recognizant of sharing that national aspiration with other denominations. The principle implied that the church order was not of divine constitution. It was a human creation. Of course the human creation was a response to the guidance of the Holy Spirit; but it nevertheless was an ordering of the church achieved in the present and designed to fit its activity. This denominational principle required *de facto* surrender of claims to be *the* church—to be the church continuous with the early church or to be the only church exemplificative of the New Testament. Methodism by the accidents of its creation and implantation in America witnessed to this principle.

Methodism's witness to this principle was somewhat clearer in America than it had been in England where as *ecclesiola in ecclesia* its claims to be part of "the Church" were not fully surrendered. In America, especially after Independence, disestablishments, and the agony of the transfer of Wesley's authority, Methodism was clearly what one critic quoting Coke called a "new plan." Indeed, it was the critics who perhaps best saw Methodism's strange role. From the Episcopalian John Kewley in the early nineteenth century to the Landmark Baptist J. R. Graves in the latter part of the century, Methodism was denounced as "merely a human device." Methodists could and would defend their episcopacy, church order and theology, invoking Providence and the Spirit. Not being the only imitators of the primitive church, experiencing their growth before American eyes, and making their pragmatic changes in Wesley's structures, Methodists were not in a good position to claim to be the unchanged church of the New Testament. They did, in the main, remain loyal to Wesley. But Wesley himself had charged them to chart their own purposive course: "They are now at full liberty simply to follow the Scriptures and the Primitive Church. And we judge it best that they should stand fast in that liberty where with God has so strangely made them free." That freedom American Methodists had exercised and continued to exercise. From what Frederick Norwood calls its "lay beginnings," through the labors of Wesley's missionaries; the early phases of organization by Rankin, Asbury, and others; the gradual elaboration of conference structures; the trials of the Revolution; and through Wesley's ordinations, abridged Articles of Religion, revised Sunday Service, and appointment of Coke and Asbury as joint superintendents, "Methodists stumbled their way from society to church."

The Methodist Episcopal Church formed at the Christmas Conference of 1784 was a denomination in the process of formation. The process of building the denomination was only just begun. The definition of episcopacy, refinement of the conference system, development of a delegated general conference, nurturing of the traveling ministry and class system, establishment through the *Discipline* of a definite shape to the denomination, creation of a Methodist Book Concern and periodicals, and the testing of the denomination in early internal and external controversies made of Methodism a church order by intention national and governed by its purpose. It was a missionary order. There were limits to this purposive or functional character. These were clearly indicated in the response to James O'Kelly, the defensiveness evidenced on a variety of issues, the authoritarianism of Asbury, and the conservatism so pronounced in the six restrictive rules of 1808. But this is only to say that the Methodists were not fully conscious of the significance of their own novelty and perhaps not a little frightened of it. Others saw this novelty and witnessed to it. In particular the United Brethren under Philip William Otterbein and the Evangelical Association under Jacob Albright, while adopting Methodist structures and procedures for Reformed and Lutheran constituencies, maintained the Pietist ideal of being *ecclesiola in ecclesia*. In time other denominations would join these three in making their structures instrumental to the spreading of scriptural holiness over the land.

Though Presbyterians, Congregationalists, Baptists, and Christians reached that stage by following different paths and by adapting and altering their own traditions, in so doing they were nevertheless replicating the Methodist pattern. As denominationalism reached maturity in the early decades of the nineteenth century, it did so as the joint testimony of distinct peoples and traditions that the Christianization of American society was to be their individual and common endeavor. That mission, as Robert Handy has so carefully shown in *A Christian America*, was the purpose of the denominations. Denominations were and denominationalism was purposive. To be sure, there were social sources for each and all. But transcending the theological and ecclesiastical differences and the social, class, and racial distinctions was a common endeavor. The denominations were instruments of the kingdom of God. Denominations were not, then, as Niebuhr argued, the end of the kingdom. They were, under the conditions of disestablishment and religious freedom, its beginning. They were not, in their earliest phases, ends but means. That they later became ends in themselves—as Niebuhr quite rightly asserts they did—was a sign that denominations, as well as the quest for the kingdom, had lost the original vision.

III

Ethnic
Denominationalism

7
Introduction

The religious denomination appears clearly in this story as a structural super-organization designed to give guidance, support, and discipline to local congregations. It was born of social necessity, quite without reference to the high doctrine of "denominationalism" which Professors Sidney Mead and Winthrop Hudson have taught us. The fulfillment of its functions required, however, a specific rationale, a permanent structure, and a leadership dedicated not only to serving the congregations but to perpetuating both the larger institution and their own place in it. Such an organization by its very nature resists sharp changes either in structure or in philosophy, and encourages an exclusive loyalty in its local units.

Timothy Smith so summarizes in the following essay the theory of denominationalism developed in his previous selection in relation to early American society. Here the theory is applied to ethnic community structures in Minnesota mining society. The denominationalism of immigrant or ethnic groups, Smith suggests, possesses the same basic features as that of the largely Anglo-Saxon evangelical mainstream: the primacy of the congregation, denominational structures that were basically voluntary organizations, polity or ideology as a cohesive agent, division and organizational rivalry occasioned by ideological conflict, competition which in appealing to ethnicity (particularity) increased ethnicity (particularism) and sectarianism, and an irrelevance eventually and ironically fostered by churchly or community-building programs (publications, education, youth activities, uniform ritual, cultural programs, a social order that met human needs from birth to death).

Particularly striking is the fact that the ethnic denominational pattern was not confined to Protestant groups nor even to religious organizations. Secular organizations—temperance and socialist societies—also evidence the denominational pattern and clearly perform denominational or ethnic functions. Even in Roman Catholicism the denominational pattern is to be found despite the appearance (and effects) of the policies of a united church and Americaniza-

183

tion. Denominational divisiveness and competition, about which much moralizing has gone on, was not a Protestant problem, nor even a Christian one. Denominations competed among themselves but also with temperance societies and with socialist organizations, each serving the ethnic interest as they sought to further their own goals.

Timothy Smith's analysis resembles H. Richard Niebuhr's in its ascription of denominationalism to social factors (ethnicity here). However, the ethnic denominationalism which constitutes an ethical failure for Niebuhr is a social necessity for Smith. The reader may want to reflect on the implications of these divergent estimations. Also worth reflection is Smith's suggestion that within the experience of ethnic social structures the sect-to-church (or denominational) process, sometimes regarded as inevitable, is reversed. This observation, in which incidentally he is joined by H. Richard Niebuhr[1] raises questions about the sometimes facile historical use of sociological ideal types. Churchly, denominational, and sectarian aspects are often involved in more complex interplay than is sometimes supposed. The reader may also want to explore efforts to relate ethnic denominationalism to the religious dimension of American society and to mainstream Evangelical Protestantism. Will Herberg's *Protestant, Catholic, Jew* (1955) and Andrew Greeley's *Denominational Society* (1972) find variant resolutions of the social irrelevance Smith posits in the long run for ethnic denominations. Herberg, writing as he was during the Eisenhower consensus, portrayed the identity- and meaning-providing functions of ethnicity and denominationalism as being assumed by three pools of religious affiliation (Protestantism, Catholicism, and Judaism) and those in turn as fostering a religion of Americanism. Greeley, self-consciously updating Herberg's analysis in order to accommodate the revived ethnicity of the late sixties and early seventies, saw the common American religion (now called Civil Religion) in conflict with denominations which as ethnic communities continue to play identity- and meaning-providing roles. Both volumes, for their social context, helpfully pursue issues that Smith raises. For further questions on Smith's essay see the introduction to his earlier essay.

---

1. Niebuhr, *The Social Sources of Denominationalism*, (Hamden, Conn.: The Shoe String Press, 1954, first published in 1929), pp. 224, 226.

7

Religious Denominations as Ethnic Communities: A Regional Case Study

Timothy L. Smith

Recent studies of the history of ethnic groups in America have produced a growing awareness that the relationships between religious institutions and ethnic identity are more complex than was earlier believed. Three factors, it seems to me, are now hindering our efforts to understand these relationships. One is the absence of analyses of the wide functional differences between congregations and denominations, the two kinds of institutions which serve the religious needs of modern democratic societies. Another is the concentration of most historical research in immigrant religion upon one ethnic group. And the third is the emphasis upon the history of either rural frontiers or large cities. In this paper, I wish to present the results of a study of the religious life of the Lake Superior copper and iron mining country, a region in which immigrants from Eastern and Southern Europe are predominant, yet one in which the newcomers of each nationality were spread widely through small towns and villages.

The scattered settlement is crucial to the story, for it made necessary the cooperative relationships among congregations which were the basis of the denominational structures. Of the fourteen towns incorporated in the mining region of northern Minnesota in 1910, for example, four—Virginia, Hibbing, Chisholm, and Eveleth—contained between seven and eleven thousand inhabitants; the remaining ten numbered between one and four thousand. A great many of the immigrants, however, lived not in such towns at all, but in neighboring mining locations. In the seventy-odd such villages which existed at one time or another on the Minnesota Ranges, nationalities were mixed, and organized

Reprinted, footnotes omitted, with the permission of Church History and the author. Footnotes available in Church History, 35 (1966), 207-26.

congregations were rare; generally, if the villagers went to church, they had to get into town. Locations and towns were alike, however, in the fact that, by contrast with the great cities in which most twentieth-century immigrants settled, they were small enough for relationships to be personal. The families along the street might be Finnish, Italian, Croatian, and Swede, but they were real persons, not strangers. Hence the church congregation, even when composed exclusively of one ethnic group, could never be coterminous with the full range of primary, face-to-face relationships which governed the immigrant family's adjustment to its new life.

The dominant class in these mining towns were Yankees, English-Canadians, and skilled English miners from Cornwall. From their ranks came the captains, foremen, and mining engineers, the doctors, lawyers, and school teachers, and the owners of larger commercial enterprises. Skilled underground miners were principally Scandinavians and Finns, the latter of whom, after 1880, were the most numerous single nationality in the region. As years went by, new arrivals from Slovenia, Croatia, Bohemia, Poland, and Italy filled up the ranks of miners and unskilled laborers. The proportions of such Eastern and Southern European immigrants increased as operations moved westward into Minnesota. There Germans and Scandinavians generally moved upward into foremen's positions or out of mining altogether, while Serbians, Montenegrins, Ukrainians, and Russians crowded into the unskilled jobs at the bottom of the ladder, especially after 1905. Labor turn-over was high. Of the 12,018 men employed by the Oliver Iron Mining Company in 1907, 84.4% were foreign-born, and half of these had resided in the United States less than two years. The census of 1910 showed that two-thirds of the foreign-born population of St. Louis County outside Duluth were from Eastern and Southern Europe, with Finns and South Slavs constituting the largest single groups.

Here, then, was a region of small towns whose population was as polyglot as Chicago, and whose economic life, like that of the great cities of America, depended entirely on giant business organizations. Its religious traditions included all major segments of Protestant, Roman Catholic,

Orthodox and Jewish faith, along with some which, like the Uniate Croatians, were almost unknown. For a time the Lake Superior region came as near as any I know to being a microcosm of twentieth-century America. The story of the emergence of religious congregations in these communities, and of the denominational super-organizations which proved so necessary to their nurture, offers some important insights, I believe, into the relationship of religion and ethnic community throughout the nation.

A visitor at Calumet, Michigan, at the turn of the century might have attended worship at Trinity Lutheran Church without realizing that the edifice was so named not in honor of the Holy Trinity, but in recognition of the three groups of Lutherans—Finnish, Norwegian, and Swedish—who had united to erect the building in 1876. The Norwegian pastor of a mixed "Scandinavian" parish in nearby Quincy had first served the Lutherans of Calumet, without regard to their national background. His successor, another Norwegian, excommunicated large numbers of Finns, however, apparently because of their devotion to the beliefs of Lars Levi Laestadius, leader during the earlier part of the century of a laymen's revival movement in Finland. But in 1876, Alfred Backman, a Finnish Lutheran pastor, came to serve the church. He formed separate congregations for each of the three nationalities, then directed the construction of the building in which they were to conduct their separate services for many years.

By the time mining operations began in Minnesota a decade later, the three national groups of Lutherans had become sufficiently self-conscious to forbid experiments in united congregations. The only exception were the Swede-speaking Finns, who were ethnically not really at home with either nationality. They eventually followed the dictates of both language and desire for status, and joined the Swedish Lutheran congregations. By 1890, moreover, it had become clear to Swedish and Norwegian newcomers that they did not have to carry the heavy burdens of church-building alone. The several Scandinavian denominations already well-established in the upper Mississippi Valley moved rapidly to supply them with the pastors, publications,

187

schools, and mission funds which they required. The Finnish congregations, by contrast, were generally independent organizations. Their founders were often laymen, and their doctrines were usually Laestadian, an event which owed as much to the necessity of lay leadership in a country where clergymen were scarce as to the fact that many of the immigrants had come from northern Finland where that doctrine had been strong. The transfer of both religious and agricultural customs was an easy one, for both had originated under frontier conditions in Finland, as landless peasants spread northward toward the Arctic Ocean.

The voluntary and independent character of these early congregations is especially evident from their close association with Finnish temperance societies. In the oldest Minnesota mining towns, temperance societies and congregations were founded together. At Ely after some years, a large segment of the membership became discontented with the Laestadian teachings and withdrew to form a new congregation. They worshipped in the temperance hall for twenty-five years, as for a time, did a third, formed in 1901 among those who wished to associate themselves with the Suomi Synod. In the towns of the Mesabi Range, however, temperance societies uniformly preceded the organization of Finnish congregations. At places like Eveleth, Mountain Iron, Chisholm, Buhl, and Hibbing, the churches met for many years in the temperance halls, and meanwhile relied upon these organizations to conduct Sunday schools, summer schools, and dramatic and social events. An Old World visitor to Ely in 1899 found the temperance hall, called the Finnish Opera House, a center for all manner of cultural activities: a lending library, a band, a dramatic club, and both Saturday and summer schools for young people.

As with congregations, however, so with temperance societies: frequent divisions within local groups prevented these organizations from becoming centers of the entire local community of Finns. At Hibbing, for example, nineteen men formed the first temperance society in 1895, and launched a full program of weekly activities which included plays, speeches and debates, and the issue of a hand-written news sheet called "Star of the Wilderness." They associated themselves at once with the National Finnish Temperance Brotherhood. Controversy soon broke out, however, over religion and rules of discipline. The national society required members to be Christians, directed their meetings be opened with prayer, and forbade dancing and gambling at cards. Debates over these issues at the national convention in 1896 prompted many local units, including the society at Hibbing, to reconstitute themselves as independent groups. Strangely, however, the new by-laws adopted at Hibbing declared that the organization was to continue on a "Christian foundation"; dancing was still forbidden, and meetings both opened and closed with prayer. Nevertheless, a minority of the members set up another society, designed to continue their association with the national brotherhood. Both local groups used the same hall for many years, and both carried on an extensive program of musical, dramatic, and educational activities. The two united with the Workers Club in 1901 to form a Finnish Library, whose holdings later on became the nucleus of the Hibbing Public Library.

As time passed, no less than four competing national organizations of Finnish temperance societies emerged. They gave a permanent institutional form, and hence a certain sectarian character, to the local divisions. The functions which they performed in assisting and guiding the activities of local units were precisely the same as those which denominations performed for local church congregations. Each gave steady and increasing emphasis to Finnishness. In 1904 the Walon Lahde Temperance Society in Eveleth initiated a regional celebration on the twenty-fourth of June, traditionally "Mid-Summer Day" in Finland. Delegates of temperance societies from most of the Minnesota Iron Range towns laid the plans, which included a vast picnic with speeches by prominent Finnish laymen and ministers, and "one or two good American public speakers." Three thousand people appeared for the day. Proceeds of the gathering went into a fund to establish a Finnish summer school at which children attending the public schools could be taught the language and history of their father's country. Thereafter, indeed, the preoccupation of both national and local societies with "education," not only in temperance but in Finnishness, was the most important aspect of their activities in any year. "You shouldn't imagine yourselves as Americans, since you are not that," Abraham Ollila told the youth of the Hibbing Temperance Societies in 1909. "You should devote yourselves to national ideals more than you have up to now. . . . Let the flame of nationalism burn, and let minds and hearts be enlightened and warmed."

Against this background, we can better understand the emergence of the several religious denominations serving Finnish Lutherans. The Laestadians, whose congregation organized at Calumet in 1872 soon adopted the name "Finnish Apostolic Lutheran Church," spread through Michigan, Minnesota, Massachusetts, and Oregon. A direct carry-over from the homeland, the chief difference in American Laestadianism was simply that the members were not, as in Finland, nominally part of a national church. What had been a movement within the church there became an independent denomination here—just as had happened to Congregationalists, Presbyterians, and Pietists long before. Such has been, in every decade, the consequence of religious diversity and the separation of church and state. The bonds of union which Laestadians forged in the new land, moreover, were the same as in the old—traveling ministers, the annual "Big Meeting," and a devotional periodical. What was new was that Finnishness now became a commitment, rather than an inheritance, a matter of conscious choice in a land where public schools and close association with diverse peoples in small towns threatened to destroy ethnic identity.

The Suomi Synod of Evangelical Lutherans was the second denomination to appear. J. K. Nikander, pastor at Hancock, Michigan, was the leader of a group of mining-region ministers who set out in 1889 to unite the congregations under their care in a national organization. At a mission meeting in Hancock that year, Nikander's sermon on "The Kingdom of God on This Earth" called for an inclusive body, not a "pure" church, one which would serve all Finnish Lutherans in America without regard to their doctrinal differences, just as did the national church of Finland. The pastors organized a consistory and drew up articles of incorporation which they filed with the county clerk of Houghton County. At that point Ino Ekman, editor of *Kansan Lehti* [*The People's Journal*], a newspaper published in Red Jacket, discovered that the articles had ignored the Michigan law requiring congregations themselves to adopt a declaration of purpose before they could be incorporated into a denominational body. Ekman then attacked the proceeding publicly, charging that the pastors wished to establish an episcopal government and to preserve in the New World the legal guarantee of their salaries which had been so much hated in Finland. Bitter public arguments ensued at the congregational meetings which the law required. In Calumet, Pastor J. W. Eloheimo had to excommunicate five hundred members before the "righteous remnant" of 200 which remained could vote for incorporation. Those excommunicated formed the "Evangelical Lutheran National Congregation of Calumet," known at first as the "People's" church, possibly in part because of the name of Ekman's journal, but perhaps more because of the similarity of the two words in Finnish meaning "national" and "peoples."

Thus the initial effort to create an inclusive fellowship of Finnish Lutheran churches produced not one but two rival organizations. The People's Church movement spread through the mining towns, gathering to itself all those who protested the episcopal tendencies of the Suomi Synod. Eloheimo moved from Calumet to Ironwood, Michigan. There, however, he fell into difficulties with his congregation, wrote a strange prophetic book, and was maneuvered out of the Suomi consistory. He then sought to organize yet another movement, the "Episcopal Fenno-American Church," but wound up in 1896 back in Calumet, pastor of the "People's" congregation whose charter members he had excommunicated six years before! Thereafter Eloheimo took the lead in the incorporation of the Finnish Evangelical Lutheran National Church. The response of local congregations to the opportunity of affiliating with one or the other of two competing denominations was, as in the case of so much of the history of denomination-founding in America, an ambivalent one. Many, as at Ely and Hibbing in Minnesota, stood aloof from formal association, but relied upon one or the other of the two organized bodies to supply preachers for them. Some who did vote to affiliate with one suffered secession by a minority intent on either preserving their independence or joining the other.

Competition served to increase the attention which leaders of the two denominations paid to ethnic identity. The Suomi Synod seemed to be acting out of loyalty to Nikander's inclusive "folk-church" principle, but the National church moved in the same direction without benefit of the rationale. From their two headquarters at Hancock and Ironwood, each published a growing body of literature aimed at the indoctrination of the young not only in religious principles but in that respect for Finnish culture which both denominations came to realize must be preserved or each would perish. The national organizations inspired programs for the training of teachers, provided guidance and encouragement to local groups when enthusiasm for summer and Sunday schools lagged, and sent missionary preachers to organize congregations in Finnish settlements where none existed before. And most important, each established a combined academy and seminary for the training of lay and clerical leaders.

The story of the two colleges deserves a separate word, for it illustrates the service which education has rendered to sectarianism in American history. J. K. Nikander's plan to form a school was set in motion immediately after the incorporation of the Suomi Synod in 1890. Proposals to locate it in St. Paul, Superior, and elsewhere proved unsatisfactory and Nikander finally opened what was called the Suomi College and Seminary at Hancock, Michigan, in the fall of 1896. The original curriculum resembled that of a progressive American high school, save for the inclusion of religion and Finnish. The first class of ministers graduated in 1906. An early emphasis upon business education, however, flourished alongside the theological program during the following decades. Finnish Americans had come to the new land in order to get ahead, and they expected the education which their church provided to give their children the tools to do so.

Similarly, the Finnish Evangelical National Church in 1900 began discussions of a school which would serve both the denomination and independent congregations. The Brooklyn, New York, newspaper, *American Kaiku* [*American Echo*] campaigned actively for the proposal, suggesting a curriculum patterned after the *Realikouluia* [Practical Schools] which were then popular in Finland. A group of 19 pastors and 16 laymen published an appeal of similar import in April, 1903. The annual convention authorized the opening of the school that fall and named it "The Finnish People's College and Theological Seminary." All students were to take two years of fundamental instruction at the high school level. Those planning for the ministry were to spend another two years in theological study, while others gave a like period to business training. The board in charge purchased a campus and a rambling building at Smithville, near Duluth, and in January, 1904, launched the sale of 50,000 shares of stock at $1.00 each to finance the venture.

Almost at once, however, members of Socialistic worker's clubs in the mining region began purchasing shares in large quantities. Four years later they took control of the institution in the name of "revolutionary Marxism" and renamed it "The Work People's College." Ironically, however, the services which the college thereafter performed for the socialists differed not one whit from those rendered earlier to the Christians: indoctrination in both faith and Finnishness, and practical business education for young people eager to get ahead in a capitalist society.

The growth of Finnish socialism, indeed, illustrates another facet of the immigrant's quest for ethnic identity. The movement reached the Lake Superior region in 1899 when Antero Tanner and other Marxist lecturers began appearing at workers' halls and temperance gatherings. When members of the temperance societies became socialists, they often sought to divert the common property to their new purposes. In Eveleth, for example, while the middle-class members of one temperance club were off on a summer's jaunt to Finland, the minority left behind voted to reconstitute themselves a socialist society and to transfer the property to the new organization. The bitter experience at

193

the People's College in Duluth was but the climactic example of such maneuvers. Thereafter, the radicals developed their own program of hall socialism, with a full range of such cultural activities as dramatics, discussion groups, music societies, and Saturday and summer schools for children and young people. Rituals for the naming of infants and the burial of the dead made the institutional substitution for the congregation complete. Even more striking, however, was the development of competing national sects of Finnish socialists, each fielding its own team of itinerant evangelists, and each armed with complete publishing, educational, and promotional programs, designed to secure the allegiance of the local workers' clubs. Their story cannot be told in this paper, save to say that by the time World War I broke out, these organizations, too, like the religious denominations, had come to stress Finnishness quite as much as socialism, in their effort to attract and hold the loyalty of their members.

In the long struggle among the church Finns, temperance Finns, and socialist Finns during these years, local divisions within each ideological camp increasingly mirrored the rivalry of the competing national organizations. Lines were by no means always clear, however. Matti Lehtonen, for example, served both as a socialist lecturer and as pastor of the Finnish Methodist Church at Nashwauk, Minnesota. He helped organize a half-dozen such congregations, with the full support of the Minnesota Conference of Methodists. Elsewhere, Suomi Synod pastors wrestled with the competing claims of their working-class and middle-class members, usually siding with the latter as a means of freeing their national group from identification with labor radicalism, so they maintained. William Rautanen, pastor at Calumet, Michigan, regretted the absence of an organized movement of Christian Socialism among American Finns, and defended the right of individual members to join unions and battle for workingmen's rights. But the common meeting-ground upon which he thought churchmen and socialists might one day stand appeared to the more doctrinaire leaders in both camps a land of never never.

Under such circumstances, the quest of an inclusive

ethnic unity among American Finns, either at local or national levels, was a hopeless cause indeed. One university professor reared in a Finnish socialist home at Chisholm in the 1920's remembers having no intimate contacts at all with church Finns, whether preachers or laymen. The Suomi Synod, which clung stubbornly to the theory that it was an inclusive communion, deferred and, by negligence, finally rejected a proposal to merge with the National church on the eve of World War I. The "folk church" concept seems, in retrospect, to have been only the vehicle by which this particular organization rationalized its steady cultivation of ethnic consciousness. Even the temperance societies became suspect to the Suomi Synod, although Rautanen was not sure whether the estrangement was due to their growing broadmindedness on such matters as dancing and card playing or to their increasingly rational philosophy. I suspect it stemmed as much from mere organizational rivalry. Certainly, the competitive and sectarian structure of the temperance groups, like that of other national organizations, dictated policies of isolation.

The most obvious generalization which this sketch of the organization of the spiritual life of American Finns reinforces is that the congregation is the primary institution in American religion. A child of both the chances and the choices of uprooted men, it is oriented to the future—dedicated to the attainment of objectives which both sermon and song may rationalize. Yet it looks backward also, providing a spiritual substitute for the kin-group left behind. Compounded thus of both hope and memory, the congregation acts to preserve as well as to refashion an ancient faith. When mobility is intensified, whether geographic or social, its usefulness in fulfilling the need for belonging, for personal identity, and for guidance in the adjustment of old customs to new conditions, becomes very great indeed. This was no more true in Red Jacket, Michigan, in 1890, than it is in suburban New Jersey in 1960.

The religious denomination appears clearly in this story as a structural super-organization designed to give guidance, support, and discipline to local congregations. It was born of social necessity, quite without reference to the high doctrine of "denominationalism" which Professors Sidney Mead and Winthrop Hudson have taught us. The fulfillment of its functions required, however, a specific rationale, a permanent structure, and a leadership dedicated not only to serving the congregations but to perpetuating both the larger institution and their own place in it. Such an organization by its very nature resists sharp changes either in structure or in philosophy, and encourages an exclusive loyalty in its local units. The immigrant denomination, thus conceived, is an ethnic sect; its activities contributed to a sharpened sense of isolation from other organizations competing for the allegiance of members of the same national group; and educational programs, so frequently regarded as broadening, contribute to this sectarian isolation.

Finally, the story of the Finnish Lutherans suggetsts that small town congregations may be different from those in large cities precisely in the fact that they are less "sectarian" than the denominations of which they are a part. The reasons seem clear: members of the congregation are involved in a host of communal face-to-face relations not only with members of their own ethnic group who belong to other denominations, but with persons belonging to other ethnic and religious groups. To illustrate the "strife of sects" in small towns, as has often been done, may simply obscure a more important source of sectarianism: the competition of national organizations for the loyalty of people whose social or ethnic backgrounds make them the prime prospects for the denomination's growth.

The immense variety of relationships between religious and ethnic identity in America becomes clearer when we turn our attention to the history of the role of the Slovenians in the Roman Catholic parishes in Lake Superior communities. In several important ways their situation contrasted sharply with that of the Lutheran Finns. Instead of one people among several communions, Catholic immigrants to the iron-mining country were many peoples in one: Slovenians, Croatians, and Italians, chiefly, with lesser numbers of Germans, Hungarians, Czechs, Poles, and, from the New World, French Canadians. Even in their homelands, moreover, the consciousness of nationality among all these but the French and the Poles was a recent and uncertain achievement. And in literacy and vocational skills, they all ranged along the bottom of the scale for immigrants in these decades. On the other hand, unlike both Finnish Lutherans and Eastern Orthodox Slavs, the Roman Catholics found an efficient and cohesive religious organization ready to serve them on their arrival in the New World. An adequate force of clergymen, operating under a carefully centralized authority, seemed determined that no migrating believer should be long out of touch with his faith.

Moreover, the Church in this region was committed to a clearcut philosophy of Americanization. Archbishop John Ireland of St. Paul stood at the head of the group of liberal Irish prelates who during these years sought to befriend labor, cooperate with the public schools, and promote social justice. In 1889, he placed one of his most loyal and tolerant priests, James McGolrick, in charge of the new Diocese of Duluth. McGolrick promptly made Father Joseph Buh, a Slovenian missionary to the Indians who had recently become pastor at the mining town of Tower, Minnesota, chancellor and vicar-general of his diocese. The move was but the first instance of the skillful and persistent policy by which these two bishops sought to bring the new immigrant into the fellowship of the Church. In every town they could count on the support of a nucleus of second-generation Irish and German settlers, many of them in business as saloon-keepers, professional men, or merchants. However willing the bishops were to compromise for a time with ethnic sentiments, their long-range goal was to make the newcomers Americans—on an Irish model, of course. Their policy appears in retrospect to have become the dominant theme of American Roman Catholic history during the first half of this century: a melting-pot church in a mosaic culture.

Finally the Slovenians, unlike any other ethnic group in American history, were preceded into the New World by priests of their own nationality. Frederick Baraga came to Lake Superior as a missionary to the Chippewa Indians in 1831. Later, as bishop of the Diocese of Marquette, he recruited pastors who welcomed French Canadian, Slavic, and Irish newcomers with a sympathy which only immigrant priests could achieve. Meanwhile, his countryman Fran Pirc carried on the Indian missions in Minnesota. Pirc returned to Slovenia in 1864 and brought back Buh, already an ordained priest, and 15 students, whom he enrolled, under Buh's care, in St. Paul Seminary. In later years Buh returned to recruit similar groups of students. Already competent in German as well as in their native Slovenian, many of these men learned Czech and Polish as well, along with the Chippewa language, so as to be able to minister to the scattered enclaves of Slavic immigrants appearing along the frontier near their Indian missions.

When, therefore, the earliest Roman Catholic congregations emerged in northern Minnesota their priests were often Slovenians, even though the parishioners were of many nationalities. Riding the spreading network of mining region railroads from his base at Tower, Father Buh said Masses regularly in schoolhouses and town halls as new communities appeared on the Mesabi Range to the south. And he supervised closely the work of the young priests who were assigned to establish parishes there. Matija Šavs, then a divinity student in St. Paul, later remembered that the first service in Biwabik was conducted in a hut thrown together in a few days. Buh preached in English, Slovenian, and French, then in Chippewa, for a few Indians had squatted in the front row. At the larger towns of Virginia and Hibbing the Irish, Germans, Italians, Poles, French Canadians, and others were together far more numerous than the South Slavs. Thus Father Mathias Bilban, ablest of the younger Slovenians, was pastor at Virginia until 1903, but gave way to an Irishman then, James Hogan. At Hibbing a Frenchman, Father C. B. Gamache, was pastor from 1895 until Hogan replaced him in 1911. In Tower and Ely, however, and thereafter in Mesabi towns such as Aurora, Eveleth, Chisholm, and Gilbert, Slovenians and Croatians comprised a majority within the parishes.

As the population of the Range towns grew, dissatisfaction with melting-pot parishes produced desultory attempts to establish national ones. While still at Virginia, Bilban erected the Holy Family Church for his parishioners at nearby Eveleth, where Slovenians were in the majority.

Religious Denominations as Ethnic Communities

When Hogan took charge of the larger parish, he built St. Patrick's Church at Eveleth "for English-speaking Catholics." Both chapels soon became independent of the Virginia church. The Italians at Eveleth, greatly outnumbered in the Holy Family parish, later took steps to establish a congregation of their own. Poles and other groups too small to hope for a national parish then had no choice but to move to St. Patrick's and learn English. Meanwhile, at Hibbing, Father John Zarrilli arrived from Italy late in October, 1905. Armed with Bishop McGolrick's blessing and endowed with promotional skills worthy of a Chamber of Commerce secretary, he awakened the first real religious enthusiasm among the Italians in that large town and its sprawling complex of neighboring locations. An Italian congregation also appeared in northside Virginia. Later on the "Polish-Slovenian" Church at Virginia proved an unsuccessful experiment in cooperation.

In smaller towns, a single mixed parish remained the rule, though the nationality of the priest often determined the current state of loyalty among the constituency. Thus Irish Father Joseph Quillin, pastor of St. John the Baptist Church in Biwabik, wrote the Oliver Iron Mining Company in 1919 that he had thirty-six "American" and one hundred and twenty "Austrian" families in his parish, but desperately needed a donation because he "received no help from the Austrians." In a similar appeal four years later the new pastor, John Jershe, a Slovenian, was able to report a much healthier situation, though it is not clear whether the "American" families shared his optimism.

Since Roman Catholic congregations could not under these circumstances serve as exclusive ethnic centers, the Slovenians fashioned a spiritual home by voluntary association in mutual benefit lodges. At Calumet, Michigan, Lodge St. Joseph, founded in 1882, preceded the organization of a separate Slovenian parish by seven years. It eventually became the nucleus of a national organization known as the "Slovene-Croatian Union," though for a long time the Croatians maintained their own associations. At Tower, Buh encouraged the organization of a Slovenian lodge shortly after he arrived there. Meanwhile the Slovenian students at

St. Paul Seminary, reacting like typical undergraduates to their minority status, conceived the idea of a national association of church-related lodges, apparently borrowing it from the Czechs, with whose parishes they were well acquainted. The students read eagerly the first issues of the Slovenian newspaper which Father Buh began publishing at Tower in 1891. Embarrassed by its antiquated grammar and careless typesetting, they volunteered to spend summers with him, helping out both with the parish and the publication of the paper, and recruiting members for Slovenian lodges there and at other mining towns. Father Buh, mindful of his non-Slavic parishioners and of his duties to the diocese, stood officially aloof from the latter effort, but privately he encouraged them and they were successful.

Two years later, delegates from several such lodges met in Joliet, Illinois, and formed a national organization, the Grand Carniolian Catholic Union, usually known as K.S.K.J., the initials of the title in Slovenian. St. Joseph's Church at Joliet was a Slovenian national parish—the only one then in existence. The pastor there, Francis S. Šušteršič, was thus free openly to support the movement and to accept the presidency of the national body; Matija Šavs, leader of the student group, was elected secretary. Local units sprang up rapidly throughout the Lake Superior region then. The sense of ethnic identity which the Church could not nurture on either local or regional levels had thus created a national association—in the sociological sense of the word, perhaps a denomination—to fulfill the same purpose. K.S.K.J. was intended "for the propagation of the faith and benefit to the Slovenian nationality." Centralization, one of the seminary students wrote, "would insure the person who moves from one locality to another, or one state to another, of affiliation with the same kind of group among his own people."

From that day forward, the affairs of lodge and church in Slovenian settlements were closely intertwined. In the national parishes which emerged at Calumet, Eveleth, Chicago, and Cleveland, an array of local lodges were responsible for virtually the whole of the congregation's social and lay activities. In mixed congregations where

Slovenians were the majority, the official parish social program was at best a limited one. Where they were a minority, the opposite sometimes happened, and some members of the lodges became so estranged from the parish as to fall an easy prey to anti-clerical or socialist agitation. Curbing radicalism was almost from the beginning one of the justifications which Slovenian priests gave for their participation in the national organization of K.S.K.J. But the longing for belonging was no doubt the greater force at work. The official organ, Buh's newspaper, carried from the beginning letters from individuals and local societies in widely scattered communities, as well as reports of parish activities in the larger centers. Lay leaders in local parishes, like Anton Nemanec, saloonkeeper, merchant, and undertaker at Joliet who succeeded Šušteršič as national president, became pillars of a self-conscious ethnic community in which priests appeared as both lords and servants. Annual conventions, at Tower, Calumet, Eveleth, and Joliet, brought lay delegates and priests together for fun, business, and fellowship, with music provided in the early years by a chorus of Slovenian divinity students from St. Paul. Buh's press issued a Slovene-English dictionary, a catechism, and, beginning in 1897, an annual almanac of Slovenian affairs which, like the newspaper, contained instructions in both citizenship and religion which were designed to ease the immigrant's adjustment to his life in the New World. But, as in the case of the Finns, denominational organization in the long run encouraged rather than restrained ethnic exclusiveness. The Slovenian Catholic group became a national sect.

Being voluntary associations, moreover, such national organizations were, as with Finnish denominations, subject to voluntary division and further sectarian development. In 1898, disagreements over the high rate of insurance claims from mining regions prompted a minority of aggrieved lodges to organize the rival "South Slovenic Catholic Union," known as J.S.K.J., with permanent headquarters at Ely. Michigan Slovenians, meanwhile, went their own way into the S.H.Z. as we have seen. More serious, however, was the threat of anti-clericalism and socialism. Young liberals from the Old Country appeared in America as early as 1894 and were making substantial inroads in the Slovenian Catholic community by the turn of the century. At the national meeting of J.S.K.J. at Omaha in 1903, arguments over the religious requirements for membership produced a secession movement. An anti-clerical monthly began publication, first in Pueblo, Colorado, but soon after in Chicago. A Socialist, Jose Zavertnik, who had recently arrived from Slovenia, became editor in 1904. He took charge of the movement to form a national association of anti-clerical lodges, the Slovene National Benefit Society, known by the initials S.N.P.J. Spread of this movement in the Lake Superior mining region was very slow, however, until the strike of 1907 created an open rupture in the parishes there. By that time, Socialists had pretty well taken over the anti-clerical movement, partly through the help of a separate organization, the Yugoslav Socialist Federation.

Bitter conflicts between K.S.K.J. and J.S.K.J. lodges and their anti-clerical rivals characterized the following years. Competition at both local and national levels required each group to expand its mutual benefit insurance program, and to develop a full range of Slovenian cultural, social, and recreational activities. This was especially so in the case of the Socialists, who had to divorce their members from the Church and its supporting lodges if they were to succeed. Library associations, singing societies, dramatic clubs, and youth organizations, much in a pattern learned from the Finns, became customary in larger centers, with their printed materials supplied, precisely as in the case of Religious denominations, by the publishers of the official newspaper organ. By World War I, the sectarianization of the two national communities of American Slovenians, one church-related and the other socialist, was so great that in the decades which followed communication between the two groups on a personal level almost disappeared.

Two by-products of the competition seem significant. Both priests and lay leaders of the church-related Slovenian lodges were prompted to maintain a pro-labor position, in order to make their opposition to Socialism effective. They had followed this policy for twenty-five years, before the mining companies discovered, at the time of the strike of 1917, that the church-related lodges might become, if properly cultivated, their allies. Scanty evidence leaves the picture confused, and the deep hostility of Slovenian workingmen to the great industrial concerns which had dominated their lives made such an outcome in fact improbable. Even after 1917, when company support for Roman Catholic church building programs began for the first time to approach the level which Protestants had enjoyed from the beginning, Slovenian congregations remained on short rations. In some cases, certainly, as at Virginia in the years between 1917 and 1921, both mining captains and Irish priests came to look upon the mixed parishes as agents of a kind of "Americanization" which differed substantially from the liberal aims which Buh and Archbishop Ireland had espoused.

Space does not permit in this paper a detailed discussion of the evidence pertaining to the Italian parishes and their affiliated clubs, nor of a half-dozen other Roman Catholic nationalities. Nor does it allow more than a word about two other ethnic groups which illustrate variant patterns: the Orthodox Serbians and the Jews. The Serbians, whose homes were scattered through a half-dozen Mesabi towns, were able to establish only one parish church, at Chisholm; but by the time they were well settled in the region railroad, street-car and automobile transportation were so efficient that on sacred days the great majority of families could appear. The warmth of fellowship which they experienced with their own kind bound the community together even in the first years, when women were scarce, and when no resident priest was available. None of them doubted that to be a Serbian was to be a member of the Serbian Orthodox Church. Jewish congregations, at Virginia, Eveleth, and Hibbing were Orthodox in practice, as befitted immigrants chiefly from Lithuania. But the scarcity of rabbis and their great distance from centers of American Jewry required them in the earliest years to develop a regional association of synagogues for mutual aid and comfort. Orthodox scruples rapidly gave way to what were in form, though not yet in theory, the customs of Reformed Jews.

Denominationalism

As for the several non-Lutheran Protestant denominations, suffice to say here that Presbyterians and Methodists, thanks to the skill and zeal of their home mission agencies, were the most flourishing. For a decade the Presbyterians, under William Bell, sought to establish a "greater Range Parish," designed to minister to the spiritual needs of immigrants in smaller towns and mining locations without demanding their conversion. Pastors of established Presbyterian congregations varied in their response to Bell's evangelism; one in Virginia cultivated an inter-ethnic fellowship. Meanwhile, the organization of Finnish Methodist churches and of the Swedish Methodist Conference testified to that denomination's readiness to fit programs to social conditions. The English-language Methodist congregations, like those of the Protestant Episcopal communion, served a strong complement of Cornish captain's families; they seem on cursory observation to have developed a feeling of identity which was almost an ethnic one as well, if we define that term broadly.

In general, neither melting-pot parishes nor melting-pot denominations seem to have been as successful as the more exclusively ethnic ones in firing the deep emotions to kinship and belonging which enabled them to mold and shape the life of the immigrant in the New World. Moreover, the experience of the Finns was repeated as other groups developed denominational organization above the level of local fellowship; these institutions, not only in their spiritual but in their cultural and educational programs as well, nurtured sectarianism. The religious and emotional weakness of the melting-pot congregation on one hand, and the long-run irrelevance of sectarianism on the other, combined to leave religious institutions at last on the fringes of the real life which the immigrant's children embraced. Instead, they placed their hopes in education and in economic ambition, found their pleasure in the round of athletic, recreational, and social events which the towns sponsored, and adopted as their own the passion for identification with American culture which became the hallmark of the region.

To American church historians, the story told here offers

three challenges of much broader significance, I think, than merely the religious history of the mining communities. The first is to study the history of both congregations and denominations in America in reference to social and institutional necessity. Was sectarianism in other communions also a by-product of denominational structures originally devised to give material and spiritual nurture to struggling congregations? If so, were the activities so often thought of as "churchly"—education, youth programs, uniform ritual, and the like—as much divisive as harmonizing influences in American Protestantism? The familiar concept of a straight-line evolution of "sects" into "churches" could scarcely survive such a discovery.

Secondly, much work lies ahead for those willing to search out the inner complexities—sociological, religious, and institutional—which characterized Roman Catholic life in twentieth-century America. Despite continuing improvement in the level of scholarship among Roman Catholic no less than Protestant church historians, we know little, yet, about anything other than the deeds and policies of the Irish leaders of the Church. When the stories of the various ethnic sub-communities within Roman Catholicism in America are fully told, with due reference to parish institutions on one hand and national organizations on the other, I suspect that our image of American Catholic history will resemble much more closely that of Protestantism. The single and exceedingly important difference will be the continued pressure of a powerfully organized hierarchy, exerted year by year upon every part of the Church, for the creation of one American Catholic faith.

The third challenge is to redefine the concept of ethnic community in American religious history in terms of social psychology, rather than national tradition. In the cases surveyed here, the Finns, Slovenians, and Croatians were divided into several different "ethnic" communities. Each one of these was made in America, and each witnessed the rapid development of a national organization, whether called a Socialist Federation, a mutual benefit society, or a denomination, which contributed heavily to its sense of exclusive identity. Such a redefinition might enable us to understand better the cohesive and persistent force of American religious movements whose membership, being composed chiefly of native-born white Protestants, does not seem at first glance to suggest an ethnic identity. Perhaps the migration of Southern Baptists to northern cities where, one suspects, not just soundness of doctrine, but the sound of the doctrine was crucial to new commitments, is an obvious case in point. I have seen dimly, and tried to record in my history of the Church of the Nazarene, similar developments among rural Wesleyans moving to the city. But much more needs to be done, I should think, before we can understand the social forces which, no less than religious belief or spiritual quest, condition the life of religion in modern industrial societies.

8
Introduction

Denominationalism in the black community has derived its centrality, nature, and role, E. Franklin Frazier suggests, from "the restricted participation of Negroes in American society," the destruction of "their social heritage and their traditional social organization," and "the influence of Christianity in creating solidarity among a people who lacked social cohesion and a structured social life."[1] The Christianization of blacks, both slaves and freedmen, which accelerated with the evangelism of nineteenth-century Christian America, filled a social-cultural void and provided a new Christian "orientation towards the world." Prior to the Civil War, blacks achieved a two-fold adaptation and application of traditional Christianity to black circumstances. In the South, blacks evolved the emotional and revivalistic preaching of Baptists and Methodists into a distinctive black spirituality and new order of the church that Frazier terms the "Invisible Institution." Freedmen, mainly in the North, found their own course to religious independence, following the course of Richard Allen, by creating black denominations modeled after their white counterparts. Black denominations (African Methodist Episcopal Church, African Methodist Episcopal Zion Church, National Baptist Conventions, and the post–Civil War Christian Methodist Episcopal Church, to use their current names) institutionalized the effective exclusion of blacks from meaningful participation in white denominations. They became, however, vehicles for distinctive black Christianity and for black aspirations for freedom. Debate rages as to whether exclusion (refuge, otherworldliness, political irrelevance) or assertion (freedom, black interests, theology of liberation) most aptly describes the part played by the denominations.

In the following selection Frazier examines the black denominations during the post–Civil War period. The two

1. E. Franklin Frazier, "The Negro Church: A Nation Within a Nation," in *The Negro Church in America* (New York: Schocken Books, 1964), pp. 85, 82, 6.

applications of Christianity to the black experience—the "Invisible Institution" and the independent black denominations—were united. These truly national denominations then undertook the care of the freedmen. This was to be the pinnacle of their influence (as it was in all probability also for white denominations). The black denominations were the primary sources and structures of social order, intimately related to efforts at economic well-being, educational agencies, and "an arena of political life." They were also the objects of blacks' deepest loyalties, refuges from a hostile world, and finally realms of other worldliness. From the height of this power and influence held by both the black denomination and the black preacher, there could be only decline. The northward and urban migration became a deluge in the early twentieth century. Urbanization with its various attendant developments—an uprooted population, the emergence of class differences, the appearance of other professionals and leaders alongside the clergy, family breakdowns, secularization, and this-world and community-oriented concerns, the duplication within the black community of the institutions of urban America—robbed the churches of their preeminence, rendered implausible the highly otherworldly traditional religious mythology, and undercut the efforts of the churches to maintain social order. While large local institutional churches appeared, they could not hold the masses, who gravitated to storefronts, cults, holiness, and pentecostal sects, where the intimacy and mythology of the South was sustained and transformed. Even the new "Black Bourgeoisie," the mainstay of denominations generally, were tempted to align with white denominations. Outside of the churches appeared new ideologies, some religious in style and content, others quite antireligious, that rivaled Christian mythology as interpretations of the black role in a white world. From the Garvey movement through the black Muslims to the black power movement, these new ideologies challenged the hold of the black denominations on black society. Hence the black denominations, bred to cultural and social dominance like their white counterparts and still marked by these significant earlier functions, have had to seek a new place. This search is now complicated by American society's tentative efforts at desegregation, the removal of precisely those conditions that gave rise to black denominations in the first place.

Frazier's pioneering studies of the black church, the black family, and the black community antedated the full impact of the Civil Rights movement, black power and black theology, the important researches in black history, slavery, and black culture of the last decade, and, of course, the new findings of the cliometricians. Frazier's findings remain viable, but there are strongly pressed alternatives. How might his assessment of black denominations require modification if important features of African religion and culture are identified in black religion, if black Christianity, even during slavery, had strong but disguised liberation commitments, if the apparent "otherworldly" preaching and song were understood as both profoundly Christian and politically significant, and if white denominations were shown to have undergone similar development? Just one example of a rather different assessment of black religion, an assessment which raises questions about Frazier's analysis may be seen in Eugene D. Genovese's *Roll, Jordan, Roll*.[2] Finally, how would an historian's treatment of the black denomination differ from Frazier's sociological account?

8

The Negro Church:
A Nation Within a Nation

E. Franklin Frazier

The "Invisible Institution" Merges
with the Institutional Church

The Civil War and Emancipation destroyed whatever stability and order that had developed among Negroes under the slave regime. An educated mulatto minister of the African Methodist Episcopal Church who went from the North to the South following Emancipation wrote:

The whole section (in the neighbourhood of Charleston, South Carolina) with its hundreds of thousands of men, women and

2. New York: Pantheon Books, 1974.
Reprinted without footnotes by permission of Schocken Books Inc. from *The Negro Church in America* by E. Franklin Frazier and *The Black Church Since Frazier* by C. Eric Lincoln. Copyright © 1963 by The University of Liverpool. Copyright © 1974 by Schocken Books Inc.

children just broken forth from slavery, was, so far as these were concerned, dying under an almost physical and moral interdict. There was no one to baptize their children, to perform marriage, or to bury the dead. A ministry had to be created at once—created out of the material at hand.

The "material at hand" was, of course, those Negroes among the slaves who had been "called to preach." In answer to the criticism that neither men nor money were available for creating a ministry, the minister just quoted wrote that "God could call the men; and that the A.M.E. Church had the authority to commission them when thus called." This represented the fusion of the "invisible institution" of the Negro church which had taken root among the slaves and the institutional church which had grown up among the Negroes who were free before the Civil War.

The most obvious result of the merging of the "invisible institution" of the church which had grown up among the slaves with the institutional church of the Negroes who were free before the Civil War was the rapid growth in the size of the Negro church organization. But there was a much more important result of this merger which is of primary concern to our study. The merger resulted in the structuring or organization of Negro life to an extent that had not existed. This becomes clear when we recall that organized social life among the transplanted Negroes had been destroyed by slavery. The traditional African clan and family had been destroyed and in the environment of the New World the development of a structured family life was always nullified by the exigencies of the plantation system. Any efforts towards organization in their religious life was prevented because of the fear of the whites of slave insurrections. Even any spontaneous efforts towards mutual aid on an organized basis was prevented for the same reasons. There was, to be sure, some social differentiation among the slaves based upon the different roles which they played in the plantation economy. But this did not result in the structuring of the social life among the slaves themselves. Among the slaves themselves one may note the germs of stratification based upon their different roles in the plantation, but no system of stratification ever came into existence that became the basis of an organized social existence.

This was all changed when the Negro became free, and it is our purpose here to show how an organized religious life became the chief means by which a structured or organized social life came into existence among the Negro masses. The process by which the "invisible institution" of the slaves merged with the institutional churches built by the free Negroes had to overcome many difficulties. These difficulties arose chiefly from the fact that there were among the free Negroes many mulattoes and that they, as well as the unmixed Negroes, represented a higher degree of assimilation of white or European culture. This was often reflected in the difference in the character of the religious services of those with a background of freedom and those who were just released from slavery. In fact, in the social stratification of the Negro population after Emancipation, a free and mulatto ancestry became the basis of important social distinctions. It should be pointed out, however, that these cultural and social distinctions were reflected in the denominational affiliation of Negroes. The Negro masses were concentrated in the Methodist and Baptist churches which provided for a more emotional and ecstatic form of worship than the Protestant Episcopal, Presbyterian, and Congregational churches. But even in the Methodist and Baptist denominations there were separate church organizations based upon distinctions of colour and what were considered standards of civilized behaviour. In the Methodist and Baptist churches in which the vast majority of Negroes were communicants, it was impractical to organize separate churches which would be congenial to the way of life of the small Negro elite. Nevertheless, some of the educated leaders were not in sympathy with the more primitive religious behaviour of the masses. The attitude of educated leaders of even Methodist and Baptist churches was expressed by a Bishop in the African Methodist Episcopal Church even before Emancipation. He opposed the singing of the Spirituals which he described as "corn field ditties" and songs of "fist and heel worshippers" and said that the

ministry of the A.M.E. Church must drive out such
"heathenish mode of worship" or "drive out all intelligence
and refinement."

Despite the difficulties, the integration of the "invisible
institution" which had emerged among the slaves into the
Negro church organization established by the free Negroes
was achieved. This provided an organization and structuring of Negro life which has persisted until the present time.
We shall begin by considering the relation of the organization of the religious life of the Negro to building up of social
control.

The Church as an Agency of Social Control

In dealing with the Negro church as an agency of control
we shall focus attention upon the relation of the church to
the Negro family and sex life during the years following
Emancipation. In order to understand the important role of
the Negro church, it is necessary to have a clear conception
of the situation which confronted organized religion. Under
slavery the Negro family was essentially an amorphous
group gathered around the mother or some female on the
plantation. The father was a visitor to the household without
any legal or recognized status in family relations. He might
disappear as the result of the sale of slaves or because of a
whimsical change of his own feelings or affection. Among
certain favoured elements on the plantation, house slaves
and skilled artisans, the family might achieve greater
stability and the father and husband might develop a more
permanent interest in his family. Whatever might be the
circumstances of the Negro family under the slave regime,
family and sex relations were constantly under the supervision of the whites.

The removal of the authority of masters as the result of the
Civil War and Emancipation caused promiscuous sex
relations to become widespread and permitted the constant
changing of spouses. The daughter of a planter family who
has idealized the slave regime nevertheless tells a story
which illustrates the disorder. "Mammy Maria," she wrote,
"came out in the new country as 'Miss Dabney,' and
attracted, as she informed her 'white children,' as much

admiration as any of the young girls, and had offers of marriage too. But she meant to enjoy her liberty, she said, and should not think of marrying any of them." Some of the confusion in marital relations was due, of course, to the separation of husbands and wives during slavery and the social disorganization that resulted from Emancipation.

The problem of monogamous and stable family life was one of the most vexing problems that confronted northern white missionaries who undertook to improve the morals of the newly liberated blacks. These missionaries undertook to persuade the freedmen to legalize and formalize their marriages. There was resistance on the part of many of the slaves since legal marriage was not in their mores. Sometimes missionaries even attempted to use force in order that the freedmen legalize their sexual unions. There were, of course, many cases in which the marriage ceremony was a confirmation of a union that was based upon conjugal sentiment established over a long period of association. Marriage and an institutional family life could not be imposed by white missionaries. Marriage and the family could acquire an institutional character only as the result of the operation of economic and social forces within the Negro communities.

A large proportion of the Negro families among the freedmen continued after Emancipation to be dependent upon the Negro mother as they had been during slavery. But the new economic conditions which resulted from Emancipation tended to place the Negro man in a position of authority in family relations. The freedmen refused to work in gangs as they had done during slavery and a man would take his wife and children and rent and operate a farm on his own account. The man or husband in the family was required to sign the rent or work agreements. Sometimes the wives were also required to sign but the husband or father was always held responsible for the behaviour of his family. The more stable elements among the freedmen who had been in a position to assimilate the sentiments and ideas of their former masters soon undertook to buy land. This gave the husband or father an interest in his wife and children that no preaching on the part of white missionaries or Negro preachers could give. But it would be a serious mistake to overlook the manner in which the new economic position of the man was consolidated by the moral support of the Negro church.

There was, of course, moral support for a patriarchal family to be found in the Bible and this fact contributed undoubtedly a holy sanction to the new authority of the Negro man in the family. However, there were more important ways in which the Negro church gave support to Negro family life with the father in a position of authority. As we have pointed out, after Emancipation the Negro had to create a new communal life or become integrated into the communities created by the Negroes who were free before the Civil War. Generally, this resulted in the expansion and complete transformation of these communities. The leaders in creating a new community life were men who with their families worked land or began to buy land or worked as skilled artisans. It is important to observe that these pioneers in the creation of a communal life generally built a church as well as homes. Many of these pioneer leaders were preachers who gathered their communicants about them and became the leaders of the Negro communities. This fact tends to reveal the close relationshp between the newly structured life of the Negro and his church organization.

The churches became and have remained until the past twenty years or so, the most important agency of social control among Negroes. The churches undertook as organizations to censure unconventional and immoral sex behaviour and to punish by expulsion sex offenders and those who violated the monogamous mores. But it was impossible to change immediately the loose and unregulated sex and family behaviour among a people lacking the institutional basis of European sexual mores. Very often the churches had to tolerate or accommodate themselves to sexual irregularities. A bishop in the African Methodist Episcopal Church in recounting the task of "cleaning up" irregular sex behaviour among the members of the church where he served said that his church became "the Ecclesiastical Court House, as well as the Church." Let us not forget, however, the control exercised by the Negro was exercised by dominating personalities. Frequently, they were the preachers who had become leaders of Negroes because of their talents and ability to govern men. Very often they were self-made men. In the Baptist Churches in which the majority of the Negroes have always been concentrated there was even greater opportunity for self-assertion and the assumption of leadership on the part of strong men. This naturally resulted in a pattern of autocratic leadership which has spilled over into most aspects of organized social life among Negroes, especially in as much as many forms of organized social life have grown out of the church and have come under the dominant leadership of Negro preachers.

The Church and Economic Co-operation

As DuBois pointed out more than fifty years ago, "a study of economic co-operation among Negroes must begin with the Church group." It was in order to establish their own churches that Negroes began to pool their meagre economic resources and buy buildings and the land on which they stood. As an indication of the small beginnings of these churches, we may note that the value of the property of the African Methodist Episcopal Church in 1787 was only $2,500. During the next century the value of the property of this organization increased to nine million dollars. The Negroes in the other Methodist denominations, and especially in the numerous Baptist Churches, were contributing on a similar scale a part of their small earnings for the construction of churches. At the same time, out of the churches grew mutual aid societies. The earliest society of this type was the Free African Society which was organized in Philadelphia in 1787. We have already noted that the Society was organized by Absalom Jones and Richard Allen, the two Negroes who led the secession from the Methodist Church. At the time the Society was organized, Negroes were migrating to Philadelphia in large numbers and the need for some sort of mutual aid was becoming urgent. The Society became a "curious sort of ethical and beneficial brotherhood" under the direction of Jones and Allen who exercised a "parental discipline" over its members. The avowed purpose of this organization was to "support one another in sickness, and for the benefit of their widows and fatherless children."

In the cities throughout the United States numerous beneficial societies were organized to provide assistance in time of sickness or death. Many of these beneficial societies, like the Free African Society, were connected with churches. These societies continued to be established throughout the nineteenth century. For example, in Atlanta in 1898 there were nine beneficial societies which had been founded from soon after the Civil War up to 1897. Six of these beneficial societies were connected with churches. The names of these beneficial societies are not without significance. At the Wheat Street Baptist Chuurch, for example, there were two beneficial societies—the Rising Star and the Sisters of Love, while at the Bethel (Methodist) Church was the Daughters of Bethel. These associations for mutual aid which were generally known as beneficial societies were often the germ out of which grew the secular insurance companies.

The role of religion and the Negro church in more elementary forms of economic co-operation among Negroes may be seen more clearly in the rural mutual aid societies that sprang up among freedmen after Emancipation. They were formed among the poor, landless Negroes who were thrown upon their own resources.These societies were organized to meet the crises of life—sickness and death; consequently, they were known as "sickness and burial" societies. The important fact for our study is that these benevolent societies grew out of the Negro church and were inspired by the spirit of Christian charity. They were supported by the pennies which the Negroes could scrape together in order to aid each other in time of sickness but more especially to insure themselves a decent Christian burial. The influence of the simple religious conceptions of the Negro folk and the Bible is revealed in the names of these mutual aid societies which continue to exist in the rural South. They bear such names as "Love and Charity," "Builders of the Walls of Jerusalem," "Sons and Daughters of Esther," "Brothers and Sisters of Charity," and "Brothers and Sisters of Love."

These "sickness and burial" societies should be distinguished from the fraternal organizations which played an important role in early economic co-operation among Negroes. Fraternal organizations like the Negro Masonic Lodge and the Odd Fellows came into existence among the free Negroes in the North as the result of the influence of the white fraternal organizations. On the other hand, Negroes began before the outbreak of the Civil War to organize fraternal organizations which reflected their own interests and outlook on life. One such secret society, the Knights of Liberty, was organized by a preacher, Reverend Moses Dickson, who was born in Cincinnati in 1824. This organization was active in the underground railroad and claimed to have nearly 50,000 members in 1856. Dickson joined the Union Army and after the Civil War he disbanded the Knights of Liberty. In 1871 he organized the first Temple and Tabernacle of the Knights and Daughters of Tabor in Independence, Missouri. The object of this secret society was "to help to spread the Christian religion and education" and its members were advised to "acquire real estate, avoid intemperance, and cultivate true manhood." At the end of the nineteenth century this society claimed to have nearly 200,000 members in eighteen jurisdictions scattered from Maine to California and from the Great Lakes to the Gulf of Mexico.

The organization and development of the Grand United Order of True Reformers provides a better example of the manner in which an organization under the leadership of a preacher fired with religious zeal played an important role in economic co-operation and the accumulation of capital. The founder of the organization was a Reverend Washington Browne who was born a slave in Georgia in 1849. During the Civil War he ran away from a new master and made his way to the North where he received a meagre education. After Emancipation he returned to Alabama where he joined a movement of the Good Templars against the whisky ring. But after observing the various benevolent and burial societies among Negroes, he decided that Negroes should have a separate organization adapted to their needs. In 1876 he succeeded in bringing together in a single organization, known as the Grand Fountain of True Reformers, twenty-seven Fountains with 2,000 members. Although he was not successful in creating a mutual benefit society, through his paper, The Reformer, he attracted the attention of the Organization of True Reformers in Virginia. He was invited to Richmond and became the Grand Worthy Master of the Virginia organization.

The True Reformers organized a variety of enterprises, including a weekly newspaper, a real estate firm, a bank, a hotel, a building and loan association, and a grocery and general merchandising store. The True Reformers took the lead in incorporating an insurance feature in its programme for the benefit of its members, an example of which was followed by the other fraternal organizations among Negroes. The insurance ventures failed because they did not have sound actuarial basis and were not under government supervision. Nevertheless, the Negro gained a certain experience and training which prepared him for his more successful business ventures.

The Church and Education

The educational development of Negroes does not reflect to the same extent as their churches and mutual aid associations the racial experience and peculiar outlook on life of Negroes. Education, that is Western or European education, was something totally foreign to the Negro's way of life. This was because, as Woodson has written, "the first real educators to take up the work of enlightening American Negroes were clergymen interested in the propagation of the gospel among the heathen in the new world." In fact, the purpose of education was primarily to transmit to the Negro the religious ideas and practices of an alien culture. In the North the strictly religious content of education was supplemented by other elements, whereas in the South limitations were even placed upon enabling the Negro to read the Bible. By 1850 there were large numbers of Negroes attending schools in northern cities. Then, too, individual Negroes managed to acquire a higher education and most of these were men who were preparing to become ministers.

This does not mean that Negroes took no initiative in setting up schools and acquiring an education. The free

Negroes in the cities contributed to the support of schools for Negro children. Generally, the support which the free Negroes provided was greater in southern cities like Baltimore, Washington, and Charleston, South Carolina, than in New York and Philadelphia. As early as 1790, the Brown Fellowship Society in Charleston maintained schools for the free Negro children. An important fact about the schools which the free Negroes maintained was that many of them were Sunday schools. On the eve of the Civil War, "There were then in Baltimore Sunday schools about 600 Negroes. They had formed themselves into a Bible Association, which had been received into the convention of the Baltimore Bible Society. In 1825 the Negroes there had a day and night school giving courses in Latin and French. Four years later there appeared an 'African Free School,' with an attendance of from 150 to 175 every Sunday." Although the Sunday schools represented before the Civil War one of the most important agencies in the education of Negroes, nevertheless the churches through their ministers urged parents to send their children to whatever schools were available.

After Emancipation the initiative on the part of Negroes in providing education for themselves was given a much freer scope. This was because of the great educational crusade which was carried on by northern white missionaries among the freedmen. As the Union armies penetrated the South, the representatives of northern missionary societies and churches sent funds and teachers in the wake of the advancing armies. The majority of the men and women or "school marms," as they were called, were inspired by a high idealism and faith in the intellectual capacity of Negroes. They laid the foundation for or established most of the Negro colleges in the South. Working with the Freedmen's Bureau which was created by an Act of Congress in 1856 to aid the freedmen in assuming the responsibilities of citizens, they also laid the foundation for a public school system for the newly emancipated Negro. It was Negroes trained in these schools supported by northern churches and philanthropy who became the educated leaders among Negroes.

Denominationalism

The schools—elementary, secondary, and those which provided the beginnings of college education—were permeated with a religious and moral outlook. The graduates of these schools went forth as missionaries to raise the moral and religious level of the members of their race. Many of the men were preachers or became preachers. A preacher who was a graduate of a Baptist college founded by white missionaries and who had helped to make the bricks for the buildings of the college, said that when he was graduated, the white president addressed him as follows: "I want you to go into the worst spot in this State and build a school and a church." This minister followed the instructions of his white mentor and established the school that provided the primary school and later the only secondary school for Negroes in the country and four Baptist Churches. This is typical of the manner in which the Negro preacher who was often the best educated man in the community took the initiative in establishing schools.

An educated and distinguished bishop in the African Methodist Episcopal Church who was the father of the most distinguished American Negro painter, wrote in his history of the Church in 1867: "For it is one of the brightest pages in the history of our Church, that while the Army of the Union were forcing their victorious passage through the southern land and striking down treason, the missionaries of our Church in the persons of Brown, Lynch, Cain, Handy, Stanford, Steward, and others, were following in their wake and establishing the Church and the school house. . . . " The work of the Negro preacher in establishing schools was especially important since the southern States provided only a pittance of public funds for the education of Negro children. When the Julius Rosenwald Fund contributed to the building of more than 5,000 schools for Negroes in the South in order to stimulate the public authorities to appropriate money for Negro schools, Negro churches played an important role in making possible the schools aided by the Rosenwald Fund. Negroes contributed 17 per cent of the total cost of the schools which amounted to over $28,000,000. They raised much of their share in this amount through church suppers and programmes under the auspices of their churches.

The impetus among Negroes to build institutions of higher education was due primarily to their need for an educated ministry. But the desire on the part of the masses for an educated ministry was far from universal. The masses of Negroes were still impressed by the ignorant and illiterate minister who often boasted that he had not been corrupted by wicked secular learning. Soon after the "invisible institution" of the slaves was integrated into the institutional church, it was feared that a schism would occur in the African Methodist Episcopal Church as the result of the conflict between the ignorant and intelligent elements in the church. Nevertheless, the African Methodist Episcopal Church succeeded in establishing a number of so-called colleges and universities. The African Methodist Episcopal Zion Church and the Colored Methodist Episcopal Church also established schools. The Baptists had to depend upon local efforts. In South Carolina the Negro Baptists who became dissatisfied with the white control of the college for Negroes finally established their own school.

The schools and colleges maintained by the Negro church denominations have never attained a high level as educational institutions. They have generally nurtured a narrow religious outlook and have restricted the intellectual development of Negroes even more than the schools established for Negroes by the white missionaries. This has been due only partly to lack of financial resources. It hardly needs to be emphasized that there was no intellectual tradition among Negroes to sustain colleges and universities. The attendance of Negro students at private colleges has reflected the social stratification of the Negro community. The children of the upper class in the Negro community have generally attended the school established by the Congregational Church and the better type of schools supported by the white Methodists and Baptists for Negroes. Nevertheless, the Negro church has affected the entire intellectual development and outlook of Negroes. This has been due both to the influence of the Negro church which has permeated every phase of social life and to the influence of the Negro preacher whose authoritarian personality and anti-intellectualism has cast a shadow over the intellectual outlook of Negroes.

An Arena of Political Life

It was inevitable that preachers who had played such an important role in the organized social life of Negroes should become political leaders during the Reconstruction period when the Negro enjoyed civil rights. The career of Bishop Henry M. Turner of the African Methodist Episcopal Church will enable us to see how these leaders in the religious life of Negroes became, after Emancipation, leaders in politics. He was born in South Carolina of free ancestry in 1834. On his mother's side he was the grandson of an African prince. He was able to acquire some education through private instruction. When fourteen years of age he joined the Methodist Church and later became a chaplain in the United States Army. After the Civil War he transferred to the African Methodist Episcopal Church in which he advanced from a position of an itinerant preacher to that of an elder. During this time he became active in politics. He organized Negroes in the Republican Party in Georgia and was elected to the Georgia legislature. Turner was expelled from the Georgia legislature when "white supremacy" was restored in Georgia and as the result of persecution he was forced to resign as postmaster of Macon, Georgia, a position to which he had been appointed by President Grant. Turner abandoned politics and devoted his life to the Church.

During the Reconstruction period a number of outstanding leaders in the Baptist and in the other Methodist denominations became outstanding as leaders of Negroes in politics. Bishop James W. Hood of the African Methodist Episcopal Zion Church was elected president of a convention of Negroes in North Carolina which was perhaps the first political convention called by Negroes after they gained their freedom. He served as a local magistrate and later as a Deputy Collector of Internal Revenue for the United States. Hood was also appointed Assistant Superintendent of Public Instruction of the State of North Carolina. These ministers who became the political leaders of Negroes were all

Republicans and shared on the whole the conservative political philosophy of that party.

It should be noted that of the twenty Negroes elected to the House of Representatives of the United States from the South during the Reconstruction period only two were preachers, but one of the two Negroes who were elected to the Senate was a preacher. Senator Hiram R. Revels, one of the two Negroes elected from Mississippi, was born a free Negro in North Carolina in 1822. He moved to the North and was ordained in the African Methodist Episcopal Church. When the Civil War broke out he assisted in organizing two Negro regiments in Maryland. He worked with the Freedmen's Bureau and, like other preachers, engaged in the establishment of churches and schools before entering politics in Mississippi. Revel's career in politics, like that of other Negro preachers was of short duration because of the re-establishment of white supremacy in the South. After elimination from politics in the South, the Negro preachers generally devoted themselves to their church though in some cases they became heads of Negro schools.

As the result of the elimination of Negroes from the political life of the American community, the Negro church became the arena of their political activities. The church was the main area of social life in which Negroes could aspire to become the leaders of men. It was the area of social life where ambitious individuals could achieve distinction and the symbols of status. The church was the arena in which the struggle for power and the thirst for power could be satisfied. This was especially important to Negro men who had never been able to assert themselves and assume the dominant male role, even in family relations, as defined by American culture. In the Baptist churches, with their local autonomy, individual Negro preachers ruled their followers in an arbitrary manner, while the leaders in the hierarchy of the various Methodist denominations were czars, rewarding and punishing their subordinates on the basis of personal loyalties. Moreover, the monetary rewards which went with power were not small when one considers the contributions of millions of Negroes and the various business activities of the churches.

223

Denominationalism

The Negro church was not only an arena of political life for the leaders of Negroes, it had a political meaning for the masses. Although they were denied the right to vote in the American community, within their Churches, especially the Methodist Churches, they could vote and engage in electing their officers. The elections of bishops and other officers and representatitves to conventions has been a serious activity for the masses of Negroes. But, in addition, the church had a political significance for Negroes in a broader meaning of the term. The development of the Negro church after Emancipation was tied up, as we have seen, largely with the Negro family. A study of Negro churches in a Black Belt county in Georgia in 1903 revealed, for example, that a large proportion of the churches were "family churches." Outside of the family, the church represented the only other organized social existence. The rural Negro communities in the South were named after their churches. In fact, the Negro population in the rural South has been organized in "church communities" which represented their widest social orientation and the largest social groups in which they found an identification. Moreover, since the Negro was an outsider in the American community, it was the church that enlisted his deepest loyalties. Therefore, it was more than an amusing incident to note some years ago in a rural community in Alabama, that a Negro when asked to identify the people in the adjoining community replied: "The nationality in there is Methodist." We must remember that these people have no historic traditions and language and sentiments to identify them as the various nationalities of Europe. For the Negro masses, in their social and moral isolation in American society, the Negro church community has been a nation within a nation.

A Refuge in a Hostile White World

In providing a structured social life in which the Negro could give expression to his deepest feeling and at the same time achieve status and find a meaningful existence, the Negro church provided a refuge in a hostile white world. For the slaves who worked and suffered in an alien world, religion offered a means of catharsis for their pent-up emotions and frustrations. Moreover, it turned their minds from the sufferings and privations of this world to a world after death where the weary would find rest and the victims of injustices would be compensated. The Negroes who were free before the Civil War found status in the church which shielded them from the contempt and discriminations of the white world. Then for a few brief years after Emancipation the hopes and expectations of the black freedmen were raised and they thought that they would have acceptance and freedom in the white man's world. But their hopes and expectations were rudely shattered when white supremacy was re-established in the South. They were excluded from participation in the white man's world except on the basis of inferiority. They were disfranchised and the public schools provided for them were a mere travesty on education. The courts set up one standard of justice for the white and another standard for the black man. They were stigmatized as an inferior race lacking even the human attributes which all men are supposed to possess. They were subjected to mob violence involving lynchings and burnings alive which were justified even by the white Christian churches.

Where could the Negro find a refuge from this hostile white world? They remembered from their Bible that the friends of Job had counseled him to curse God and die. They remembered too that Samson when blinded had torn down the Temple and destroyed himself along with his tormentors. Had not one of their leading ministers in his disillusionment and despair cried out against the flag of the nation he had served in the Civil War, "I don't want to die under the dirty rag." But the Negro masses did not curse God and die. They could not pull down the Temple upon the white man and themselves. They retained their faith in God and found a refuge in their churches.

The Negro church with its own forms of religious worship was a world which the white man did not invade but only regarded with an attitude of condescending amusement. The Negro church could enjoy this freedom so long as it offered no threat to the white man's dominance in both economic and social relations. And, on the whole, the Negro's church was not a threat to white domination and aided the Negro to become accommodated to an inferior status. The religion of the Negro continued to be other-worldly in its outlook, dismissing the privations and sufferings and injustices of this world as temporary and transient. The Negro church remained a refuge despite the fact that the Negro often accepted the disparagement of Negroes by whites and the domination of whites. But all of this was a part of God's plan and was regarded just as the physical environment was regarded. What mattered was the way he was treated in the church which gave him an opportunity for self-expression and status. Since the Negro was not completely insulated from the white world and had to conform to some extent to the ways of white men, he was affected by their evaluation of him. Nevertheless, he could always find an escape from such, often painful, experiences within the shelter of his church.

IV

Transformation

9

Introduction

"That peculiar institution, the American denomination, may be described as a missionary order which has turned to the defensive and lost its consciousness of the invisible catholic church." So observes H. Richard Niebuhr in the following selection from *The Kingdom of God in America*. In it Niebuhr puts the denomination and denominationalism within that powerful dynamic in American Protestantism, the kingdom of God. The kingdom, the expectation of the millenium as others have confirmed,[1] was that end towards which American Protestantism labored. The denomination, according to Niebuhr, was a religious institutionalization of that end. But like all attempts to embody, articulate, or institutionalize the religious impulse, the denomination was a betrayal as well as a conservation of the end, the kingdom. The various religious institutions, or denominations, were made into their own ends, to be promoted, defended, conceptualized as though they were the kingdom to be sought. The shift from a dynamic, ecumenical, evangelical movement to a divisive, confessionally conscious, defensive, apologetic institution was but part of the larger transformation of the kingdom of God into convention. Legalism, ecclesiasticism, denominationalism, divisiveness, imperialism, ritualized and mechanical revivals, a moralism in service to American bourgeois society, and faith in progress belong together as institutionalizations of the kingdom. Each in its own way an effort to conserve aspects of the kingdom-of-God movement, they were nevertheless betrayals of that movement. The language Niebuhr uses to describe the change leaves little doubt as to his evaluation of it—petrification, creeping paralysis, confining, confusion, externalization, capitulation, self-congratulatory, self-

---

1. Illustrative are James F. Maclear, "The Republic and the Millennium," in *The Religion of the Republic*, pp. 183-216; Robert T. Handy, *A Christian America* (New York: Oxford University Press, 1971); Perry Miller, *The Life of the Mind in America* (New York: Harcourt, Brace & World, 1965); Ernest Lee Tuveson, *Redeemer Nation* (Chicago: University of Chicago Press, 1968); Alan E. Heimert, *Religion and the American Mind* (Cambridge, Mass.: Harvard University Press, 1966).

confident, self-righteous. The judgment is tempered some-what by Niebuhr's insistence that institutionalization and its effects are inevitable in religion. The fact remains that for those religious movements involved in the American evangelical quest for the kingdom, denominationalism, that is, the denominational form of the church, represents compromise, betrayal, and violation of that quest. The various evangelical denominations, despite their vaunted distinctions, share their most vital characteristics—movements united in the quest for the kingdom, each in its own way an institutionalization of that quest, commonly related to the other aftereffects of that quest: legalism, confessionalism, American imperialistic nationalism, moralism, ritualized revival, and progress. The de-nominationalism of the evangelical churches for Niebuhr, as for Hudson and Mead, can be treated as a single reality.

The view of denominations given earlier by Niebuhr in *The Social Sources of Denominationalism* is in apparent conflict. The accent in *Social Sources* is on the divisions in Christianity that denominationalism produces, a divisive-ness caustically denounced. The forces seen as productive of denominations (and hence one is led to conclude of the overall pattern, denominationalism) are also several. The various social factors constitutive of modern society are regarded not as the rationale for the religious movements themselves, but as the forces which channel the movements and create religious divisions. Class, nationalism, sec-tionalism, immigration (ethnicity), and racism cause the vital religious impulses to course through different (social) channels. Denominationalism is seen as a sociological and secular matter, the result of the differentiation of Christianity by its "conformity to the order of social classes and castes."[2]

Niebuhr himself contrasts the view of American Christian-ity given in *The Kingdom of God in America* with that of *Social Sources*. Not content with American Christianity treated as institutions or with the inattention given the force, unity, and faith of the movements that became institutions, Niebuhr explored with great dexterity the unifying motif in American Protestantism—the kingdom of God. The depic-tion of the denomination in the two books, however, is consistent. It is, as he notes in *The Kingdom of God in America*, a "halting place" of a dynamic movement; the language of "compromise" applied to it in *Social Sources* still applies.[3] What *The Kingdom of God in America* does

2. Niebuhr, *The Social Sources of Denominationalism* (Hamden, Conn.: The Shoe String Press, 1954, first published in 1929), p. 25.

3. Niebuhr, *The Kingdom of God in America* (New York: Harper & Brothers, 1937), pp. x, xiv.

alter is the social source or social context of American evangelical denominationalism. Niebuhr depicts the pursuit of the kingdom as a unifying goal for the evangelical movements well into the nineteenth century. This evangelical empire from which the denominations emerge was an informal evangelical Protestant establishment.[4]

It is fruitful to place the analysis of social factors of *Social Sources* in relation to the evangelical empire and to see the denominationalism of those groups excluded from the evangelical empire (by nationality, class, race, section) as dialectically related to the denominationalism produced by the evangelical empire itself. In those terms the evangelical denominationalism of part II of this volume and Niebuhr's *Kingdom of God in America* and ethnic denominationalism of part III and *The Social Sources of Denominationalism* are dialectically related. A new utility for Niebuhr's volumes with two possible interpretations can be derived. One employs Niebuhr's language of compromise for the denomination. Evangelical denominationalism (*Kingdom* and parts of *Social Sources*) is successor to the building of the kingdom and influenced by the social factors that fed that enterprise. Ethnic denominationalism (*Social Sources*, remaining parts) establishes social identity for groups denied full inclusion in the evangelical empire. The other reading uses the conception of denominationalism of part II. It conceives of evangelical denominationalism as instrumental to the building of the kingdom (*Kingdom*). Ethnic denominationalism, or, more broadly, confessionalism, is represented by the whole of *Social Sources*, all denominations being so defined when either in initial stages or later their reason for being is defined in terms of themselves, their congregations, polity, traditions, theology, or interests. One denominationalism has its essence without; the other has its within. This latter reading raises the fundamental question concerning Niebuhr's view of religious institutions. Do they, as he argues, spell the death of religious vitality? Is denominationalism *per se* the termination of vital religion? Are the religious movements in quest of the kingdom by definition something other than denominations? Are denominations the halting places of dynamic Christianity?

4. See the essays by Sidney Mead, Russell Richey, Elwyn Smith, and Martin Marty included in this volume. Robert Handy's *Christian America*; Martin E. Marty's *Righteous Empire* (New York: Dial Press, 1970); James F. Maclear's " 'True American Union' of Church and State: The Reconstruction of the Theocratic Tradition," *Church History*, 28 (1959), 41-62; and Elwyn A. Smith's "Voluntary Establishment of Religion," *The Religion of the Republic*, ed. Elwyn A. Smith (Philadelphia: Fortress Press, 1971), pp. 154-82 also describe this voluntary Protestant establishment.

9

Institutionalization and Secularization of the Kingdom

H. Richard Niebuhr

The Kingdom of God in America is neither an ideal nor an organization. It is a movement which, like the city of God described by Augustine in ancient times, appears in only partial and mixed manner in the ideas and institutions in which men seek to fix it. In that movement we vaguely discern a pattern—one which is not like the plan of a building or any static thing, but more like the pattern of a life, a poem or of other things dynamic. It is a New World symphony in which each movement has its own specific theme, yet builds on all that has gone before and combines with what follows so that the meaning of the whole can be apprehended only as the whole is heard. If one listens only to measures and phrases and bars, no pattern can be apparent.

The first symphonic movement developed the theme of the sovereignty of God in many variations. There were discords and clashing of cymbals and some solo flights by wayward players in the orchestra, yet all were carried by and united in the persistent strains of the first violins. The second movement began with the theme of Christ's kingdom for which the first part had prepared the listeners. Sometimes only a fragment of the theme was sounded; a counter-theme of human kingdoms was developed; the movement was interrupted by rumbling kettledrums suggestive of internal strife. Yet the unity of the composition was maintained as crude instruments, fashioned in the backwoods and played by amateurs, reasserted the theme of the dominion of the Lord. The third movement was allegro.

Institutionalization and Secularization of the Kingdom

Though it began with forewarnings of doom a strain of hope lifted itself out of the morbid sounds and grew in power and completeness until it dominated the great polyphony of New World life.

Our allegory fails us at many points. The kingdom of God in America is not wholly describable in terms of movement. For there were pauses in the process, moments of petrifaction when the living current was frozen into rigidity. And there was loss of memory; what had gone before was forgotten and men began to move without remembrance of their point of departure or of their plan of march.

I. Institutionalizing the Kingdom

Professor Henri Bergson has described religion as "the crystallization, brought about by a scientific process of cooling, of what mysticism had poured, while hot, into the soul of man." [1] The statement is subject to many criticisms. since it may be objected that the term "religion" is as applicable to the dynamic process as it is to the crystallized product, that the process of cooling is not always scientific, that prophetism more than mysticism represents the dynamic element in Christianity, and that the molten fluid is poured into the social life rather than into individual souls. Nevertheless the philosopher of vitalism has described a process which had become unintelligible to modern men when it was set forth in the traditional terms of gospel and law, but which is a very real part of all religious life.

The occasional crystallization or institutionalization of the kingdom of God movement is apparently inevitable. The prophets' conviction of the divine sovereignty as a living reality, their experience of judgment and hope of salvation were conserved by legal Judaism in such fashion that the vitality of prophetic faith was denied. The living Christianity of the apostolic period was made concrete in the rituals, organizations, disciplines and creeds of the Greek and Roman churches. The religious renaissance of the twelfth and thirteenth centuries came to a stop in scholastic theology and ecclesiastical institutions. What happened in the earlier eras was repeated in the history of European Protestantism. On the Continent the Reformation came to its conclusion with the establishment of state churches, systems of pure doctrine and conventionalized Christian conduct. The "glorious revolution" in England marked the beginning of the Georgian era in church as well as state. What had occurred elsewhere with monotonous regularity could not be prevented in America. Here also Puritanism and Quakerism, the Awakening and the revivals, poured white-hot convictions into the souls of men, only to have these cool off into crystallized codes, solidified institutions, petrified creeds.

Such phenomena of institutionalization always have an ambiguous character. On the one hand they are genuine efforts to conserve for post-revolutionary generations the gains made by a revolutionary movement. By reducing prophetic ethics to a code Judaism was enabled to teach it to the children who had not seen the Lord with Isaiah nor heard with Amos the thundering approach of the hosts of wrath. By committing that code to the watchful care of a professional group it could enforce the conduct called for by the seers. Henceforth the nation had been made secure against lapsing again into the idolatry and disloyal conduct which had called forth the protests of Hosea and Jeremiah. So also the creeds, rites, offices and discipline of the early Christian churches made it possible for them to lead second generation Christians into the communion with the Father and the Son which their parents had received as a surprising gift, and to the experience of forgiveness and brotherly love which had come as a revolutionary event into the lives of the early disciples. The same thing is true of the later crystallizations of Christian movements. They all consolidated the gains of revolutionary epochs and put them into forms that could be transmitted to children and children's children. Without such stabilization and conservation the great movements would have passed like storms at sea, leaving behind them nothing but the wreckage of the earlier establishments they had destroyed.

Yet institutions can never conserve without betraying the movements from which they proceed. The institution is static whereas its parent movement had been dynamic; it confines men within its limits while the movement had liberated them from the bondage of institutions; it looks to the past, the movement had pointed forward. Though in content the institution resembles the dynamic epoch whence it proceeded, in spirit it is like the state before the revolution. So the Christian church, after the early period, often seemed more closely related in attitude to the Jewish synagogue and the Roman state than to the age of Christ and his apostles; its creed was often more like a system of philosophy than like the living gospel. Post-Reformation Lutheranism and Calvinism resembled, in their efforts to control belief and conduct and in their self-assured bearing, the Catholicism with which they fought. It is ever so, in politics and in learning no less than in religion. The situation is not explicable in terms of a philosophy of progress which maintains that "they must upwards still and onwards who would keep abreast of truth." For the failure of the institution is not simply due to its inability to keep pace with a changing cultural environment; frequently it is more adaptable to its setting than the revolutionary movement had been. It seems rather to lack inner vitality; it is without spontaneity and the power to originate new ideas; it is content with past achievement and more afraid of loss than it is hopeful of new insight or strength; it is on the defensive. Institutions, however, differ not only in spirit from their parent movements; they tend also to change the content which they are trying to conserve. When the great insights of a creative time are put into the symbolic form of words, formulas, and creeds, much must always be omitted. The symbol is never the reality and it is subject to progressive loss of meaning; in time it often comes to take the place of the experience to which it had originally pointed. So by limitation and loss of symbolic reference, and by the substitution of the static for the dynamic, institutions deny what they wish to affirm and become the antithesis to their own thesis. The antithesis is never complete; something is always conserved, but much is lost and repudiated.

This universal process from which there seems to be no escape in time is illustrated by the history of the kingdom of God in America at more than one point. Something of the tendency toward petrifaction manifests itself, indeed, throughout the movement; a downward drag accompanies the whole aspiration as those who are ever fearful of disaster attempt to halt the march and to establish safe camping places. At two points, however, the tendency toward institutionalization becomes particularly manifest: first, in the time of second and third generation Puritans and Quakers and second, in the period after the Awakening and the revivals.

The conservative interest showed itself in the earlier period in the adoption of the Half-Way Covenant and of Stoddardeanism by Puritans and of birthright membership by the Society of Friends. Apart from the political consid- erations which made the first of these measures desirable, all three of them represented genuine efforts to make available for new generations the church fellowship which their fathers had enjoyed and to maintain the influence of faith in the sovereignty of God and in the kingdom of Christ.[2]

Moreover they were necessary for children who, having been bred in the doctrines and discipline of the church, could not be expected to receive the faith with the ardor their parents had manifested nor to experience in a second birth what had in their case been given them in large part with the first. The revolution was past and it was not wise to expect of the post-revolutionary generation the same reconstruction of life which a revolutionary time had required. Still, the effect of these measures was to convert the society of the loyalists of the kingdom into a complacent organization with convictions less and less pronounced and a discipline less and less rigorous. The sovereignty of God was no longer the dynamic activity of the being who created, judged and saved mankind in every moment of time; it was now rather the rule of his laws, while the kingdom of Christ came to mean either the present church on earth or heaven with its eternal rewards.

The typical representative of post-revolutionary Puritanism was Cotton Mather, who is so often and so unfortunately used as an example of Puritanism itself. Good conservative that he was, much of the old loyalty to the divine sovereignty is manifest in him; yet in what perverted form! Parrington has written that "in the egocentric universe wherein Cotton Mather lived and labored the cosmos had shrunk to the narrow bounds of a Puritan commonwealth whereof Boston was the capital and the prosperity of the North Church the special and particular object of divine concern."[3] The statement may be paraphrased with respect to the kingdom of God, for this had been reduced for Cotton Mather to the dominion of the English Reformation, and of that Reformation Boston was the chief glory. "Boston," he exclaimed, "thou hast been lifted up to heaven!"[4] He looked to the past, to the incomparable institutions of the fathers, to the Sabbath day ordinances, the Congregational order and discipline, and the laws of the commonwealth. With all his eagerly displayed learning he defended the established order which, in his estimation, came nearer to perfection than any other Christian society in the world. Not only had the kingdom of God become an institution but the reign of Christ had become a habit. The law written upon the inward parts was for Cotton Mather an inscription to be endlessly studied in a state of hypochondriac introspection. His *Essays To Do Good*[5] are a classic example of inverted moralism. Here all attention is directed toward the self and its moral culture. The brave objectivism of the early Puritans which demanded only that God's will be done is turned into febrile subjectivism which evermore asks whether the heart of the doer is good. The message of the kingdom of Christ is translated into a new, spiritualized version of the law, as exacting in its demands, as minutely defined and hedged about and as full of temptations to Pharisaism as any external legal code ever was. Against the codified, formalized and institutionalized conceptions of the sovereignty of God and the kingdom of Christ secular liberalism was bound to rebel. The Yankee spirit with its objective common sense offered a happy alternative to this ingrown Puritanism.[6] Yet it was Edwards rather than Franklin and the Great Awakening rather than the rational enlightenment which really broke the fetters of petrified Puritanism and restored dynamic to the Christian church.

The fate which overtook the earlier movement could not be evaded, however, by its successor. The Awakening also lapsed into slumber as the attempt was made to conserve the

237

gains which it had brought. At the beginning of the nineteenth century the standing order in Connecticut, represented especially by Timothy Dwight and Lyman Beecher, reproduced the spirit of Cotton Mather, though the content of their creed was Edwardean. As the century went on the process of crystallization continued; the creeping paralysis extended from Connecticut to the frontiers, until all of the orders of American "friars" had become denominations and all the denominations began to defend their glorious past, their creeds and conventions. Compared with the movement out of which it proceeded this institutional faith was characterized above all by the absence of the sense of crisis which had always been present in the movement. Stated positively, the conventional faith was marked by the conviction that the crisis was past and that the main concern of men should be the conservation of its fruits.

Edwards, Hopkins, Whitefield, Finney knew the sovereignty of God as the present activity and initiative of the being on whom every man in every moment was infinitely dependent. The sovereign God of Lyman Beecher and his colleagues is an absentee monarch who declared his will in a remote past and caused it to be recorded in irrefrangible laws. To live under the sovereignty, as these church leaders seem to conceive it, is to love not in relation to divine being but in obedience to law. They would interpret the fall of an apple from the tree not as due to the attraction of the large mass for the small but as an act in obedience to the law of gravity. At all events in religion they define the decrees of God as "his determination to create a universe of free agents, to exist forever under the perfect laws of his moral government, perfectly administered; for the gratification and manifestation of his benevolence, for the perfect enjoyment of all his obedient subjects: with all that is implied therein and all the consequences foreseen." [7] The sense of critical immediate relations between man and the Being of beings has been lost in the feeling that man is responsible for keeping certain laws. Moreover these laws are conceived to have been once and for all established in nature and published in the Bible, so that the latter comes to be a book of statutes rather than an aid to the understanding of God's living will.[8] It is not only the Bible which mediates the moral government of God, for the religious institutions founded upon that statute book may claim to represent his sovereignty also. Lyman Beecher tends to identify the moral law of God with the law of New England Puritanism and the latter with the law of the United States.

> Our own republic [he declares] in its Constitution and laws is of heavenly origin. It was not borrowed from Greece or Rome, but from the Bible. Where we borrowed a ray from Greece or Rome, stars and suns were borrowed from another source—the Bible. There is no position more susceptible of proof than that, as the moon borrows from the sun her light, so our Constitution borrows from the Bible, its elements, proportions and power. It was God that gave these elementary principles to our forefathers, as the "pillar of fire by night, and the cloud by day," for their guidance. All the liberty the world ever knew is but a dim star to the noon-day sun which is poured on man by these oracles of heaven.[9]

Beecher reserves his most glowing praise for the laws of New England. "Behold," he exclaims, "their institutions, such as the world needs and attended as they have been by the power of God, able to enlighten and renovate the world."[10] The church organization of New England is "the noblest edifice ever reared by divine and human cooperation";[11] "the Sabbath is the great organ of the divine administration—the only means provided by God to give ubiquity and power to his moral government."[12] So Beecher rallies men to "the standard which our fathers reared" and "to institutions of heaven, provided to aid us in fleeing the wrath to come."[13]

When the sovereignty of God has been reduced to a code of laws established in the past all the ideas connected with it at a time when it was experienced as living reality become unintelligible. To an Edwards, aware of infinite dependence on the Being of beings, God's absolute agency in all things is a glorious and self-evident truth, while it is equally self-evident that man must and does struggle to respond to the divine initiative. When God's sovereignty has become a law and the living relation a mechanical one, the dialogue between God and man is dissolved into a statement of incompatible doctrines. Man, it is said, is completely determined; man, it is claimed, is free to obey or disobey. The dialectic becomes a debate in which men shout their dogmas at one another and sometimes make slight concessions, such as that God does not wholly determine man or that man is not quite free; and such concessions are called "improvements in divinity." What could be truly said of a living process becomes untrue or unintelligible when it is asserted of the petrified product. Institutionalized faith, seeking to conserve the insights of prophetic experience, reduces the sovereign God to a law and his activity to that of fate. So the divine determinism of an Edwards becomes fatalism in his successors.

In similar fashion the post-revival period confined the kingdom of Christ within the walls of the visible church. "The church as a collective body," says Beecher, "is the organ of God's moral administration—a chartered community, formed for the special purpose of giving efficacy and perpetuity to the revealed laws of the divine government"; it is the executive arm of God's moral government, even as the Bible is the legislative organ. It is "the divine practical system for accomplishing the salvation of the world"; it is an association for "mutual defense and increased efficiency in the propagation of religion."[14] Here we have that very definition of the church of which dynamic Protestantism had been afraid; the church has become a self-conscious representative of God which instead of pointing men to him points them first of all to itself. Naturally it turns to the defensive under the circumstances; now it must justify and praise itself, its gospel and its faith, instead of living in the forgiveness of sin, doing its work and making its confession.

In the area of practice the institutionalization of the kingdom of Christ became even more fateful. The evangelization movement had attempted to conserve and develop the results of conversion by organizing converts into societies, by requiring these to exercise supervision over their members and by encouraging them to undertake further evangelization. Such societies reflected the peculiar interests, prejudices and convictions of leaders or of social groups, and were as different from one another as Franciscans were from Dominicans or as both were from Jesuits. Under the influence of the Awakening and the revivals divisions also took place in the established churches. Yet there was a great deal of hearty cooperation and it was definitely understood that the organization of churches or societies was quite secondary to the common work of extending the kingdom of Christ. Moreover the various groups and leaders were conscious of participating in a single great movement, though their work lay in different areas among people of varying traditions and was advanced by different methods. The social divergences between the churches or societies were not sufficient to conquer this sense of community.[15] Speaking of the first Awakening Leonard W. Bacon remarks that in "the glow of the revival the Continent awoke to the consciousness of a common religious life" and, since the movement was international in origin as well as in effect, American Christians became highly aware under its influence of the ecumenical character of the faith. The effect of the second revival was similar; American religious life, though divided among many groups, took on a common pattern, exhibited a common interest and was inspired by a common hope.

With the cessation of the movement and the turn to institutionalism the aggressive societies became denominations, for that peculiar institution, the American denomination, may be described as a missionary order which has turned to the defensive and lost its consciousness of the invisible catholic church. These orders now confused themselves with their cause and began to promote themselves, identifying the kingdom of Christ with the practices and doctrines prevalent in the group. Though the content of the institutionalized faith seemed to be like that of the movement, its spirit was utterly different. As Congregationalists and Presbyterians became self-conscious and more aware of their differing heritages than of their common task they dropped their plan of union and entered into competition with each other. The missionary enterprise, home and foreign, was divided along denominational lines; every religious society became intent upon promoting its own peculiar type of work in religious education, in the evangelization of youth, in theological education, in the printing and distribution of religious literature. Cordial relations, such as had existed between Lutherans and Reformed, between the latter and the Congregationalist and Presbyterian churches, and among revival groups on the frontier gave way to keen competition. With the loss of the sense of the common task in proclaiming the kingdom of Christ, sectional, racial and cultural differences assumed increasing importance. The more attention was concentrated upon the church the greater became the tendency toward schism. It is difficult to assign a date to this development of institutionalism. In New England Congregationalism it reappeared during the Jeffersonian period; in general it manifested itself particularly in the fourth decade of the century and from then on became increasingly important as the impetus of the original movement was progressively lost.[16]

The institutionalization of the kingdom of Christ was naturally accompanied by its nationalization. For with attention directed to the self with its peculiar advantages, heritage and mission, with the turn from aggression and confession to defense and apologetic and with the increasing confusion of church and world, it was natural that contact with ecumenical Christianity should be lost. The old idea of American Christians as a chosen people who had been called to a special task was turned into the notion of a chosen nation especially favored. In Lyman Beecher, as in Cotton Mather before him, we have seen how this tendency came to expression. As the nineteenth century went on the note of divine favoritism was increasingly sounded. Christianity, democracy, Americanism, the English language and culture, the growth of industry and science, American institutions— these are all confounded and confused. The contemplation of their own righteousness filled Americans with such lofty and enthusiastic sentiments that they readily identified it with the righteousness of God. The crisis of the kingdom of the Christ was passed; it occurred in the democratic revolution, or in the birth of modern science, or in the evangelical revival, or in the Protestant Reformation. Henceforth the kingdom of the Lord was a human possession, not a permanent revolution.[17] It is in particular the kingdom of the Anglo-Saxon race, which is destined to bring light to the gentiles by means of lamps manufactured in America. Thus institutionalism and imperialism, ecclesiastical and political, go hand in hand.

As the kingdom of Christ is institutionalized in church and state the ways of entering it are also defined, mapped, motorized and equipped with guard rails.[18] Regeneration, the dying to the self and the rising to new life—now apparently sudden, now so slow and painful, so confused, so real, so mixed—becomes conversion which takes place on Sunday morning during the singing of the last hymn or twice a year when the revival preacher comes to town. There is still reality in it for some converts, but, following a prescribed pattern for the most part in its inception and progress, the life has gone out of it. It is not so much the road from the temporal to the eternal, from trust in the finite to faith in the infinite, from self-centeredness to God-centeredness, as it is the way into the institutional church or the company of respectable Christian churchmen who keep the Sabbath, pay their debts promptly, hope for heaven and are never found drunk either with sensual or with spiritual excitement. What happened to conversion is strikingly indicated by a somewhat curious book written in the eighteen-thirties for the instruction of English Christians by an American clergyman, Calvin Colton. He distinguishes between two sorts of revivals, "one when the instruments are not apparent; the other when the instruments are obvious." The former simply come; one waits for them as for rain, and this, he says, "till a few years past, was the more ordinary character of revivals of religion in America. ... It is only within a few years, that the promotion of revivals by human instruments, has to a considerable extent been made a subject of study, and an object of systematic effort." Now revivals "are made matters of human calculation, by the arithmetic of faith in God's engagement." God may work when his people sleep but he never sleeps when his people work.[19] The Great Awakening had become a method for rousing God from slumber. The method which Colton naively set forth, and which indeed Finney had tended to prepare, continued to develop until it reached its climax in "Billy" Sunday's manipulation of mass suggestion. In a new form the institutionalism and sacramentalism against which Protestantism had originally rebelled asserted themselves. Church and religion were confused with the center and fountain of being, and their means of grace became the sole instruments through which God was allowed to work. Moreover the new ecclesiasticism was less beautiful and often less wise than the old had been.

Moralistic ideas were closely associated with this mechanical conception of conversion. To be reconciled to God now meant to be reconciled to the established customs of a more or less Christianized society. As the Christian church became the protector of the social mores so its revivals tended to become instruments for enforcing the prevailing standards. As it became increasingly clear how perilous the use of liquor was in democratic and industrial society the revival was used especially to combat this evil. Men were now saved not from the frustration, conflict, futility and poverty of life which they sought to escape in the saloons; they were saved from whisky. And the revivals were sometimes used in less evidently useful ways, to enforce the codes of capitalist industry, to overcome the rebellion of workers and to foster the bourgeois virtues on which the success of the industrial system depended.

Petrifaction also assailed the life of hope. As the sovereignty of God was institutionalized in laws, the kingdom of Christ in denominations and means of grace, so the strain toward the coming kingdom and the hope of its coming were transformed into a moral sanction or into a belief in progress. As a hope of the individual the coming kingdom became an otherworldly event not organically related to the present. Hell became a prison to which a divine judge committed the citizens who had failed to observe the laws, and heaven a reward for good deeds done. Punishment and reward were as externally related to life as monetary wages are to labor and fines to misdemeanors. The doctrine of crisis became an instrument for enforcing the mores of a Christian, democratic bourgeois society. As is the habit of unskillful parents and legislators, the preachers of this defensive faith increased their threats and made their promises the more alluring the worse the behavior of the children became; and the greater the threats and promises the more doubtful of their fulfillment were the children. If the crisis was thought of in terms of the end of all mundane things it was again dealt with in the mechanical and literalist fashion of those who had forgotten the reality while retaining the symbol. Doubtless there was a good deal of genuine awareness of the critical character of human life in the Millerite movement and in later millenarian fundamentalism, but on the whole they seem to have been more interested in symbols than in meanings and their preparation for the coming kingdom was usually as irrelevant to the actual issues of life as was the crisis itself.

Insofar as the kingdom was conceived in social terms the faith in its coming was transformed into a belief in progress. The judgment was really past. It had occurred in a democratic revolution. The life now lived in the land of promise was regarded as the promised life and no greater bliss seemed possible for men than was afforded by the extension of American institutions to all the world. That America itself would need to meet the ever coming kingdom as a judgment upon itself, or that the American church would ever need to pass through new catastrophes and resurrections, was not even remotely suggested. The self-congratulatory tone appeared even in the youthful Bushnell, who took it for "granted that complete Protestantism is pure Christianity," while Protestantism in its complete form is congregationalism and congregationalism is the author of republicanism. "We are the depositaries of that light," he cried, "which is to illuminate the world."[20] Whether conceived in political or ecclesiastical or economic or cultural terms, the coming kingdom is never regarded as involving both death and resurrection, both crisis and promise, but only as the completion of tendencies now established.

When the social gospel appeared at the end of the nineteenth century this institutionalized view of the coming kingdom was one of its ingredients. Since the social gospel movement was a multifarious thing, it may be truer to say that one of the parties which called for the application of Christianity to the social life had in mind above all the conservation and extension of American political and ecclesiastical institutions. Many of the reformers seem to have been interested at this point. In the days of the slavery conflict they had indicated little interest in slaves, but a profound concern for the conservation of institutions threatened by the political power of the slaveholder and a great desire to extend their own patterns of life over the whole country. Now they often seemed less interested in the worker than in winning him to the church, that is, of using the social gospel as a means for the maintenance of the institution. As reformers they turned, when persuasion failed, to political means, in order that good social habits of temperance and Sabbath observance might be maintained. As propagandists they sought the extension of democratic institutions—if necessary by recourse to military force—in order that all the world might share in the blessings of the kingdom of God on earth.

In these and other ways the faith in the kingdom was institutionalized. Having achieved some construction it became content with its achievements and displayed a self-confidence and a self-righteousness which could not but call forth reaction on the part of those who discerned how relative and confining were the institutions which claimed universal validity as well as heavenly origin.

V

A Perspective

10
Introduction

Andrew Greeley in *The Denominational Society* argues that the denominations are the supporting structure or framework of American society. He calls it, accordingly, "a denominational society." For him the denominations are belonging-, meaning-, and identity-providing ethnic groups. This is the genius of American religion:

American religion is vigorous precisely because it is denominational . . . It is able to be pluraform precisely because it is pluralistic. American religion, in short, is successful because American religious denominations are ethnic groups. The secret of the survival of the organized churches in the United States . . . is their ability to play an ethnic, or at least quasi-ethnic role in American society.[1]

H. Richard Niebuhr was no less convinced of the decisive character of such social factors as race, nationality, class, caste, and region—what in Greeley's scheme have 'ethnic' qualities—in the existence and functioning of denominations. In his now classic *Social Sources of Denominationalism* Niebuhr observed that

the denominations, churches, sects, are sociological groups whose principle of differentiation is to be sought in their conformity to the order of social classes and castes. It would not be true to affirm that the denominations are not religious groups with religious purposes, but it is true that they represent the accommodation of religion to the caste system. They are emblems, therefore, of the victory of the world over the church, of the secularization of Christianity, of the church's sanction of that divisiveness which the church's gospel condemns.[2]

What Greeley acclaims as the "secret of survival" Niebuhr denounces as "the moral failure of Christianity."

1. Greeley, *The Denominational Society* (Glenview. Ill.: Scott, Foresman, 1972), pp. 1-3; 108.
2. Niebuhr, *The Social Sources of Denominationalism* (Hamden, Conn.: The Shoe String Press, 1954, first published in 1929), p.25.

Denominationalism

The two judgments resemble the two meanings of "skeleton" that Martin E. Marty explores in the following selection "Ethnicity: The Skeleton of Religion in America." Ethnicity has been a skeleton in the closet for those like Niebuhr who saw or sought unity, consensus, or uniformity in American life. For those like Greeley who have honored or espoused the pluralism, particularities, and conflicts of American life, ethnicity has been skeletal, but in the sense of "'the supporting framework,' 'the bare outlines or main features' of American religion." Marty's explorations of different treatments of ethnicity provide perspective on the important assessments of denominationalism by Niebuhr and Greeley. Marty does not bond denominationalism to ethnicity as does Greeley (or to social factors as does Niebuhr). Ethnicity is seen as more basic, decisive, and structural than denominations. Nevertheless, throughout the essay Marty attempts to relate ethnicity to the denominations (as well as to the religion of individuals and to various versions of a common religion).

Marty's typology of approaches to ethnicity with variables of individual religion, denominations, ethnicity, secularism, and common religion also classifies approaches to denominations. It serves to identify what is deemed "basic" in various interpretations of American religion. The reader is provided with some of the basic interpretive options, options that apply to discussion of denominationalism as well as to American religion generally. The essay also functions as a bibliographical essay, introducing some of the important literature within each of the types. For this reason the footnotes containing the references are reproduced.

Marty's essay serves as a reminder of, and raises some basic issues in, the study of religion. Whether denominations or some other religious phenomena are in view, certain questions are inescapable. They may be treated explicitly or left as unexamined presuppositions, but they remain. What in fact is the nature of religion? How is religiousness manifested? How does this religiousness inform everyday life and intersect society and social structures? What space and time are afforded religion within contemporary society? What construction is to be placed on secularization, societal differentiation, civil religion, and ethnicity? The position taken on such questions substantially affects whether denominations are viewed as basic or derivative, authentic or inauthentic, vital or dead, functional or dysfunctional, important or insignificant religious forms. Marty's essay brings into play some of the larger questions in the interpretation of denominationalism.

10

Ethnicity:
The Skeleton of Religion
in America

Martin E. Marty

"The story of the peopling of America has not yet been written. We do not understand ourselves," complained Frederick Jackson Turner in 1891.[1] Subsequent immigration history contributed to national self-understanding. Eighty years later historians have turned their attention to a second chapter in the half-told tale of the peopling of America. They have begun to concentrate on the story of the regrouping of citizens along racial, ethnic and religious lines, and of their relations to each other in movements of what have come to be called "peoplehood."[2]

Peoplehood and Tribalism

First, the realities of black power, black religion, black theology and black churchmanship inspired historians of religion in the 1960s to explore hitherto neglected elements in the make-up of spiritual America. The murder of integrationist leader Martin Luther King and the publication of separationist Albert Cleage, Jr.'s *The Black Messiah* in 1968 were signs of a developing sense of "peoplehood" among blacks as well as of what Cleage called the "religiocification" of a black revolution. Ties to the African religious past and to other spiritual forces outside America were regularly stressed: "We must seek out our brothers in all of Asia and Africa."[3]

The black revolution triggered or was concurrent with other expressions of peoplehood. The American Indian frequently stated his case in religious terms and even provided a metaphor for understanding all the movements: people came to speak of the presence of "a new tribalism."[4] Meanwhile, many Jews resisted being blended into the

From *Church History*, 41 (1972), 5-21. Reprinted by permission.

American mixture. They reinterpreted their community around two particular historical events, the Holocaust and the formation of modern Israel; their new self-consciousness resulted in "the retribalization of the Jew."[5] This change was accompanied in America by some retreat from interfaith conversation on the part of Jews and some questioning as to whether the common "Judeo-Christian tradition" was anything more than a contrivance.[6] The ghetto walls had largely fallen, but the suburban Jew had not fully resolved his questions of identity and mission.

"Peoplehood" movements brought to view the 9.2 million Americans of Spanish descent, including the newly assertive Chicanos, chiefly in the southwest. "Chicano describes a beautiful people. Chicano has a power of its own. Chicano is a unique confluence of histories, cultures, languages, and traditions. ... Chicano is a unique people. Chicano is a prophecy of a new day and a new world."[7] In the northeast, particularly in New York City, almost a million Puerto Ricans, representing the first airborne migration of a people, stamped their distinctive claims on the consciousness of a nation.[8]

Americans of Eastern Orthodox descent made moves to recover their heritages. Orientals in San Francisco protested school busing because integration might threaten their people's heritage. Chinese and Japanese all across the country became subjects of curiosity by their non-Oriental contemporaries who showed interest in Eastern religion, in Yoga or Zen. Nationalist separatist groups in Quebec gathered around French culture and Catholic faith in neighboring Canada and provided local examples of a world-wide neo-nationalism.

The racial and ethnic self-consciousness of what had been called the "minority groups" led to a new sense of peoplehood among the two groups which together made up the American majority. One of these clusters came to be called "white ethnic," its members, "ethnics." They took on new group power at a moment when paradoxically, as students of *The Real Majority* pointed out, "ethnics are dying out in America and becoming a smaller percentage of the total population."[9] The actual decline was from 26 percent of the population ("foreign stock") in 1940 down to an estimated 15 percent in 1970. Austrians, "Baltics," Czechoslovakians, German Catholics, Hungarians, Italians, Poles and other heirs of earlier immigration from Europe were often led to see a common destiny despite their past histories of separation and often of mutual suspicion or hostility. Most of them were of Roman Catholic backgrounds, members of a church which in its Second Vatican Council taught its adherents to think of themselves in the image of "The New People of God." [10] In America they wanted also to be a people with identity a people of power.

Finally, there is "One of America's greatest and most colorful minority groups."

They came here on crowded ships, were resented by the natives and had to struggle mightily for every advance they made against a hostile environment. Despite these handicaps, despite even a skin color different from the native Americans, this hardy group prospered and, in prospering, helped build the nation. They fought in her wars, guided her commerce, developed her transportation, built her buildings. The debt that the country owes to this particular group of immigrants can never be over-estimated. In short, like most American minority groups, they made good citizens.

"The only thing different about the group is that it is the one traditionally viewed as the 'American majority.'" The minority group just described by Ben J. Wattenberg and Richard M. Scammon is "White Anglo-Saxon Protestant," further qualified today as "native-born of native parentage." [11] The acronym and designation WASP-NN in the 1960s represented only about 30 percent of the population. It was divided into 60 percent urban and 40 percent rural, 35 percent southern and 65 percent non-southern communities and included great inner variety. But its critics tended to lump all WASPs together, and increasing numbers of Americans accepted membership in this "people." Among them are large numbers "who happen to be both Anglo-Saxon and white, but whom none would think to describe in terms of WASP power structures. For these particular Protestants (in rural Appalachia, for example) also happen to be exploitable and as invisible as any of America's other dispossessed minorities," and are sometimes themselves referred to as a separate people."[12]

Despite internal variety, at least as late as the 1960s, "the white, Anglo-Saxon Protestant remains the typical American, the model to which other Americans are expected and encouraged to conform."[13] One of the most significant events in the recent study of the peopling of America has been the growing sense, however, that WASPs are a minority themselves. They have at least lost statistical bases for providing a national norm for ethnic self-understanding.

Race, Ethnicity and Religious History

These good years for peoplehood have given rise to whole new historical and social inquiries concerning "ethnicity." The term ('obs., rare') once meant "heathendom," "heathen superstititon."[14] Today it is coming to refer to participation in "an ethnic group—racial, religious, or national" in origin.[15] In this essay, "racial" is a species of the genus "ethnic." People may have authentic or only imaginary ties to a common place of origin, as Max Weber noted.[16] Thus when a non-churchgoing American of Swedish descent is listed as a WASP and accepts that designation, his part in an "Anglo-Saxon" people relates only to an imagined common origin with some Englishmen.[17] Two American Italians who share actual ties to common birthplaces in Europe present a more obvious case for membership in an ethnic group. Yet in practical life and in the world of the politicians or analysts the Swedish WASP and the Italian will tend to be treated as equally legitimate participants in the lives of their people.

The new movements of peoplehood and the expressions of ethnic and racial consciousness—almost all of them marked by claims of "chosenness"—caught many Americans off guard. I shall argue that professional students of religion in America for the most part had become committed after the middle of the twentieth century to theories of interpretation, models and paradigms of inquiry which led them to neglect, gloss over, or deliberately obscure the durable sense of peoplehood in the larger American community. This also left many members of the fraternity ill-prepared to tell the stories of those who shared new styles of ethnic consciousness.

If that argument can be established, we may properly speak of ethnicity as the skeleton of religion in America. In a plea for historically-informed ethnic studies and in an account of the history of the neglect of ethnic groups, Rudolph J. Vecoli says: "Ethnicity in American historiography has remained something of a family scandal, to be kept a dark secret or explained away."[18] This suggests two dictionary images. One is that of "a skeleton in the closet," which is "a secret source of shame or pain to a family or person." The other is that of "a skeleton at the banquet," a "reminder of serious or saddening things in the midst of enjoyment." Equally seriously, ethnicity is the skeleton of religion in America because it provides "the supporting framework," "the bare outlines or main features," of American religion.

When the new particularism was first asserted in the 1960s, students had been enjoying their realization that consensus-minded America no longer seemed to be "tribal." (Tribes, as Lord Bryce pointed out long ago, possessed distinctive and localized religions. "Religion appeared to them a matter purely local; and as there were gods of the hills and gods of the valleys, of the land and of the sea, so each tribe rejoiced in its peculiar deities, looking on the natives of other countries who worshipped other gods as Gentiles, natural foes, unclean beings.")[19] In the midst of the enjoyment, tribalism reappeared. Black messiahs, black madonnas, the black Jesus, "the Great Spirit," the Jewish identification with the land and soil of Israel and charges that white Gentile America had been worshipping a localized self-created deity suddenly disturbed the peace. The issues of ethnicity and racism began to serve as the new occasions for a re-examination of the assumptions and often hidden biases of students of American religion.

Observers and Advocates of a Common Religion

For the sake of convenience, these students can be divided into two broadly-defined schools. Members of the first seek some sort of spiritual "sameness," if not for the whole family of man, then at least for the whole American people. In the Protestant historical community this search is a kind of enlargement of the nineteenth-century evangelical vision typified by the words of Lyman Beecher in 1820:

The integrity of the Union demands special exertions to produce in the nation a more homogeneous character and bind us together with firmer bonds. . . . Schools, and academies, and colleges, and habits, and institutions of homogeneous influence . . . would produce a *sameness* of views, and feelings, and interests, which would lay the foundation of our empire upon a rock. Religion is the central attraction which must supply the deficiency of political affinity and interest.[20] [emphasis mine]

Another spokesman of this tradition was theologian Charles Hodge, who in 1829 claimed that Americans were overcoming Europe's problem of disunity by becoming one people, "having one language, one literature, essentially one religion, and one common soul."[21]

In the course of time that vision had to be enlarged so that it could accommodate other Americans though many of these others have regularly complained ever since that Protestant views of "sameness" and "essentially one religion, and one common soul" were superimposed on non-Protestants. Many Roman Catholics, on a somewhat different set of terms, also affirmed a religious nationalism that transcended their particular creed.[22]

Philip Schaff in 1855 observed continuing immigration and looked ahead to see that a

process of national amalgamation is now also going on before our eyes in America; but peacefully, under more favorable conditions, and on a far grander scale than ever before in the history of the world. America is *the grave of all European nationalities*; but a *Phenix grave*, from which they shall rise to new life and new activity. . . .

Then he added, in a still rather ethnocentric line not often quoted with the rest of the paragraph, that this would be "in a new and essentially Anglo-Germanic form."[23] Later, Frederick Jackson Turner, the historian who had wanted the "peopling of America" to be studied for the purposes of national self-understanding, chose to concentrate on the frontier. He argued that "in the crucible of the frontier the immigrants were Americanized, liberated, and fused into a mixed race, English in neither nationality or characteristics." [24] His successors came to expect that a spiritual fusion would accompany the amalgamation of peoples.

Through the years the seekers of spiritual sameness of oneness and ethnic fusion or assimilation had to include the physical presence and spiritual strivings of ever more varied peoples. Those who advocated what John Dewey in 1934 had called *A Common Faith* [25] made little secret of their desire to overcome particularisms of religion, race and class. For some this desire may have been born of weariness over all tribal-religious warfare; for others, it grew out of conscious philosophical choices about reality, religion and nation.

In this spirit at the beginning of this period sociologist Robin M. Williams, Jr., wrote during 1951 that "Every functioning society has, to an important degree, a *common* religion. The possession of a common set of ideas, rituals, and symbols can supply an overarching sense of unity even in a society riddled with conflict." [26] A year later, at the end of a long book on denominational varieties in American religion, J. Paul Williams moved beyond Robin Williams in the quest for a common national faith. He spoke of it as a "societal religion." Williams favored teaching democracy as a religious ultimate, mildly criticized men like Walter Lippmann for having been content to describe it merely as a "public philosophy" when it ought to have been termed a religion, and called moreover for "spiritual integration." [27]

The dean of American church historians throughout this period, Sidney E. Mead, gave a generally positive interpretation of "the religion of the democratic society and nation" (over against "the religion of the denominations"). While he clearly retained a Lincolnian sense of judgment over against idolization of the nation, he also agreed with G. K. Chesterton's observation that America is the "nation with the soul of a church," and that it was "protected by religious and not racial selection." [28] The question of racial or ethnic selection played only a very small part in Mead's thought. He was critical of those who stressed religious and theological particularity at the expense of the idea of the nation's "spiritual core." Mead promoted Ronald Osborn's suggestion that "a common type of faith and life . . . common convictions, a common sense of mission . . . could and should be the goal for Americans."[29]

One did not have to be a promoter of the search for "sameness," "oneness," or a "common faith" or religion in order to point to their development after mid-century. Mead singled out Winthrop Hudson, Will Herberg and Martin Marty as three definers of societal religion who withheld consent from it because of interests in religious and theological particularity. It was true that during the Eisenhower era many had been critical about a national "Piety along the Potomac" just as during the Nixon era there are complaints against a "religion of the East Room of the White House." These referred to the new, currently sanctioned expressions of common national faiths that were perhaps adhered to by a national majority,[30] but which many members of the liberal academic community rejected.

Most of the intellectuals' affirmations of a generalized American religion came during and shortly after the brief era when John F. Kennedy seemed to be portraying a new spiritual style for America. It was in this mood and at this moment that Robert N. Bellah in 1966 attracted a latter-day market for the term "Civil Religion in America." This was "at its best a genuine apprehension of universal and transcendent religious reality as seen in or, one could almost say, as revealed through the experience of the American people."[31]

The defenses of the common vision as against the particular contention were based on historical observations of good moments in past American expressions of religious "sameness." They also revealed philosophical commitments toward the higher unity. Most of the defenders overlooked ethnic and racial factors because these usually reinforced senses of difference. Rudolf J. Vecoli believes that "the prevailing ideology of the academic profession" which has been the "prime article of the American creed" has been a "profound confidence in the power of the New World to transform human nature." Vecoli related this to Hector St. John Crevecoeur's eighteenth-century discernment of a "new race of men," a "new man," this American, who, "leaving behind him all his ancient prejudices and manners, receives new ones from the new mode of life he has embraced, the new government he obeys, and the new rank he holds. Here individuals of all nations are melted into a new race of men. . . ." The result of this faith has been an "assimilationist ideology." [32] In the nineteenth century Ralph Waldo Emerson, among others, kept this faith alive. Let immigrants come: "The energy of Irish, Germans, Swedes, Poles, and Cossacks, and all the European tribes— and of the Africans, and of the Polynesians,—will construct a new race, a *new religion*, a new state, a new literature. . . ." [33] Regularly throughout American history, those who failed to be assimilated or who stressed separate racial, ethnic, or religious identities were embarrassments. Ethnicity became the skeleton in the closet and had to be prematurely pushed aside and hidden from view.

The Analysts and Defenders of Particularity

The other line of interpretation has been dedicated to the love of what the philosopher Leibnitz and the historian Marc Bloch spoke of as "singular things." [34] Some representatives of this approach may have shared a concern for or belief in ultimate unity, but at least they recognized that pluralist terms for life in the civil order must be found. Thus in 1958 Father John Courtney Murray S. J., classically summarized the matter: "Religious pluralism is against the will of God. But it is the human condition; it is written into the script of history. It will not somehow marvelously cease to trouble the City." [35]

The historians and analysts who dealt more critically with "sameness," "oneness," and "common" religion in America after mid-century ordinarily devoted themselves to the religious shape of this pluralism. Only as the result of the racial upheavals and the new ethnic consciousnesses which were manifested during the 1960s have some of them begun to perceive again that ethnicity has been the skeleton, "the supporting framework" of American religion. These historians and other observers have seen that racial, ethnic, class, partisan, religious and ideological conflicts in America have countered or qualified the homogenizing ideals that earlier held together the "consensus" schools of history. Some of them have begun to try to cope specifically with the ethnic pluralism that is also part of "the human condition."

Sometimes spokesmen for ethnic or racial pluralism and separatism have attached ideological commitments to their observations. Out of myriad possibilities the word of Thomas H. Clancy can be regarded as representative. Clancy quoted Daniel Patrick Moynihan, who was one of the first to speak of the failure of assimilationist or "melting pot" theories to explain the American situation. Wrote Moynihan: "The sense of general community is eroding, and with it the authority of existing relationships, while, simultaneously, a powerful quest for specific community is emerging in the form of ever more intensive assertions of racial and ethnic identities." Adds Clancy: "Black nationalism caused the white ethnics to remember what they had been taught to forget, their own origins." Thus came his own theology of "unlikeness":

The year 1970 is the date when the drive for group rights became more important than the struggle for individual rights. (In the demonstrations and rallies of the future, most signs will bear an ethnic adjective.) . . . For a long time now we have been exhorted to love all men. We have finally realized that for sinful man this is an unrealistic goal. The saints and heroes among us will still face the challenge in a spirit of unyielding despair. The rest of us will try first to love our own kind. This is the year when 'brother' and 'sister' began to have *a less universal and hence truer meaning.*[36] [emphasis mine]

Of course not all historians who tried to make sense of racial and ethnic particularism have shared this creed, but it is the common affirmation of many spokesmen for "differences" over against "sameness" in civil and religious life.

The two general approaches just described can be best studied by reference to several prevailing models—many of them defined by sociologists—which are regularly used for historical explorations and contemporary analyses of the shape of American religion.

Sameness through Common Secularity

First, some advocates of "sameness" have chosen a *secular* interpretation of American religious life. In this view the belief is expressed that there will be progressively less religion in society. Secular men will unite on the basis of some sort of emergent godless, homogenizing, technological and political scheme. The result will be a global village marked by non-religious synthesis for world integration.[37] The "secular theologians" of the 1960s shared this creed, as did many working historians.[38] In the view of British sociologist Bryan Wilson, participation in American church life could itself be called secularization, because on the legal basis of the nation's formal secularity "religious commitment and Church allegiance *have become* elements in the American value system." Wilson presupposed or observed that "the common values" embodied in religious institutions and the secular American Way of Life were rather simply congruent with each other.[39]

Seymour Martin Lipset, also writing in this frame of mind, dealt in passing with racial and ethnic groups and explained their continuing appearance in terms of cultural lag: "American religious denominations, like ethnic groups, have experienced collective upward mobility. . . ." On these terms, contemporary

Negro religious behavior resembles that of the nineteenth-century lower status migrant white population. The Catholics have taken on the coloration of a fundamentalist orthodox religion comparable in tone and style, if not in theology, to the nineteenth-century evangelical Protestant sects.[40]

Because distinctive religious symbols have been connected with almost all the recently recovered movements of peoplehood, racial and ethnic, their spokesmen would not have been content to see themselves on Lipset's escalator. They would resist and stress their distinctive symbols ("Afro-American," "Amerindian," "Chicano," and the like) rather than accommodate themselves to the secular trend of "the common values" of American life or simply be an element in the scheme of "upward collective mobility."

Civil Unity, Religious Privacy

A second line of interpretation is close to the secular one. It simply says that a man's beliefs are *private* affairs and that these have little common or civic consequence. Ideological support for this view is deep in the American tradition. While Thomas Jefferson supported the idea that those moral precepts "in which all religions agree" could be supportive of civil order, he believed differing private religions to be a societal luxury: "It does me no injury for my neighbor to say that there are twenty gods, or no God."[41] One could be for sameness and for a common faith independent of private religious opinions. Religion, said philosopher Alfred North Whitehead in 1926, is "what the individual does with his own solitariness."[42] Religion, for William James in 1903, had meant *"the feelings, acts, and experiences of individual men in their solitude."*[43]

These views find support in the conditions of modern urban and industrial life, says social theorist Thomas Luckmann. He claims that "the most revolutionary trait of modern society" is the fact that "personal identity becomes, essentially, a private phenomenon." Religion, now housed in specialized institutions and religious opinions, has become "a private affair." Each person selects a world of significance from a variety of choices. "The selection is based on consumer preference, which is determined by the social biography of the individual, and similar social biographies will result in similar choices." "Individual religiosity in modern society receives no massive support and confirmation from the primary institutions."[44] Families, sect participation and the like are of some help, but cannot provide much support for community. Luckmann, unfortunately, does not dwell on ethnicity or race as religious factors in this context.

The new advocates of peoplehood, however, would contradict these pictures. "The new tribalism" accuses the American majority of having forced people to lose their identities by throwing all into the private sphere. One Indian summed it up long ago: "You are each a one-man tribe." Another said: "The question is not how you can Americanize us but how we can Americanize you."[45] Whether or not they succeed in the effort, the new ethnic and racial recoveries are designed to supplant the private interpretation of identity and religion, and historians at the very least have to explore these claims at a time when, as Luckmann and others point out, denominational and sectarian involvement supply little of either.

Religious, Not Ethnic, Pluralism

The third model for religion in America, the *pluralist*, moves the discussion to the center of the debate over "sameness" versus "unlikeness" on national *versus* ethnic-racial and religious lines.

The religious pluralist interpretation was born in the face of the problem of identity and power which increased as ethnic origins of Americans became progressively more remote and vague. In a sense, it served to push the skeleton of ethnicity into the closet. Thus Gerhard Lenski in 1961 condensed the thought of Will Herberg, the best-known representative of this view at mid-century:

Earlier in American history ethnic groups [provided community and identity] and individuals were able to enjoy this sense of communal identification and participation as members of the German, Polish, Italian, and other ethnic colonies established in this country. Today such groups have largely disintegrated, but many of the needs they served continue to be felt. In this situation, Herberg argues, Americans are turning increasingly to their religious groups, especially the three major faiths, for the satisfaction of their need for communal identification and belongingness.[46]

Herberg himself in 1955 had deplored the "sameness" or "common religion" schools, but he recognized the presence of a common faith in the "American Way of Life" as the ultimate. Identification with Protestant, Catholic, or Jewish religions were paths for reaching it.[47] E. Digby Baltzell, a student of the WASP establishment, observed in 1964 that "religious pluralism is replacing the ethnic pluralism of the earlier era."[48] Historian Arthur Mann, ten years earlier, had seen that in the matter of pluralism and a single religion of democracy "American Catholicism, American Protestantism, and American Judaism appear like parallel shoots on a common stock."[49] John Cogley, after hosting a tri-faith conference on pluralism in relation to common religion in 1958, reported with favor on the response of one participant. This man had learned "that the free society of America means more than an agreement to disagree; it is posited, rather, on the idea that Americans will disagree in order to agree."[50]

Ethnic and racial pluralism, however, did not go away just because religious pluralism was able to serve some social purposes during the religious revival of the 1950s. Religionists themselves could not agree on the three-faith interpretation. Thus, Orthodox theologian John Meyendorff overstated the case somewhat when he said in 1960 that the Orthodox had later come to be recognized as a fourth "official" American faith.[51] Lenski, who asked no ethnic questions when he studied Detroit religion, did find that Herberg's single "Protestantism" had had to be divided and understood on black/white lines, at least. The religious revival eventually waned, and many people in a new generation no longer found it possible or desirable to define themselves in terms of one of three religions. Most of all, ethnic and racial reassertion did provide identification and community for the "different," who were dissenters against a common faith for all Americans.

Many Denominations, One Religion

The fourth interpretation has to be taken more seriously because of its obvious appropriateness on so many levels. This is an application to the whole of American Christianity by others of Sidney E. Mead's classic statement that *denominationalism* is the shape of Protestantism in America. "Denominationalism is the new American way in Christianity," wrote Karl Hertz.[52] Catholicism is also regarded as a denomination by historians. Judaism, too, is formally denominationalized.

At first glance it may seem to make little sense to say that the denominational interpretation tended to be favored by those who looked for a common religion. After all, denominations had been invented in order that they might protect peoples' differing ways of looking at religious ultimates without permitting society to disintegrate. It turns out that they seem to have been clever but almost accidental inventions. They served to channel potential conflict out of possibly violent racial or ethnic spheres into harmless and irrelevant religious areas. Where are the dead bodies as the result of persistent denominational conflict?

In effect, argue the viewers of a single American community, denominationalism works just the opposite way. Two illustrations, one from a man who favors a secular and the other a religious scheme for seeing America, in that order, will serve. British sociologist Bryan Wilson, as we noted above, posited "secularization as the experience of Christianity" in America. In a long chapter he then discussed "Denominationalism and Secularization." Denominationalism is "an aspect of secularization." Using an interpretation which stressed class distinctions, Wilson saw "the diversity of denominations . . . as the successive stages in the accommodation of life-practice and ethos of new social classes as they emerged in the national life." And denominational diversity "has in itself promoted a process of secularization." The religious choices offered people effectively cancel out each other. Denominations exist and even thrive, but when people accept the ground rules of denominational civility they telegraph to others that society's ultimate values are being bartered outside the sects, if anywhere.[53]

Sidney Mead's religious interpretation works to similar effect. While the churches accepted denominationalism as a pattern which would guarantee their own integrity and relevance, in practice the opposite has happened. The competitive element in sectarian life has worked against the truth claims and the plausibility of the denominations. Those who seek religious affiliation of any sort cannot avoid denominations, though it is true that they need not necessarily repose their ultimate concerns in denominational formulations. In this context Mead includes one of his rare references to nationality and racial backgrounds:

[There has been] a general erosion of interest in the historical distinction and definable theological differences between the religious sects. Increasingly the competition among them seems to stem from such non-theological concerns as nationality or racial background, social status, and convenient accessibility of a local church. Finally what appears to be emerging as of primary distinctive importance in the pluralistic culture is the general traditional ethos of the large families, Protestant, Roman Catholic, and Jewish. If this trend continues, the competition inherent in the system of church and state separation, which served to divide the religious groups in the first place, may work eventually to their greater unity.[54]

By the end of the paragraph, then, the ethnic skeleton has been placed back in the closet, and trends toward higher unity prevail in Mead's world.

The matter was not resolved so easily, however. Denominational distinctiveness remained durable, as Charles Y. Glock in 1965 showed in an essay on "The New Denominationalism."[55] Glock, basing his assertions on his findings of a population sample in California, disagreed with both Will Herberg on the theme of a "common religion" and with Robert Lee on there being a "common core Protestantism." Glock is probably correct: great numbers of Americans *do* want to be loyal to their denominations. The interdenominational Consultation on Church Union, which would cluster and merge denominations, attracts little support. Non- and inter- and para- and counter-denominational, ecumenical ventures do not prosper. Despite this, it would be easy to overstress the importance of denominational pluralism.

For one thing, the denominations are divided down the center in a kind of two-party system. The differences on vital issues (such as racial and ethnic matters) are expressed within and not between denominations, as Jeffrey Hadden demonstrated in 1969.[56] What is more, on matters of deepest significance, even where denominational names have been useful, denominational designations reveal little. For example, black religion was denominationalized, but sectarian bonds have meant almost nothing across racial lines. Millions of southern blacks have been Baptist, but there was until recently almost no contact between them and southern Baptists, the largest white Protestant group in America. The racist has looked at the Negro as a black, not as a Methodist or a Protestant. The black American has had little choice between church bodies when he wished to look for differences in attitudes among them. "Denomination mattered little, for support of the racist creed ran the gamut from urban Episcopalians to country Baptists," wrote David Reimers concerning the late nineteenth-century situation.[57]

Even among whites, ethnic lines usually undercut denominational interests. WASPs, for instance, once established a line-crossing mission to "Catholic Immigrants." Theodore Abel wrote in 1933 that "in general the work among Catholic immigrants is carried on with the aim of promoting Americanization and breaking down the isolation of immigrants from American society by bringing them into the fellowship of the Protestant Church." In the fifty years before 1933 between fifty and one-hundred million dollars had been spent on the cause. But

The mission enterprise has failed to realize the main purpose for which it was instituted. It has failed to accomplish to any significant degree the evangelization of Catholic immigrants and their descendants, and it has not achieved the control that it sought of directing the process of their adaptation to American life. No movement toward Protestantism has taken place as a result of these missionary efforts.[58]

That report dealt with a half-century during which Protestants had been notably missionary, expansionist and devoted toward transforming remote churches. But at home, ethnic factors served to frustrate such motives or achievements. Black, Indian, Chicano, white ethnic and other movements of peoplehood found neither the denominational shape nor the nation's soul to be as effective for promoting identity and power as they found race or ethnicity, which was still—or again—the skeleton or supporting framework for their religion.

A Common Religion

The fifth major line of interpretation has been implied throughout. In it "sameness," "oneness," and a "common faith" found their home in a societal or civil religion that informed, infused and inspired virtually the whole population. How does it fare in a time of new peoplehood or "new tribalism"? Its expression is complicated and compromised. At the very least it must be said that the racial or ethnic group "refracts the national cultural patterns of behavior and values through the prism of its own cultural heritage," as Milton Gordon put it.[59] The black child in the ghetto or the Amerindian youngster may engage in ceremonies of civil religion. But they may think of something quite different from the world of the white child's Pilgrims or Founders when they sing of a "land where my fathers died." This is the land where their fathers were enslaved or killed. The symbols of societal religion can be used in more ways than one by separate groups.

Most of the movements of racial and ethnic consciousness have found it important to oppose militantly the symbols of civil religion. Historian Vincent Harding in 1968 defined Black Power itself as "a repudiation of the American culture-religion that helped to create it and a quest for a religious reality more faithful to our own experience."[60] An Indian does not want the white man's religion. The Chicano detects the Protestant work-ethic in the calls for his participation in a common civil religion. The white ethnic at his American Legion hall relates to civil religious symbols in a different way than does the Jewish member of the Americans for Democratic Action. The young WASP counter-cultural devotee rejects all American civil religion. The delineations of civil religion themselves are never universal in origin, content, ethos, or scope; they are informed by the experience of the delineators' own ethnic subcommunities. Robert N. Bellah's and Sidney E. Mead's views are unexplainable except as expressions of particular WASP traditions. Orientals, Africans, Latin Americans ordinarily would neither bring Bellah's and Mead's kinds of questions nor find their kinds of answers in civil religion. As British observer Denis Brogan wrote concerning Bellah's

essay, "The emblems, the metaphors,
might have put it) of public civil religi
when those symbols are used by Ca
Orthodox, ..."[61] It is precisely this fea
attempts at rejection of civil religion and
the part of so many ethnic and racial gr

In summary, it would appear that the fi
interpreting American religious "samen ... —the secular,
the private, the pluralist, the denominational, and the
common-religious—apply appropriately only to the white
and largely generalized Protestant academic circles where
they originated. Other ethnic-racial-religious complexes can
be only occasionally and partially interpreted through these.

Ethnic and Racial Themes Reintroduced

To suggest that ethnic and racial themes have to be
reintegrated into the schemes for posing historians' questions is not to say that these should displace the others. The
secular tendencies in America will probably not be successfully countered by the new religious practices of minority
groups. Many people can find identity in the private sphere
without explicit reference to ethnic and racial religious
motifs. Protestantism, Catholicism, Judaism may long serve
to identify practitioners of a common American religion.
Denominationalism may indeed be the shape, and civil
religion the soul, of American religion—just as ethnicity is
its skeleton or supporting framework. But as the most
neglected theme until recently, racial and ethnic particularity deserves compensatory interest and inquiry.

Numerous benefits could result from such an effort.
Concentration on religious dimensions of peoplehood could
lead to a more accurate portraying of the way things have
been—that is always the first goal of the historian. Historians
in the once-majority traditions, WASP and white ethnic
combined, can re-explore their own assumptions and may be
able to discern the ethnic aspects in what they had earlier
regarded as their universal points of view. The theories
seeking "sameness" and "oneness" tended to be based on a
kind of optimistic and voluntaryistic spirit. Ethnic-racial
recovery should help historians deal more adequately with

...ed, predestined, tragic and even violent elements in ...ion in America.

WASP Histories as Ethnic Expressions

In any case, WASP and white ethnic American historians would be able critically to revisit their own older traditions, traditions which were once racially and ethnically self-conscious, for better and for worse. When WASP is seen not as the norm but as an ethnic minority among minorities, the racial special pleading of the fathers appears in a different light. Robert Baird, whom many regard as the first historian of American religion, in 1843 insisted that "our national character is that of the Anglo-Saxon race," and he ranked other ethnic groups downward from Anglo-Saxon.[62] Baird began his history with reference to the differences of Indian, Negro and other non-Anglo-Saxon peoples and kept them in mind consistently as he measured them in the light of his own racial norm.

Not only WASPs were particularists. Baird's counterpart, John Gilmary Shea, the father of American Catholic historiography, was a spokesman for the Irish minority, and Catholic history has been consistently marked by ethnic distinctives.[63] Philip Schaff, a continental "outsider," had to invent artificial ways to blend his German-Swiss background with the Anglo-American dominant strain. Daniel Dorchester in 1890 criticized the German and Irish influx as people of "low habits and ideas, retaining supreme allegiance to a foreign pontiff, or controlled by radical, rationalistic, materialistic, or communistic theories. . . . Can Old World subjects be transformed into New World citizens?"[64] Even Leonard Woolsey Bacon, a man of ecumenical temperament and a devotee of religious "sameness," spoke during 1898 in terms of "masterful races" in American white Protestantism.[65]

Josiah Strong—shall the historians' fraternity claim him?—was explicitly racist in his accounting of American religion in the 1880s and 1890s. For Strong, the Anglo-Saxon's religion was "more vigorous, more spiritual, more Christian than that of any other." It was destined to "dispossess many weaker races, assimilate others, and mold the remainder, until, in a very true and important sense, it has Anglo-Saxonized mankind."

If I do not read amiss, this powerful race will move down into Mexico, down upon Central and South America, out upon the island of the sea, over upon Africa and beyond. And can anyone doubt that the result of this competition will be the 'survival of the fittest'?[66]

The themes of WASP ethnicity and superiority which had been explicit in the nineteenth century became implicit and taken for granted in the twentieth. The assimilationist ideal took over. In 1923 Peter Mode could write that "American Christianity has . . . no racial coloring and its Americanization as yet has been a process void of racialism," a suggestion about America that would be incomprehensible to most of the world. Instead, said Mode, American Christianity has taken its character by having been "frontierized."[67] Joining the frontierizing-sameness school was William Warren Sweet, who dealt at length with slavery, but most of whose energies were devoted to the white Protestant mainline churches as normal and normative. Sidney E. Mead changed the topic to denominationalism and a common national religion without picking up much interest in non-WASP religion.

On the other hand, Robert Handy's recent *A Christian America: Protestant Hopes and Historical Realities*[68] is one of the first important attempts by a WASP to come to terms with the WASP particularism which once had paraded itself as universalism. Handy stresses ethnic, racial and other conflict-inducing questions over against the interpretations which derived from the mid-century "sameness" and "oneness" schools.

The Future of Tribal Confederation

Even though the future is not the historian's province, it is sometimes asked whether it is worth scholars' efforts to re-tool so that they can henceforth include the ethnic and racial questions. The assimilating, blending, melting processes do remain and are accelerating. There are few new immigrants. The children of old ones intermarry and expose themselves to common value systems in education and through the media or by travel; they move out of vestigal ghettos. Perhaps the attention to the quest for identity through ethnic and racial communities will pass again as soon as certain needs have been met. The political and psychological use of WASP terms such as "white ethnics" and "WASPs" may soon be exposed as inauthentic, and the new and artificial ethnic coalitions may break apart. Maybe the focus on peoplehood has been only a fashion, a passing fancy, one which can be a partial setback in the quest for expressions of a common humanity.

If the ethnic factor remains strong, certainly there will be times of crisis when a sort of "tribal confederation" will be instinctively and informally convoked so various peoples can get together and affirm their common, not their separate, symbols. The historians can then stand ready to interpret both the past interplay between conflicting particularities and homogenizing concordant elements in national life and the considerable assets and liabilities of each.

Whatever happens, however, it seems clear that not all of men's needs can be met by secular interpretation and private faith, by tri-faith or conventional denominational life or by a common national religion. New particularisms will no doubt continue to arise, to embody the hopes of this "people of peoples." Meanwhile, when spokesmen for the oldest of American peoples, the American Indian, assert that they wish to Americanize the rest of the nation and that they would like to teach their fellow citizens the merits of life in tribes, these other citizens could appropriately reply: "In some senses, we never left home."

NOTES
Foreword

1. Denominations are treated as self-contained units. Denominational histories are too numerous to cite. This approach groups discrete denominational histories or descriptions together to explain the denominational pattern or denominationalism. Representative are Thomas Branagan, *Concise View of the Principal Religious Denominations in the United States of America* (Philadelphia, 1811); Israel Daniel Rupp, *He Pasa Ekklesia, An Original History of the Religious Denominations at Present Existing in the United States* (Harrisburg, 1849); Peter Douglas Gorrie, *The Churches and Sects of the United States* (New York, 1850); Joseph Belcher, *The Religious Denominations of the United States* (Philadelphia, 1857); Philip Schaff, et al., *The American Church History Series*, 13 vols. (New York: Christian Literature Company, 1893–1897); Frank Spencer Mead, *Handbook of Denominations in the United States* (5th ed., Nashville: Abingdon Press, 1970; published since 1951); J. Paul Williams, *What Americans Believe and How They Worship* (New York: Harper & Row, 1952); Frederick M. Mayer, *The Religious Bodies of America* (3rd ed. St. Louis: Concordia Publishing House, 1958).

2. This has been a major preoccupation of the discipline, building on the pioneering labors of Max Weber and Ernst Troeltsch. Accordingly, the literature on typology and religious organization is immense and beyond summary here. Of help are H. Richard Niebuhr, *The Social Sources of Denominationalism* (Hamden, Conn.: The Shoe String Press, 1954; first published in 1929); Liston Pope, *Millhands and Preachers* (New Haven: Yale University Press, 1942); D. A. Martin, "The Denomination," *British Journal of Sociology*, 13 (March 1962), 1-14; Thomas F. O'Dea, *The Sociology of Religion* (Englewood Cliffs: Prentice-Hall, 1966); J. Milton Yinger, *The Scientific Study of Religion* (New York: The Macmillan Co., 1970); Benton Johnson, "Church and Sect Revisited," *Journal for the Scientific Study of Religion*, 10 (Summer 1971), 124-137; Bryan R. Wilson, "Religious Organization," *International Encyclopaedia of the Social Sciences*, 13:428-36 and the several works by Wilson on sectarianism.

3. The importance, role, and function of voluntary associations in democratic societies and American society in particular have been much discussed in political science and sociology especially since the appearance of Alexis de Tocqueville's *Democracy in America*, 2 vols. (New York: Vintage Books, 1941; first translated in 1835). Voluntarism in religion, the voluntary church, and the church as voluntary association have been familiar themes in the treatment of denominations and denominationalism. Robert Baird's *Religion in America*, ed. Henry Bowden (New York: Harper &

Row, 1970), originally published 1843, 1844 and Philip Schaff's *America* ed. Perry Miller (Cambridge: Harvard University Press, Belknap Press, 1961) originally published in 1855, pioneered in and popularized the approach. Recent examples are James Luther Adams (see D. B. Robertson, ed., *Voluntary Associations* [Richmond: John Knox Press, 1966], a valuable illustrative collection, for the bibliography of Adams's writings and a discussion of the importance of voluntary associations for Adams by James D. Hunt, "Voluntary Associations as a Key to History," pp. 359-73); James Gustafson, *Treasure in Earthen Vessels* (New York: Harper & Brothers, 1961) and *The Church as Moral Decision-Maker* (Philadelphia: Pilgrim Press, 1970); Milton B. Powell, ed., *The Voluntary Church* (New York: The Macmillan Co. 1967); and J. Roland Pennock and John W. Chapman, eds., *Voluntary Associations* (New York: Atherton Press, 1969).

4. The burgeoning field of organization studies has been adapted for the study of religious institutions by research departments and consultants for denominations and applied for programmatic, developmental, efficiency, management, or reform purposes to congregations and bureaucracy. There has been surprisingly little effort to build theory for the study of denominations and denominationalism. The isolated exceptions are most helpful: H. Paul Douglas and Edmund deS. Brunner, *The Protestant Church as a Social Institution* (New York: Institute for Social and Religious Research, 1935); James Gustafson (see note 3); Paul M. Harrison, *Authority and Power in the Free Church Tradition* (Princeton: Princeton University Press, 1959); David Moberg, *The Church as a Social Institution* (Englewood Cliffs: Prentice-Hall, 1962); and Gibson Winter, *Religious Identity* (New York: The Macmillan Co., 1968).

5. In the last few years ethnicity and ethnic studies have been very much in vogue. Ethnicity is seen by some as the most basic social factor, displacing, for instance, class. A case for denominations as ethnic groups is made by Andrew Greeley in *The Denominational Society* (Glenview: Scott, Foresman and Co., 1972). Essays by Timothy Smith and Martin Marty in this volume explore the relation between ethnicity and denominationalism.

6. Niebuhr, *The Social Sources of Denominationalism*, p. 25.

7. Marty, *Righteous Empire* (New York: Dial Press, 1970), pp. 67-68.

8. Some readers may feel that the volume's focus serves to perpetuate the consensus religious historiography that depicted American religion primarily in terms of the Puritan-Evangelical experience. Since this book does not pretend that the focus is the only one available, in fact insists on the importance of alternative approaches, and clearly does not intend to comprehend religious organization in general, this criticism would seem unwarranted.

9. See note 2.

Chapter 5

Evolution of the Denomination Among the Reformed of the Middle and Southern States, 1780–1840

1. George Potts, *An Address . . . (Philadelphia, 1826)*, pp. 31-32.

2. Presbyterian Church in the United States of America, *Constitution* (Philadelphia, 1797), p. 417.

3. Sidney E. Mead, *The Lively Experiment; The Shaping of Christianity in America* (New York: Harper & Row, 1963), p. 107.

4. Presbyterian Church in the United States of America, *Constitution*, pp. 467-68.

5. *Ibid.*

6. Presbyterian Church in the United States of America, *Minutes of the General Assembly* (Philadelphia, n.d.), I, 12 (hereafter *MGA*). The General Synod of the Reformed Dutch Church also wrote Washington, but that letter was not recorded in the minutes. Reformed Dutch Church in the United States of America, *Acts and Proceedings of the General Synod* (New York, June 1789), p. 200 (hereafter *APGS*).

7. *MGA*, I, 9-10; 46-47.

8. Presbyterian Church in the United States of America, *Constitution*, p. 116.

9. *Ibid.*, p. 372.

10. Reformed Dutch Church in the United States of America, *Constitution* (New York, 1793), p. 116.

11. *MGA*, I, 195-96.

12. *Ibid.*, 196-97.

13. *Ibid.*, p. 197.

14. Jacob J. Janeway, *Address of the Board of Mission* (Philadelphia, 1816), pp. 21-23, 7; *MGA*, I, 633.

15. *MGA*, I, 146-147, 157.

16. *Ibid.*, p. 420.

17. *Ibid.*, p. 502.

18. *Ibid.*, p. 593-94. For similar statements on the societies on a synodical level see *Synod of New York and New Jersey, Extracts from the Minutes*, 1809, pp. 6-7; 1812, p. 54; 1814, p. 71; 1815, p. 77.

19. Reformed Dutch Church in North America, *Acts and Proceedings of the General Synod* (New York, 1823), p. 36; 1826, pp. 32-36. See also *APGS*, 1834, pp. 270-72. By this latter date the American Home Missionary Society and The American Education Society were not favored and are conspicuously absent from the list. For support of the societies by the Associate Synod of North America see *Acts and Proceedings of the Associate Synod of North America*, 1822, p. 10.

20. John Holt Rice, *A Discourse delivered before the General Assembly of the Presbyterian Church in the United States of America* (Philadelphia, 1820), pp. 5-23.

21. Whitney R. Cross, The Burned-over District: The Social and Intellectual History of Enthusiastic Religion in Western New York, 1800–1850 (Ithaca, N. Y.: Cornell University Press, 1950), pp. 55-76.

22. Religious Monitor, VI (1829–1830), 180-85, 470-71, 483-84.

23. Ibid., XI (1834–1835), 273.

24. Christian's Magazine, I (1831), 85-86.

25. Christian's Magazine, III (1834), 348-49; V (1836), 128-29, 341, 373-81.

26. Magazine of the Reformed Dutch Church, III (June 1828), 95.

27. APGS, June 1833, pp. 235-36.

28. Magazine of the Reformed Dutch Church, III (April 1828), 28-30; III (May 1828), 59-62; III (June 1828), 90.

29. Ibid., III (September 1828), 189.

30. APGS, June 1831, pp. 367-69; June 1832, pp. 60, 71-73, 75; June 1833, p. 207; June 1830, pp. 294-99; June 1831, pp. 375-79, 381-84; June 1832, pp. 88, 90; June 1834, p. 327; June 1832, p. 90, 92-95; October 1832, p. 140; June 1836, pp. 525-26.

31. MGA, II, 261, 296, 301.

32. Quoted in Archibald Alexander, The Pastoral Office (Philadelphia, 1834), pp. 13-14.

33. Joshua Wilson, Four Propositions Sustained Against the Claims of the American Home Missionary Society (Cincinnati, 1831), pp. 4-9.

34. For a minute of the convention see Moore, History of the Huron Presbytery (Philadelphia, 1892), pp. 78-79.

Chapter 6

The Social Sources of Denominationalism: Methodism

1. H. Richard Niebuhr's Social Sources of Denominationalism (Hamden, Conn.: The Shoe String Press, 1954, first published in 1929) is generally acknowledged as the standard statement on denominationalism. Some of what is said here is directed against Niebuhr's treatment of denominationalism. It should be noted however, that this paper is concerned with issues that are really implicit in Niebuhr's analysis and that his basic arguments are not under review. Niebuhr's theologically informed sociology, despite the title, does not seem to concern itself with denominationalism as a form of the church. Rather he seems to be concerned with the divisions in Protestantism and the factors of caste and class that explain their origin and perpetuation. He assumes the Weber-

Troeltsch church-sect typology and the sect-to-church (denomination) movement. His concern is to bring into view the less-than-ideal dynamics which are productive of the ideal types. This work, widely admired by historians, is more useful for its explanation of specific denominations and their social sources than for the perspective provided on denominationalism per se.

2. Robert Baird, *Religion in America* (New York: Harper & Brothers, 1844); H. Richard Niebuhr, *The Kingdom of God in America* (New York: Harper & Brothers, 1937); James F. Maclear, "'The True American Union' of Church and State: The Reconstruction of the Theocratic Tradition," *Church History*, 28 (1959), 41-62; Elwyn A. Smith, "The Voluntary Establishment of Religion," *The Religion of the Republic*, ed. Elwyn A. Smith (Philadelphia: Fortress Press, 1971), pp. 154-82; Martin E. Marty, *Righteous Empire* (New York: Dial Press, 1970); Robert T. Handy, *A Christian America* (New York: Oxford University Press, 1971). The very important essay by D. A. Martin "The Denomination," *British Journal of Sociology*, 13 (March 1962), 1-14, presents a similar portrayal of the denomination. Martin does not, however, relate the pragmatism or instrumentalism of the denomination to the end which legitimized the pragmatism, namely, the building of the kingdom. Since the end of the kingdom was what kept the tendencies toward relativism, politicization, divisiveness, and other human exploitations of religion in bounds, this omission is signifcant. To no small degree, it would seem to me, does the cynicism about the compromises of the denomination found in sociological literature derive from this oversight. To no small degree, also, do present difficulties in the denominations derive from their loss of the higher purpose and larger unity which once defined them and made them more than bureaucracies.

Chapter 9
Institutionalization and Secularization of the Kingdom

1. Bergson, *The Two Sources of Morality and Religion* (New York, 1935), p. 227.

2. F. H. Foster, *A Genetic History of New England Theology* (Chicago, 1907), pp. 31f.

3. Vernon Louis Parrington, *Main Currents in American Thought* (New York, Harcourt, Brace, 1927–30), I, 107.

4. "The Bostonian Ebenezer," published as an appendix to Book I of *Magnalia Christi Americana*.

5. *Bonifacius: An Essay upon the Good that is to be devised and*

designed by those who desire to answer the great end of life, etc.
(Boston, 1710). Later published in many editions under the title
Essays To Do Good.

6. Parrington, op. cit., I, 125ff.

7. Lyman Beecher, Works (Boston, 1852), I, 287f.

8. Cf. Beecher's sermons, "The Bible a Code of Laws," Works, II,
154ff., and "The Government of God Desirable," II, 5ff.

9. Works, I, 189f.

10. Ibid., I, 322.

11. Ibid., II, 219.

12. Ibid., I, 332f.

13. Ibid., II, 106, 110f. On the mind of New England in this period
cf. Henry Adams, History of the United States in the Administration of Thomas Jefferson (New York, 1930), Book I, chap. 3.

14. Beecher, Works, II, 222, 223, 228.

15. Leonard Woolsey Bacon, A History of American Christianity
(New York, 1897), chaps. 11 and 12, p. 175.

16. R. E. Thompson, A History of the Presbyterian Churches in
the United States (New York, 1895), pp. 95ff.; W. W. Sweet,
Methodism in American History (New York, 1933), pp. 332ff., also
pp. 272, 309, 325, 332; Rufus Jones, The Later Periods of Quakerism
(London, 1921), I, 435ff., 488ff.; Bacon, op. cit., 292ff.

17. Typical expressions of this spirit may be found in Lyman
Beecher, Works, I, 324ff.; Horace Bushnell, The Crisis of the Church
(Hartford, 1835), and An Oration . . . on the Principles of National
Greatness (New Haven, 1837); Henry C. Fish, "The Earth Tributary
to Christ's Kingdom," National Preacher, Ser. III, Vol. IV, no. 11
(Nov., 1865) and other sermons in that collection; Josiah Strong,
The New Era, or the Coming Kingdom (New York, 1893), and
Expansion Under New World Conditions (New York, 1900).

18. Cf. Nathaniel Hawthorne, "The Celestial Railroad," "Mosses
from an Old Manse.

19. Calvin Colton, History and Character of American Revivals of
Religion (2nd ed., London, 1832), pp. 2-7.

20. Bushnell, The Crisis of the Church, pp. 9, 10, 14.

Chapter 10

Ethnicity: The Skeleton of Religion in America

1. Quoted in Lee Benson, Turner and Beard: American Historical Writing Reconsidered (Glencoe, Illinois: The Free Press, 1960),
p. 82.

2. Milton M. Gordon, Assimilation in American Life (New York:

Oxford University Press, 1964), popularized the concept of "peoplehood," which is the "sense" of an ethnic, racial, or religious group. The word turns up frequently in literature on ethnicity and new movements. Sometimes these movements, among them Women's Liberation, the New Left, "the counter culture," and the like, speak of themselves in the terms of "peoplehood," but this essay restricts itself to study of those groups which have at least a minimal claim on some sort of common ethnic origin and orientation. Significantly, the term worked its way into *Webster's New International Dictionary* during the 1960s; it did not appear in the second edition (1960) but is present in the third (1969): "Peoplehood: the quality or state of constituting a people; also: awareness of the underlying unity that makes the individual a part of the people."

3. The literature on black religion is rapidly expanding; Hart M. Nelsen, Raytha L. Yokley, and Anne K. Nelson, *The Black Church in America* (New York: Basic Books, Inc., 1971) is an excellent anthology on every major aspect of the subject. The suggestion that 1968 was a watershed year in black religious consciousness appears in this book, pp. 17 ff. Cleage is quoted on p. 18 and Bishop Herbert B. Shaw, speaking of ties to Asia and Africa, on p. 21. James H. Cone, *A Black Theology of Liberation* (Philadelphia: J. B. Lippincott, 1970) is a representative charge that most of what had previously been seen to be a generalized and universal theology in America is actually an expression of "whiteness." See also James J. Gardiner, S. A. and J. Deotis Roberts, Sr., *Quest for a Black Theology* (Philadelphia: Pilgrim Press, 1971).

4. Vine Deloria, *We Talk, You Listen* (New York: Macmillan, 1970) was a widely noticed expression of new American Indian assertiveness; it included an explicit suggestion that our impersonal, homogenized America should relearn the tribal model from the original Americans.

5. Richard L. Rubenstein, "Homeland and Holocaust" in Donald R. Cutler, *The Religious Situation: 1968* (Boston: Beacon, 1968), p. 45.

6. Arthur A. Cohen, *The Myth of the Judeo-Christian Tradition* (New York: Harper and Row, 1970), was written to help "break through the crust of harmony and concord which exists between Judaism and Christianity" and to help "destroy that in both communities which depends upon the other for authentication" (p. vii). Cohen believes that the myth of the common tradition was largely devised in America in the face of a secular religiosity; it induced two faiths to "join together to reinforce themselves in the face of a common disaster" (p. xix).

7. Armando B. Rendon, *Chicano Manifesto* (New York: Macmillan, 1971), uses figures (p. 38) from a survey taken in November, 1969; 9.2 million persons claiming Spanish descent would represent 4.7 percent of the population. Three quarters of this number were native born; the rest were immigrants, with half coming from Mexico. See also p. 325.

8. Joseph P. Fitzpatrick, *Puerto Rican Americans: The Meaning of a Migration* (Englewood Cliffs, New Jersey: Prentice-Hall, 1971) is a brief but comprehensive survey of the situation of this minority.

9. Richard M. Scammon and Ben J. Wattenberg, *The Real Majority* (New York: Coward-McCann, 1970), p. 66. Andrew M. Greeley, *Why Can't They Be Like Us? America's White Ethnic Groups* (New York: E. P. Dutton, 1971) introduces this conglomeration of hitherto separate ethnic forces. He also points to the fact that in part because its members spoke English and were Catholic the large Irish immigrant group does not fit easily into "the white ethnic/white Anglo-Saxon" Protestant combination. Nor, it might be added, did Germans and Scandinavian Protestants, who did not speak English.

10. References to the Church as "the new people of God" can be found throughout Walter M. Abbott, S. J., ed., *The Documents of Vatican II* (New York: Guild Press, American Press, Assoc. Press, 1966). In actual practice, ethnocentrism, competing ethnic subcommunities, and isolated or rival "national" parishes throughout American history have blurred the vision of their being a single "people of God."

11. Ben J. Wattenberg and Richard M. Scammon, *This U.S.A.: An Unexpected Family Portrait of 194,067,296 Americans Drawn from the Census* (New York: Doubleday, 1965), pp. 45f.

12. David Edwin Harrell, Jr., *White Sects and Black Men in the Recent South* (Nashville, Tennessee: Vanderbilt University Press, 1971), p. viii.

13. Lewis M. Killian, *The Impossible Revolution* (New York: Random House, 1968) p. 18. Richard L. Means, in *The Christian Century*, 78 (August 16, 1961), pp. 979-80, began to discuss the significance of *Anti-Protestant Prejudice*, a theme which subsequently received increasing attention, and which may serve to cause more WASPs to affirm the self-designation they had once shunned—if the experience of other more obvious victims of group prejudice is to be repeated in this instance. See also Peter Schrag, "The Decline of the Wasp," in *Harper's* Magazine, April 1970. While the WASPs "still hold power, they hold it with less assurance and with less legitimacy than at any time in history. . . . One can almost define their domains by locating the people and

institutions that are chronically on the defense. . . . For the first time, any sort of settlement among competing interests is going to have to do more than pay lip service to minorities and to the pluralism of styles, beliefs, and cultures. . . . America is not on the verge of becoming two separate societies, one rich and white, the other poor and black. It is becoming, in all its dreams and anxieties, a nation of outsiders for whom no single style or ethic remains possible. . . . We will now have to devise ways of recognizing and assessing the alternatives. The mainstream is running thin."

14. This definition and two subsequent definitions of "skeleton" are from the Oxford English Dictionary.

15. Charles H. Anderson, *White Protestant Americans: From National Origins to Religious Group* (Englewood Cliffs, N.J.: Prentice-Hall, 1971), p. viii. "Every American, as we shall use the term, is a member or potential member of an ethnic group—racial, religious, or national in origin."

16. See Max Weber, "Ethnic Groups," Translated by Ferdinand Kolegar, in Talcott Parsons, *et al.*, *Theories of Society*, Vol. 1 (Glencoe, Ill., The Free Press, 1961), pp. 305 ff. "Any aspect or cultural trait, no matter how superficial, can serve as a starting point for the familiar tendency to monopolistic closure." "Almost any kind of similarity or contrast of physical type and of habits can induce the belief that a tribal affinity or disaffinity exists between groups that attract or repel each other." "The belief in tribal kinship, regardless of whether it has any objective foundation, can have important consequences especially for the formation of a political community. Those human groups that entertain a subjective belief in their common descent—because of similarities of physical type or of customs or both, or because of memories of colonization and migration—in such a way that this belief is important for the continuation of non-kinship communal relationship we shall call 'ethnic' groups, regardless of whether an objective blood relationship exists or not." "Behind all ethnic diversities there is somehow naturally the notion of the 'chosen people,' which is nothing else but a counterpart of status differentiation translated into the plane of horizontal coexistence. The idea of a chosen people derives its popularity from the fact that it can be claimed to an equal degree by any and every member of the mutually despising groups."

17. Charles H. Anderson, *op. cit.*, pp. 43 ff. locates Swedes with WASPs. "They have been granted WASP status on the basis of their successful adaptation to Anglo-Saxon America. In a sense even today Scandinavians are second-class WASPs; nevertheless, Scan-

dinavians know that it is better to be a second-class WASP than a non-WASP in American society."

18. Rudolph J. Vecoli, "Ethnicity: A Neglected Dimension of American History," in Herbert J. Bass, *The State of American History* (Chicago: Quadrangle, 1970), pp. 70 ff. sets the stage for the present essay on religious historiography.

19. Quoted in Carlton J. H. Hayes, *Nationalism: A Religion* (New York: Macmillan, 1960), pp. 20f. Hayes provides one of the best analyses of the dimensions of national cultural religions in Chapter XII, pp. 154 ff.

20. Lyman Beecher, *Address of the Charitable Society for the Education of Indigent Pious Young Men for the Ministry of the Gospel* (Concord, Mass., 1820), p. 20.

21. Charles Hodge, "Anniversary Address," in *The Home Missionary*, Vol. II (New York, 1829), p. 18.

22. Dorothy Dohen, *Nationalism and American Catholicism* (New York: Sheed and Ward, 1967) brings testimony of numerous nineteenth-century Roman Catholic leaders on this subject.

23. Philip Schaff, *America: A Sketch of Its Political, Social, and Religious Character* (Cambridge, Mass.: The Belknap Press of Harvard University Press, 1961), p. 51.

24. Quoted by Vecoli, *op. cit.*, p. 75.

25. John Dewey, *A Common Faith* (New Haven, Conn.: Yale University Press, 1934). While the book uses the term "God," it is non-theistic and advocates an imaginatively-based synthesis or unification of values in which the many take part.

26. Robin M. Williams, Jr., *American Society: A Sociological Interpretation* (New York: Knopf, 1951), p. 312.

27. J. Paul Williams, *What Americans Believe and How They Worship* (New York: Harper and Row, 1962), pp. 477-592. The first edition appeared in 1952.

28. See especially Sidney E. Mead, "The Nation with the Soul of a Church," *Church History*, Vol. 36, No. 3 (September 1967), pp. 262 ff. Williams quotes Mead with favor, *op. cit.*, p. 479, in reference to the religion of the democratic society *versus* the religion of the denominations.

29. Sidney E. Mead, "The Post-Protestant Concept and America's Two Religions," in Robert L. Ferm, *Issues in American Protestantism: A Documentary History from the Puritans to the Present* (Garden City, New York: Doubleday, 1969), pp. 387 f. Following Paul Tillich's distinction, it might be said that Mead affirmed "the catholic substance" in a common national religion because he trusted the presence of "the protestant principle" of prophetic protest. Those Mead criticized tended to stress "the

protestant principle" even where they affirmed the common faith because they feared that its "catholic substance" could be idolized or imposed on people.

30. William Lee Miller, *Piety Along the Potomac: Notes on Politics and Morals in the Fifties* (Boston: Houghton Mifflin, 1964); Stephen C. Rose, *Sermons Not Preached in the White House* (New York: Baron, 1970).

31. Robert N. Bellah, "Civil Religion in America" reprinted by Cutler, *op. cit.*, pp. 331 ff., especially p. 346. The paper was first presented at a conference in May, 1966, before the liberal academic community had largely turned its back on the Johnson administration. After the escalation of the Vietnamese war, the rise of the New Left and the intensification of black power movements, this community was somewhat less congenial to the expressions of a national religion once again.

32. Vecoli, *op. cit.*, pp. 74 f. Crevecoeur first published his *Letters from an American Farmer* in 1782.

33. Quoted by Stuart P. Sherman in *Essays and Poems of Emerson* (New York, 1921), p. xxxiv.

34. Marc Bloch, *The Historian's Craft* (New York: Vintage, 1964), p. 8. Such a "thrill of learning singular things" was not characteristic of Leibnitz, who tried to transcend variety and pluralism. Over against this, William James posed *A Pluralistic Universe* (New York: Longmans, Green, 1909), which may be seen as the philosophical grandfather of the American schools which tolerate or encourage particularisms.

35. John Courtney Murray, S. J., *We Hold These Truths: Catholic Reflections on the American Proposition* (New York: Sheed and Ward, 1960), p. 23.

36. In *America*, January 9, 1971, pp. 10 f.

37. Secular and religious approaches to world integration are sketched by W. Warren Wagar, *The City of Man: Prophecies of a World Civilization in Twentieth-Century Thought* (Boston: Houghton Mifflin, 1963).

38. For a review of secular theologians' positions, see Martin E. Marty, "Secularization in the American Public Order," in Donald A. Giannella, *Religion and the Public Order*, Number Five (Ithaca: Cornell University Press, 1969), pp. 33 f. and "Secular Theology as a Search for the Future," in Albert Schlitzer, C. S. C., ed., *The Spirit and Power of Christian Secularity* (Notre Dame, Ind.: University of Notre Dame Press, 1969), pp. 1 ff.

39. Bryan Wilson, *Religion in Secular Society: A Sociological Comment* (Baltimore, Maryland: Penguin, 1966), pp. 40 ff. and 121.

40. Seymour Martin Lipset, *The First New Nation: The United*

States in Historical and Comparative Perspective (New York: Basic Books, 1963), pp. 151 f.

41. Jefferson to J. Fishback, September 27, 1809, in Albert Ellery Bergh, *The Writings of Thomas Jefferson* (Washington, 1905), XII, 314-316; the second reference is quoted by Anson Phelps Stokes, *Church and State in the United States* (New York: Harper and Brothers, 1950), Vol. I, 335.

42. Alfred North Whitehead, *Religion in the Making* (New York: Macmillan, 1926), p. 58.

43. William James, *The Varieties of Religious Experience: A Study in Human Nature* (New York: Longmans, Green, 1903), p. 31.

44. Thomas Luckmann, *The Invisible Religion: The Problem of Religion in Modern Society* (New York: Macmillan, 1967), pp. 97 f., 105 f. While Jefferson, Whitehead and James often advocated private limitations of religion, Luckmann merely observes it and regards it as a burden for moderns seeking an identity.

45. Quoted in Edgar S. Cahn, ed., *Our Brother's Keeper: The Indian in White America* (New York and Cleveland: World, 1969), pp. 184, 175.

46. Gerhard Lenski, *The Religious Factor: A Sociological Study of Religion's Impact on Politics, Economics, and Family Life* (Garden City, New York: Doubleday, 1961), p. 11.

47. Will Herberg, *Protestant-Catholic-Jew: An Essay in American Religious Sociology* (Garden City, New York: Doubleday, 1955), pp. 88-102. Lenski and Herberg did not regard the common religion of America with favor. Among those who did were Horace M. Kallen, in *Secularism Is the Will of God* (New York: Twayne, 1954) and Duncan J. Howlett, though they treated secularism or humanism as *The Fourth American Faith* (New York: Harper and Row, 1964), which still had to contend for place with Protestantism, Catholicism and Judaism. Samuel A. Mueller, "The New Triple Melting Pot: Herberg Revisited," in *Review of Religious Research*, Vol. 13, No. 1 (Fall 1971), suggests that a new set of categories should be "white Christian, white non-Christian, and black." He bases this on a sociological study of lines between these and Herberg's three groups in the matters of "marriage, friendship, residence, occupations, and politics."

48. E. Digby Baltzell, *The Protestant Establishment* (New York: Random House, 1964), p. 53.

49. Arthur Mann, "Charles Fleischer's Religion of Democracy," in *Commentary*, June 1954, p. 557.

50. John Cogley, ed., *Religion in America: Original Essays on Religion in a Free Society* (New York: Meridian, 1958), p. 9.

51. John Meyendorff, *The Orthodox Church: Its Past and Its Role in the World Today* (New York: Pantheon, 1960), p. 107.

52. Mead's essay is reprinted in Sidney E. Mead, *The Lively Experiment: The Shaping of Christianity in America* (New York: Harper and Row), 103 ff. Karl Hertz writes on denominationalism in "Some Suggestions for a Sociology of American Protestantism" in Herbert T. Neve and Benjamin A. Johnson, *The Maturing of American Lutheranism* (Minneapolis, Minnesota: Augsburg, 1968), pp. 36, 42.

53. Bryan Wilson, op. cit., pp. 47, 51.

54. Sidney E. Mead, *The Lively Experiment*, pp. 132 f.

55. Charles Y. Glock and Rodney Stark, *Religion and Society in Tension* (Chicago: Rand McNally, 1965), pp. 86 f.

56. Jeffrey K. Hadden, *The Gathering Storm in the Churches: The Widening Gap Between Clergy and Laymen* (Garden City, New York, 1969), especially Chapter IV, "Clergy and Laity View the Civil Rights Issue."

57. David Reimers, *White Protestantism and the Negro* (New York: Oxford University Press, 1965), p. 29.

58. Quoted in Benson Y. Landis, *Protestant Experience with United States Immigration, 1910–1960* (New York: Church World Service, 1961), pp. 12 f.

59. Gordon, op. cit., p. 38.

60. Vincent Harding, "Black Power and the American Christ," in Floyd B. Barbour, *The Black Power Revolt: A Collection of Essays* (New York: Collier, 1968), p. 97.

61. Denis W. Brogan, "Commentary," in Cutler, op. cit., p. 357.

62. Robert Baird, *Religion in the United States of America* (Glasgow, 1843); see Chapter VI, p. 35 ff.

63. John Gilmary Shea, *The History of the Catholic Church in the United States* (New York, 1886–92), four volumes.

64. Daniel Dorchester, *Christianity in the United States* (New York: Hunt and Eaton, 1890), p. 765.

65. Leonard Woolsey Bacon, *A History of American Christianity* (New York: Scribners, 1898), p. 292.

66. Josiah Strong, *The New Era; or The Coming Kingdom* (New York, 1893), pp. 54-55; *Our Country: Its Possible Future and Its Present Crisis* (New York, 1885), pp. 178, 174-175.

67. Peter Mode, *The Frontier Spirit in American Christianity* (New York: Macmillan, 1923), pp. 6, 7, 14. Mode-Sweet-Mead represent a University of Chicago succession which is most familiar to me. See also William Warren Sweet, *The Story of Religion in America* (New York: Harper and Brothers, 1930); another student in this tradition, along with Robert T. Handy (see note 68), is

Winthrop S. Hudson, whose *Religion in America* (New York: Scribner's, 1965) pioneered at least in its sense of proportion, since it devoted much attention to black Protestantism, Judaism and other non-WASP religious groups.

68. New York: Oxford University Press, 1971. For another attempt to isolate WASP history and to treat WASPs as an ethnic group, see Martin E. Marty, *Righteous Empire: The Protestant Experience in America* (New York: Dial, 1970).

Contributors

E. Franklin Frazier (d. 1962) was until retirement Professor and Head of the Department of Sociology, Howard University. His publications include *The Negro Family in the United States* (1939), *The Negro in the United States* (1949), *Black Bourgeoisie* (1957), and *The Negro Church in America* (1963).

Fred J. Hood is Associate Professor of History, Georgetown College. He is author of "Revolution and Religious Liberty: The Conservation of the Theocratic Concept in Virginia," *Church History*, 40 (June 1971) and "Quantitative Analysis in the Study of American Religious History," *Journal of the American Academy of Religion* 43 (June 1975).

Winthrop S. Hudson holds a joint appointment as Professor of History at the University of Rochester and Professor of Church History in Colgate Rochester/Bexley Hall/Crozer. Among his publications are *The Great Tradition of the American Churches* (1953), *American Protestantism* (1961), *Nationalism and Religion in America* (1965), and *Religion in America* (1973).

Martin E. Marty is Professor of Modern Church History at The University of Chicago Divinity School and Associate Editor of *The Christian Century*. Of his books, the ones most immediately related to this volume are *The New Shape of American Religion* (1959), *The Modern Schism* (1969), *Righteous Empire* (1970), and *Protestantism* (1972).

Sidney E. Mead is Professor Emeritus in the School of Religion and the Department of History, University of Iowa, and author of *Nathaniel William Taylor, 1786–1858* (1942), *The Lively Experiment* (1963), and *The Nation with the Soul of a Church* (1975).

H. Richard Niebuhr, until his death in 1962 Sterling Professor of Theology and Christian Ethics at Yale

University, is the author of *The Social Sources of Denominationalism* (1929), *The Kingdom of God in America* (1937), *Christ and Culture* (1951), and *The Purpose of the Church and Its Ministry* (1956).

Russell E. Richey, Associate Professor of Church History, Drew University, is co-editor of *American Civil Religion* (1974) and author of "Did the English Presbyterians Become Unitarian?" *Church History,* 42 (March 1973) and "The Origins of British Radicalism: The Changing Rationale for Dissent," *Eighteenth-Century Studies,* 7 (Winter 1973/74).

Elwyn A. Smith is currently Consultant for Continuing Education for Church Professionals in Florida and Assistant Minister at the Garden Crest Presbyterian Church in St. Petersburg. He is associate editor of the *Journal of Ecumenical Studies,* editor of *Church-State Relations in Ecumenical Perspective* (1966) and *The Religion of the Republic* (1971), and author of *The Presbyterian Minister in American Culture* (1962) and *Religious Liberty in the United States* (1972).

Timothy L. Smith, Professor of History at The Johns Hopkins University, is author of *Revivalism and Social Reform* (1957), *Called Unto Holiness: The Story of the Nazarenes* (1962), and co-author of *Anonymous Americans* (1971).